Rekindling Your Spirit:

Messages to Live By

Rekindling Your Spirit:

Messages to Live By

❧❧

William Gorvine

Eagle Press

Published in association with Tabby House
Manufactured in the United States of America
Library of Congress Catalog Card Number: 96-096323
ISBN: 0-9651703-0-6

Cover design: Tracy Hall

Eagle Press
P.O. Box 512376
Punta Gorda, FL 33951
(941) 575-7239

To my wife, Enid,
for her unstinting encouragement and support
throughout this spiritual odyssey of mine.

Introduction

I think a brief explanation of who I am and how this work came about would be helpful to the reader. I am a graduate of Harvard College (magna cum laude, Phi Beta Kappa) and Harvard Law School. I worked in government for the U.S. Atomic Energy Commission, in industry for a major defense company, and in private practice for a large law firm for a total of forty years before retiring. My education and experience have been rationally and analytically oriented, and I have led a very conventional life.

I became interested in matters of the human spirit some thirty years ago while trying to find meaning in the death of my only son. (Happily, twenty months later, we were blessed with another son, Bill.) Charlie was diagnosed at the age of five with Wilm's Tumor, a form of kidney cancer. After a gallant two-year battle, involving several operations and apparent periods of remission followed by the agony of another recurrence, he died a week after his seventh birthday. His death left my wife and me devastated and his two sisters, ages eight and five, upset and confused. Why would a loving and benign God do something like this? Thus began an exploration into the not-entirely-respectable world of psychic phenomena, with the full knowledge that all-too-many practitioners in this field were phonies. Among other works, I read about the remarkable accomplishments of Edgar Cayce, the Sleeping Prophet, and much of the material dictated by Seth to Jane Roberts while she was in a trance state. I became convinced that psychic capabilities were both real and natural—at least for other people. I also met and became good friends with a genuine practicing psychic. Nevertheless, if anyone had told me that I would some day be channeling messages from beings in the spirit world, I would have laughed at him.

After retiring to Punta Gorda, Florida, my wife and I took a course called Developing Your Psychic Capabilities taught by Sandy Anastasi. The underlying theme, which I agreed with, was that we all have psychic capabilities, but for most of us they remain undeveloped and therefore, like unused muscles, tend to atrophy. The course was designed to show us how to exercise those hitherto-unused muscles and included such items as how to communicate with your spirit guide (we all have them from birth!), automatic writing, and the use of a pendulum for divination.

When we got to the automatic-writing segment of the course, mine seemed to be clearer and to come more easily than some of the other students. I then got the idea that instead of holding a pencil to paper and allowing my hand to be guided—an approach that consumed a lot of time and energy—I would sit at my computer in a meditative state and try to do the equivalent. I inquired of my spirit guide whether this would be an acceptable alternative and got a manually written, "Yes."

When I sat down at my computer in a meditative state, I was surprised to find that instead of individual words laboriously spelled out, I was receiving complete thoughts in sentence form. My job was to type these thoughts (messages) on my computer as I received them. Since I was in a meditative state with my eyes closed nearly all the time, I did the typing by touch and cleaned it up later. (Since I am not a very good touch typist, I had to open my eyes and check from time to time to make sure the typing was not so bad that I wouldn't be able to clean it up later. The spell checker on the computer also helped.)

As I kept getting more and more thoughts, sometimes very rapidly, I concluded that what I was really doing was more in the nature of channeling rather than automatic writing. Though in a mediative state, I still had control over my body; no other entity had temporarily taken it over and was using my physical attributes (e.g. voice or fingers) to communicate his messages—as compared with some trance channelers. The thoughts I received passed through my own consciousness and were typed by me, using my own vocabulary and syntax for the most part.

At first I wondered if what I was receiving came to me from my own subconscious, but I came to the conclusion that the messages were too profound for that to be the case. I decided that the source of the messages was another entity, my spirit guide, whom I met while in a meditative state. He is a wise, loving, compassionate, very old Native American with a charming sense of humor, who uses the name "Seneca" in his communications with me.

My conclusion was confirmed about nine months into my personal odyssey when, on August 29, 1993, I encountered another spiritual entity. He appeared beside Seneca as a blinding light shimmering around a human figure. When I asked, Seneca told me that the other entity had come to help guide me, that he was "far more advanced" than Seneca himself and that he had no name that was pronounceable to humans. However, the other entity has allowed me to call him "Michael" and told me that some day he might tell me his real name. Since that time, both Seneca and Michael have always appeared together but it is Michael who does most of the talking. Nothing Michael has said to me in any way contradicts material that I had previously received from Seneca. Quite the contrary.

Seneca and Michael told me early on that these messages were intended for the benefit of all humankind and that they would tell me when to make the messages public. For my part, I have found them to be messages of hope and encouragement, even amidst the many problems that afflict us in this world.

To avoid unnecessary repetition and confine the messages to their substantive content, I have deleted most of the introductory greetings and closing expressions of love and blessing (unless there was something in an individual one that might be of help to others). I have also deleted those portions that were entirely personal to me, my family or my friends, unless I thought that a particular item of personal information might be helpful to others as well. In those cases, where friends were involved, I substituted fictitious names. I have deleted Sessions 17 and 27 because they were entirely personal. I have used italics to emphasize those portions of a message that I considered to be of particular importance or interest to a reader. Since neither Seneca nor Michael used italics (or equivalent) in their messages, the choice of passages to italicize is mine, not theirs.

I have not tried to organize the information into categories or chapters based on subject matter. Instead, I decided that the best approach would be to present these messages to you just as I received them, in the same sequence and with the same flavor. I did add what seemed to me to be appropriate titles to the various messages. However, for the benefit of those who might want to find what has been said on individual subjects, I have tried to include a fairly detailed index.

WILLIAM GORVINE

April 1996

PART I

SENECA

Initial Contact

Session 1 - November 2, 1992

The world is changing as spirit is expanding its role versus material. We are ushering in a new age—a good age, a spiritual age when spirit and materiality will be harmonized. What should you do to prepare for this? Study, learn, be open but protected. You will see marvels that you thought could not exist. No, it's not the end of the world as you know it. But there will be a great awakening to the importance of the inner life. More later.

Message for People Seeking Spiritual Growth

Session 2 - November 4, 1992

I said I would give you more information later. What kind of information would be most helpful to people seeking spiritual growth and development? *A reminder that today is just a passing fancy and that what happens here is simply preparation and training for greater tasks.* Once you learn that, you will cease to strive so violently, yes violently, for material success. You will become more aware of the importance of the inner being, its eternal nature and its significance as the real you. Continue to work and study. A yearning for spiritual growth will stand you in good stead. It will help you to follow what your conscience tells you about how to deal with fellow humans and all of God's creation. That itself leads to growth. Think about what you are supposed to be learning in this lifetime. The clues are there, from your own experiences, both good and bad. Each of us has a particular mission/lesson to learn in a particular lifetime and if we don't learn it, we have to come back and do it again. But eventually we get it right. So there is always hope, no matter what the existing conditions of this life may be.

Eventually we all move on to a higher plane, though it may take some of us longer than others. Just like school. We all move ahead at our own pace, depending on our learning ability and how much we apply ourselves.

I look forward to seeing the expressions on your faces when you come to realize what your potential truly is. *Never forget that you partake of the divine.* It sometimes gets covered with garbage but the diamond is still there waiting to be discovered. We here love humanity and want to help you progress. We can't do it for you but we are always available to help. As you have been told, *you are never truly alone—unless you want to be. Never unloved or abandoned. If it seems that way sometimes, it means there is a lesson for you to learn from that experience. God does not punish; He teaches!* With that message of hope and encouragement—until next time.

Living Your Belief System

Session 3 - November 5, 1992

I am glad that we have made this kind of contact because there is a great deal of information that needs to be passed on. If you continue to work at it, you can be a clear channel for us to help earth people to progress spiritually.

W. G.: What guidance do you wish to offer us at this time?

Seneca: First, try to absorb what I have already said. You may already know it but living it is still something quite different. It represents a real mouthful to put into practice these precepts. But if you do it, your life on earth will be much different—more calm and serene and bright with the knowledge that you are advancing, which after all is what you are here for. We smile indulgently whenever we see one of our earth brothers take our information seriously and act on it. All this information is of course meant for all, not just you. I know that you know that but I wanted to make it absolutely clear that this is not just a private conversation.

W. G.: Can you give us some specifics about how our world here will be changing over the next ten or twenty years?

Seneca: I think I'll wait a little bit for that. You have to start with fundamentals and while you're off to a good start, you are still just a beginner. Have patience. It will all come in good time, when we think you are ready for it, and perhaps when the world will be more receptive.

Keep practicing. I think you will be a worthy ally in this venture. And you will gain from it. I don't mean materially but I do mean spiritually. You may even get to skip a grade at school. Ha. Ha. Stay with the fundamentals for now and try to put this belief system of yours that I summarized for us earlier into practice in living your life there. *As you well know, intellectual knowledge is by no means enough. That's just the beginning. Living your belief system is what counts. Knowing but not living gets you nowhere.*

We will begin to make a great deal of progress soon. You are getting a good start in using your computer for this purpose. It makes it possible for me to send you whole thoughts, ideas, etc. rather than just individual letters or simple messages. We can thus communicate with you while using much less energy than would otherwise be required, so we can spend more time together with less drain on your energy and ours.

I look forward to our next conversation. Remember, I don't need sleep so I am here to help you whenever you call on me, not just with automatic writing but in many other ways as well. Together we will figure out what those other ways are. Good-bye for now.

The Divine Plan

Session 4 - November 8, 1992

W. G.: Do you wish to continue our discussion?

Seneca: Oh, we still have a great deal to talk about. We haven't scratched the surface of things you and all mankind should know about the world of spirit and how we interact with the material world—to try to uplift you so that you can ultimately realize your full potential.

Where to start? Let's start with the divine plan. There are so many levels that it is hard to communicate them to the necessarily limited human mind/intelligence. After all, your present training program is in the material world, the world of things, so your awareness of spirit is much attenuated. But don't worry, you all will get there. I can't repeat that too often.

All living things have a spark of the divine about them, or they wouldn't be alive. Nonliving objects are of course also part of God's creation but they don't have that little spark in them. If they did, they would also be alive in the sense that we know life—that is, able to reproduce their own kind.

This really means that all life is precious, even low forms of life that you as humans may find distasteful. They all have a purpose and are part of the plan. You need maggots and other (to you) unattractive species in order the help keep the natural order in balance. *So stop and think before you deprive anything of its life.* This doesn't mean that you shouldn't eat plants or even animals because you need food to live and the plants and animals have as one of their purposes to provide it. But don't waste, don't kill unnecessarily and do what you can to replenish the bounty that nature bestows upon you. In that general respect, the Native Americans have the right idea. *You may take what you need but you are not intended to be the exploiters of nature. Rather you are intended to live in harmony with nature—and ultimately with each other.* I don't want to hold my breath on the latter because you still have a long way to go before overcoming your violent, competitive, xenophobic tendencies. But you will, eventually.

The plan is to have you continue to go to school until you have learned what you must—you could call it "purified your soul"—and then you become a co-creator with God. No, you don't sit around playing harps and wearing halos. There is too much work to be done for that. Remember, this is a continuing process and, once an individual reaches enlightenment, by whatever name you may choose to call it in your various religious traditions, you then have to help the rest on their journey to the same end result. So don't worry about being bored when you get through school; I can assure you that you won't be. And the joy and satisfaction that you will get from helping humans grow in knowledge, love and understanding will be ample reward.

I try to give you something new in each of our conversations but I emphasize that you must always go back and reexamine our prior conversations because there are nuggets in each of them that you are meant to live by. They aren't hard to pick out. But again, it comes down to living, not just knowing. I'll probably be repeating this many times as we continue with your education but it can't be overemphasized.

Our conversations and your growing knowledge of spirit and God's plan are no substitute for living your belief system, which is a good one. All people must come to the point of living the noble features of their belief systems. *None of you has a monopoly on truth, yet all your systems have much truth in them. Winnow out the most basic features of traditional religions and you will see how much in common they really have.*

Earth—The Schoolhouse

Session 5 - November 16, 1992

Your knowledge is still imperfect but I will try to prepare you for what is to come. The world as you know it will eventually end when it is no longer needed as a schoolhouse. By then all humankind will have evolved to a higher plane of spiritual growth so the schoolhouse can then be abandoned.

Until then it behooves you to cherish the earth as your temporary home—both for yourselves and for those who come after you. School will not be out when you pass on. The resources of this earth, while enormous, are nevertheless limited—and you have no idea when they will no longer be needed. Neither do I for that matter—sounds like the "need to know" principle applied here. But I really don't need to know this in order to do my job—and neither do you. Do what you know to be right in your relationships with the earth and all that dwell upon it, and let the duration of the earth's existence as such take care of itself.

You people of earth always seem to want to know dates and times when future things will happen—and I don't mean who will win the World Series or the fifth race. You give much too much significance to time, which after all is merely a construct, a man-made one at that. You have to think in linear terms because the material world is structured in such a way that you must approach it that way in order to survive in it. But don't ever lose sight of the fact that it is nothing more than a convenient construct. It really doesn't exist—not in our world or in spirit worlds in general.

The fact that past, present and future are one doesn't mean that everything is preordained. Free will will always be an essential part of the total picture. Free will means the power of choice but it also carries with it the responsibility for the choices made. Religious traditions which speak of God as having given man free will and thus making him little less than the gods—angels?—are correct. That is why earth is both a school and a halfway house on our path back to union with the Divine— whether it is called enlightenment, heaven, paradise, or any other comparable name. It is our ultimate goal. As I said before, it is then that we become co-creators with God, not just harp players.

You once were told that prayer was the most powerful force in the universe. I remember that you were surprised at the time because you didn't really believe it in your conscious mind. However, you had opened up enough of your higher self or communicated with a guide so that this nugget of truth was passed along to you. Now you really believe it but I don't think you practice it often enough. Remember, it can be done at any time and place and it doesn't have to take long. You don't have to be in a church, synagogue, mosque or ashram (I didn't want to leave anybody out) to pray. Prayer has tended to become formalized and too confined to church or equivalent. But it is nothing more than communication by you with God, by whatever name you may choose to call Him. I assure you He doesn't care about names, only about deeds and attitudes. So talk often to God because you then invite Him to talk back.

That is true of most of us in the spirit world who are trying to help humanity progress. I've been looking after you for a long time but I wouldn't, maybe couldn't, initiate a conversation with you, at least not consciously. You had to initiate the conversation and then I could come forth with ideas, advice, etc. But you had to want me to. We do not force help upon you. You have to want it and ask for it. And isn't that a pretty good short summary of what prayer is?

When you pray, don't just concentrate your attention on what you want or need. God knows that very well. Just be quiet and listen for the small, still voice within you that provides you with answers.

Love and Other Subjects

Session 6 - November 23, 1992

You already know that the most powerful force in the universe is prayer. Now the next most powerful force is love—not erotic or sexual love but the more lasting and unselfish kind. To be able to love is one of God's greatest gifts to mankind. It is what will transform humanity from a series of fierce, competitive and violent beings into a harmonious, caring whole. That is still a long way off in terms of your time—but it will come.

I have much to pass on to you but I must do it at a rate that you can handle and comprehend. Since I am sending you thoughts rather than just words, you must have some understanding in order to be able to set them down. Just sending you words to write down won't really do the job. You need to understand them if they are to be meaningful to the rest of mankind.

What are the things you consider important to know about your evolving world? Unfortunately they are more mundane and materialistic than spiritual, and my job is to try to help you on the spiritual path. So that's what I intend to talk about, even though many of you would rather hear about something else.

Love for all human beings, respect for opinions that differ from yours, and a sense of the interrelationship among all elements of creation are necessary prerequisites to spiritual growth. You know that you were not meant to be masters of the earth but stewards. And you, all of you everywhere, have done a pretty poor job of it. You could expect to be fired when the boss returned and saw the kind of job you had been doing. But it is never too late to change. That is what we count on as we observe human development. You *can* change. You *can* adapt. You can be marvelously innovative when you put your minds and hearts to it. *It is important that you stop despoiling the earth.* Sure, people need to eat and live reasonably well, but that does not excuse the wasteland you have made of too much of the earth. *Work together now to preserve what remains of this small planet or you will pay a much higher price than you can now imagine!* That is not intended as a threat but merely an observation based on what we see ahead.

Yes, you are your neighbor's keeper. I don't mean it literally because, in the last analysis, each of us must assume responsibility for himself or herself. But you are your neighbor's keeper in the sense that you must always treat him with consideration and fairness and come to his aid when he needs you. It works both ways and he must do likewise for you. You don't necessarily even have to like him but the duty remains anyhow.

You would like to know about other realms? There are as many as there are stars in the sky. And they all lead to the ultimate objective— reunion with your divine nature—but they all go about it in vastly different ways. When you finish with life on earth, therefore, and move on to other realms, you can be sure that you will never be bored. There will always be useful work to be done. I never could understand how you Christians could ever portray heaven as a place where you do nothing but play harps and praise God. Boy, is that anthropomorphic! God doesn't need that kind of stroking or appeasement. You should have learned that long ago but the notion still seems to persist in many of your religious traditions.

Astral travel is very real. It is a wonderful way by which you can travel anywhere, not just to other parts of this material world but to other planes as well. It helps, however, to know where you want to go, and that is difficult if you don't really know what's out there. Maybe I can help relieve some of that ignorance. There are levels in which spirit plays an increasingly large role and body an increasingly small role. There are levels in which all is spirit, but spirit functions on a whole series of levels of its own, from fairly low to extremely high. I, Seneca, am pretty well up the line but by no means at the top level. I've still got a great deal to learn but I also learn by helping you. You can partially prepare yourselves for these higher realms by putting more emphasis on spirit and less on materiality while you are still on the earth plane. It will give you a head start toward your spiritual future—and speed your path.

Reincarnation and Karma

Session 7 - November 27, 1992

You would like to know what the status of your soul is between incarnations and whether you choose the circumstances of your next birth. As spirit between incarnations, you know much more than when you are in the flesh. Therefore, even a person who has performed badly while on earth knows that he has not grown spiritually from that experience and may choose to relive it so that he can do better next time. In that sense he has a choice. But it is also true that he must progress in order to be promoted to a higher realm and in that sense he does not have a choice. He must overcome the obstacles that separate him from union with the Divine one way or another.

On the earth plane, that can only be accomplished by living in the flesh and living the kind of life that will take him spiritually beyond the human plane. On other planes we grow spiritually in different ways but here on earth you show your degree of enlightenment by how you live— not what you profess but how you live it. The unbeliever who truly cares for all God's creation makes far more progress than the so-called believer who thinks he truly believes but who does not carry these beliefs over into his life style.

When you are in spirit between incarnations, you go to school also. There is always so much more to learn and so much more to do. The range of knowledge and wisdom is infinite and therefore we never complete our studies. But some of us can get so far that we do actually become co-creators with God of this universe that we live in—and that is so vast as to be literally incomprehensible to the limited human understanding. You simply aren't equipped to comprehend it. It's the same as your eyes being able to see only visible light and missing the enormous range of the electromagnetic spectrum. It's not a matter of fault or inferiority. You just aren't constructed so as to understand the full range of the cosmos.

Reincarnation is definitely real and has been a part of many belief systems for thousands of years. Take it as a given—it's real. You know that your own sense of fairness has told you long ago that the concept of one life of a mere sixty or seventy or eighty years, followed by final judgment unto eternity, simply doesn't make sense. That notion really represented a power play among the religious leaders of the time when belief in reincarnation was being attacked and ultimately anathematized. More and more people on earth, in the western world, are coming to appreciate the reality of reincarnation and the message of hope that goes with it. *We are here to learn and grow in holiness, not to be punished because we may sometimes be slow learners.* The school analogy I gave you before is still applicable. We keep doing it until we get it right. And as some of you may recall, repeating a grade in school because you didn't pay attention or didn't bother to do your homework isn't very pleasant. So it is with lives on earth.

Yes, karma goes with reincarnation and is the net result of past lives' good or bad deeds. It's something like a profit and loss column that ends up in a given lifetime with a bottom line profit or loss. If a profit, then you can expect that the good net karma will be very helpful in your next life on earth. If a net minus, then you've got more obstacles to overcome in your next dance around the floor. It's really very simple and straightforward. And the interesting, and maybe surprising, thing about it all is that *you yourself are the bookkeeper, not some outsider, not even God Himself.*

You want to know something about earth changes? There will be some pretty drastic ones within the next twenty years or so, not necessarily catastrophic but enough to get your attention. And that is really what they are supposed to do. Why all the terrible killing in Africa and what was Yugoslavia? It shows that too many people still do not know how to handle freedom. They abuse it. They abuse it to wreak vengeance on other people just because they are different. They fail to recognize that there is great strength in diversity—that people are not the product of cookie cutters. People who are still so unenlightened can only remain at peace among themselves under the repressive aegis of a dictatorship. What a shame! It may be that they will end up with such a dictatorship since they have shown that they are not yet able to master the responsibilities that go with freedom. It will be their choice, though not a conscious one.

Happiness

Session 8 · December 2, 1992

I have a great deal to impart to you. Some of it you will not want to hear but it is important to mankind that you listen.

What shall we discuss? Happiness? You had said you were interested in that subject. OK. Happiness is what you make it. Again, like most real things, it comes from within. You can never achieve happiness, even on the earth plane, just by having an abundance of material things. Your son saw that in India where he met a good many very poor people who were nevertheless happy. They were poor materially but rich spiritually. They knew that the material world was a very temporary, and even dangerous, world because it is too easy to become trapped—or maybe lured—into the false belief that it really counts. *Look within yourself for real, lasting, meaningful happiness. No one else can give it to you— but by the same token, no one else can take it away from you. All is encompassed by you!*

You find it hard to believe that, I know. But eventually you will be convinced. You are on the right road and you will get there. But we have plenty of time—since there really isn't any such thing. Ha ha.

As you come to recognize your own divine spark, so you will also recognize that the same divine spark is also present in every other human being, including people you don't like and (this is harder) including people who do bad things in this world. That same divine spark, though perhaps to a lesser degree, is also present in every living being in the universe—after all, they are also part of God's creation. And even inanimate objects have a connection to each of you, because they too are part of God's creation.

You have heard of the Gaia concept—that the earth is a living organism in its own right. Well, it's true but you don't go far enough. The whole universe is a living organism! We are all part and parcel of one another. You wouldn't intentionally cut off your own hand, would you? Well, if you recognize the entire universe as a living organism of which we are all a part, then you will not despoil the earth or any other planets you may encounter, because you will understand that it is like cutting off your own hand.

We are getting into some good stuff here. Someday you may actually publish this material, even though there has already been quite a bit of similar material already published. We'll see whether it is needed when the time comes.

As for personal advice, you need to meditate more regularly and frequently, not just before you contact me but to achieve your own clarity of thought. It also helps to meditate on these messages—I almost called them "teachings" but that sounds a bit stuffy or pompous. Meditating on the messages helps you to internalize them and therefore makes it more likely that you will live them. And as you know, and I regularly repeat, living is what counts; knowing is not enough.

W. G.: After we leave the earth plane, do we go to some other material world and resume lives there on something like another material plane?

Seneca: No. This is the only material plane for you. You keep reincarnating here until you have progressed far enough to be able to proceed further in spirit alone. While other parts of the universe have intelligent life on them, and they are making their own way to the same ultimate end objective, they are not human beings as such. Only here do human beings exist in a material world.

When you advance enough to be able to proceed further as spirit alone, you still have a great deal to accomplish. There are many levels of spirit before union with the Divine—maybe not as many levels as in the Masonic lodges (thirty-three there, I think)—but quite a few. You move up the line as you learn, help others and become increasingly more spiritual. For now, I think that's enough on that subject—just a brief overview to give you some perspective.

The path itself is really rather simple to understand, though much harder to actually follow (let the split infinitive go). But more meditation will make it easier for you to follow it because it will help keep you from being deluded by the charms of the material world to the extent that you forget why you're here and what you are supposed to accomplish. Meditation not only clears your mind but it also helps to clear your body. The serenity that accompanies deep meditation is a wonderful healing and restorative medicine for the stresses that the body inevitably encounters in this life. Try to do it regularly. While this advice is personal to you, it also applies to the rest of mankind as well. The rewards of meditation far outweigh the time and effort involved. So do it!

W. G.: What about the monastic life that many people all over the world adopt in their search for holiness?

Seneca: What is the saying—different strokes for different folks? I myself happen to believe that the challenge is greater in the midst of the material world than it is in a cave or a monastery, so the benefit gained is also greater. It is much harder to live a life of caring and compassion for your fellow creatures, especially people, in the middle of Los Angeles or New York than on a mountain top. Nobody is trying to run over you at eighty miles an hour on a mountain top. But some people are better adapted to the monastic life and that is fine, especially if they also serve as teachers for the rest of you. Living on the mountain top, they are less likely to be led astray and their teachings are therefore less likely to be corrupted. On the other hand, their remoteness from the material world may make their teaching too esoteric and therefore less effective. Your friend, Yeshe, was a beautiful example of one who combined the best of both approaches. He had the holiness of the true monk, together with the wisdom and courage to adapt his teachings to the way of life of the western world and thus have so much more influence.

Native American Tradition

Session 9 · December 4, 1992

What shall we talk about today? You expressed an interest in the Native American tradition, partly because you know that is my background and partly because in at least one prior life it was yours as well. Native American tradition was and is still very nature-oriented. It was a kind of combination of animism and shamanism. They intuitively recognized that spirit was not the sole prerogative of man. They know that animals have spirits, as do all living creatures. To that extent they had a big leg- up on western man, who had come to believe or been led to believe, by misinterpretations of Judeo-Christian traditions, that man was the master of nature, rather than just the steward. They never had much of a theology. They tended more to live their key beliefs rather than philosophize about them. Theology wasn't important to them. Living was. And again, to that extent, they were farther along than western man with his learned dialogs occurring simultaneously with his cruel behavior, especially toward his fellow man whom he has been enjoined to love.

I say to all of you today that theology is not important! Your limited human minds cannot understand complete, unvarnished truth. And you don't need to in order to accomplish the spiritual growth that you are supposed to achieve on the earth plane. Theology has actually turned out to be a terribly divisive force in your world. It has separated you and produced hatred among sects that follow different theologians. That is exactly the wrong direction to go in. Unity is what you are seeking. Unity with each other, and ultimately unity with the Almighty. As I've said before, He doesn't care what name you give Him, and you all have a piece of the truth. But I tell you flatly, it is your human arrogance that lets you imagine that any of you has the complete truth–or some kind of monopoly on it. Eastern religions also have their own shortcomings and their various adherents also have many of these terrible hatreds—witness the Hindus and Moslems in what was India. But at least the eastern religions tend to be more inclusive while your western religions tend to be more exclusive. You can learn much from the eastern religions, but without taking on their own bad habits.

I don't want to leave you with the impression that Native Americans were examples of Rousseau's "noble savage." They weren't. They were all too human. They fought with each other, they committed many atrocities against each other as well as against the white man, and many of their tribal rites of initiation were painful and primitive. *But they did have a more profound understanding of the relationship between man and nature.* They gave thanks to the spirit of the animal that they killed for food, clothing and shelter and they never wasted anything. Now their situation is tragic on reservations. They are a forgotten people and that is wrong. Governments should do something about it but I do not see that happening in any kind of near-term future. For your treatment of Native Americans, particularly repeatedly breaking solemn treaties with them in response to pure greed, Americans must bear a heavy burden of guilt—karma that will require much to compensate for. Again, Americans are not the only ones who have oppressed and exploited native populations but I just don't want you feeling so self-righteous because the U.S. was not a colonial power as such. In your own way you were.

I don't really want to talk about Native American traditions as such. There are plenty of good books on the subject. My focus is on what is needed for spiritual growth and development, regardless of where it originated. In one sense, I am trying to string together for you what I perceive as the best features of the various religious traditions that I may know something about, in order to provide you with guidance for your spiritual life. As your guide, Bill, that is my job. But the same information may be helpful to many others who are also seekers so I attempt to disseminate the guidance for you in a form that may have wider application, if that should later seem to be constructive.

✿✿✿✿

She [referring to a person we had been discussing] has in recent months made more progress in spiritual growth than she had in many years previously. Spiritual growth is also a great aid to self-esteem and it is doing wonders for hers. After all, when you know who you really are, that you have a share in the Godhead if you could only realize it, how can you not have great self-esteem? Of course, I mean self-esteem in the best sense of the word, not to be compared with the cockiness that goes with success in the material world.

You want to know about God? You want me to sound like another theologian? After what I said before? Not a chance. People should not be asking those kinds of questions—e.g., about God's characteristics and attributes and whether male or female (to be facetious). *People should instead focus their attention on what it takes to achieve reunion* with God. *That's the substantive question, and the only one that matters. And that involves living, not talking, philosophizing or knowing!* So keep your eye on the right ball so that you don't strike out and have to keep coming back here until you finally learn what's really important.

I'll finish this little sermon by repeating that *the path is simple but following it truly is hard.* There are too many distractions and diversions—intellectual, financial, emotional. But that is where the self-discipline comes into play. If you can steer clear of the distractions and can remember that this material world is only a way station—and a temporary and maybe illusory one at that—then you can make enormous progress in a single lifetime.

What about those who say, "I like it here on earth. How do I know that the next step will be better?" If you like it that much, of course you can keep coming back again and again. Nobody forces you to move on. You can repeat the third grade indefinitely if you're dumb enough to want to. Only you decide that you want to progress—nobody else. That's your free will in operation again. Have you forgotten that you have it—even if you choose to use it foolishly? But I must point out that next time you come back here, you may come back in a much less enjoyable capacity than this time, but that's your risk to choose. I can also tell you that the next level, when you are able to function as pure spirit, is so much better and richer and more fulfilling that I can hardly find adjectives to describe it. But it's your choice to make.

Seneca Discusses Several Subjects

Session 10 - December 7, 1992

What would you like to talk about tonight? The tragedies that you see on the day's news—Somalia, India–Pakistan, the Israeli-occupied West Bank? *Man's inhumanity to man has a long karmic history behind it.* How it all started I do not know but it has been going on for many hundreds, even thousands of years. It all stems from fear—fear of people who are not just like us. It is an understandable condition but one that must be eradicated before mankind can progress to where it must go in order to escape the cycle of death and rebirth here on earth. *You must look on differences as sources of strength, not as causes for fear, and therefore hatred.* I've said it before but it cannot be repeated too often. When people start paying attention to this very simple truth, then I won't have to keep repeating it so much.

I sometimes think you on earth need some kind of outside threat—like Orson Welles' little green men from Mars—to make you appreciate your common humanity. Race, color, language, ethnic background—all pale into insignificance when confronted by a truly different life form. Can't you understand that what unites you is infinitely more significant than what divides you? Well, you're not going to be seeing any little green men so you have to get to that point all by yourselves. Until you do, there will continue to be much misery in your world—so terrible and unnecessary but of your own doing.

You ask why we do not act to stop this senseless killing. The answer is simple. We are here to guide and help you but we do not interfere in your decision-making or your free will. We will not; we may not. *You on earth make your decisions for good or otherwise—but remember, you must also live with the consequences of those decisions.* The law of karma is real. It is no bogeyman to keep you from misbehaving. It is as straight-forward as Newton's law that every action has an equal and opposite reaction. That's all karma is—the law of cause and effect.

W. G.: How can we overcome these terrible inclinations in our-selves?

Seneca: I would recommend regular meditation, prayer for enlight-enment and compassion, and an awareness of your own behavior and mental attitudes. Then live what you know to be right! Within you all you know what is right. All you have to do is do it! That takes a lot of self-discipline and that is what you all must work on.

✺ ✺ ✺ ✺

I appreciate the fact that you try to stay away from mundane or personal matters when talking with me because you know that my mission is spiritual growth and development. But I am still mindful of your human concerns and intend to continue looking after you in those areas as well. I have been doing that since you were born and I don't intend to abandon you now, especially since we have made this wonderful contact and I can use your consciousness to send my messages to the whole world—or at least to any who will listen. So don't be afraid to ask me about your legitimate human concerns. I don't give out winning lottery numbers but you know better than to ask that kind of nonsense anyhow. Remember that I am your guide and that is a very personal relationship.

What other profound thoughts would you like to hear tonight? Is there any importance to sacrifices, offerings, prostrations or other acts of humility? Not in themselves, but only in that they serve to remind the person making the offering of the great mystery with which he is interacting. It helps to put us in the proper frame of mind. Again, God or Divinity, or the Universe if you prefer, has no need to be "buttered up," but these gestures of respect help to produce in you a suitable awe in the presence of God—and hopefully a reminder that you yourselves partake of that awesome divinity if you can only get past the garbage that obscures that knowledge and its resulting behavior.

How about study? Study will of course help your *intellectual* understanding but it will not by itself do anything for your *spiritual* understanding. Don't misunderstand this to mean that I don't place great value on study and learning. You can't have too much. What I am trying to say is that study and intellectual knowledge are not a substitute for living a path that you know to be right for you. I've said it before and I repeat it—knowledge is splendid but it is not enough. Living your belief system every moment of every day of your life is what counts! In fact, an excessive concentration on study and knowledge can be a trap because it can mislead you into thinking that you have achieved the goal merely because you understand what the goal is. So, as long as you can avoid the trap of intellectual arrogance, the more knowledge you can acquire, the better.

W. G.: My son and I have talked about psychic capabilities and whether it is a diversion from the path to make use of them. What are your thoughts?

Seneca: Psychic capabilities are a natural gift that all mankind possesses but has managed to suppress quite successfully for centuries. Your whole western cultural bias and educational structure have been and still are oriented toward development of the left brain, the logical, analytical half of your brain. So development of psychic skills in the present day is still quite limited in the west but expanding rapidly. The good thing about it is that it reminds you that you are far more than just flesh and blood—that the physical, material world in which you live is only a small piece of reality, rather than the whole of it. That is a most healthy change from the standard views of so many of your scientists and engineers. But the purpose of acquiring psychic skills is to help you progress spiritually, including by helping others.

Since your son has set foot down another path, he is quite right not to be diverted toward the acquisition of psychic skills for their own sake. That would be a waste of his time and energy, and actually detrimental to his search. For you and your wife, it is fine to pursue these skills as you deem appropriate because you know enough already to use them properly—to help others and not for self-aggrandizement. After all, your use of a kind of automatic writing with a computer has made it possible for us to reach this initial stage of communication, where I can send you complete thoughts and sentences, not just laboriously sending you individual letters and words for you to copy slowly by hand. Now there is a psychic skill that is being used to serve a spiritually constructive purpose. So it all comes down to purpose and motive.

By the way, the Mahayana Buddhist tradition that your son finds so appealing is one of the most profound and deeply moving religious traditions. The Boddhisatva concept, in which an enlightened being voluntarily gives up the bliss of Paradise in order to help his less fortunate human brothers and sisters, is a manifestation of love so pure and transcendent that it almost defies description. Not even that great Master, Jesus, remained with his people forever by continually reincarnating here on earth to help mankind achieve spiritual enlightenment. It is a noble tradition and your son will do it proud, once he achieves the necessary self-discipline.

ಞಲ

The Nature of Reality

Session 11 - December 13, 1992

What would you like to discuss today? The nature of reality! That's quite a mouthful. We couldn't begin to cover that in one short session. But I'll try to hit the highlights and maybe we can come back to it at a later time. Reality means many different things to different people. Also, there are many different kinds of reality. For instance, your material world is very real to you and the spirit world is unreal to many. Even to those of you to whom it is real, it still seems to be lacking in substance, like a kind of ghost world. But that isn't really the case, if you will pardon the pun. Is the world of dreams real? Of course, even though that reality disappears when you wake up. The same can be said for the person whom you call insane because he cannot make the transition between another real world of his and your material world that he also shares. *All experience is real. The big secret is that we live on many levels of reality, and somewhat simultaneously.* I say "somewhat" because when you are dreaming, your consciousness is in one reality while your body is in another. But they are not actually competing because in that situation your bodily reality is quiescent. You can't be fully in more than one reality at a time, even though time is still only a human construct.

When you die, you give up your bodily reality but move on to a spirit reality that is far richer and more alive than you could have anticipated while in a material reality. Everything is faster because you are not then hampered by a heavy, lower-vibrational material body. So communication can take place with the speed of thought and travel is like the astral travel that some of you have tried for short trips. You get where you're going mighty fast, don't you? That's what the spirit world—or at least what I'm familiar with—is like. Much more varied, more colorful and without the same kinds of conflicts that you encounter on earth because of your ambitions and competitiveness.

As I have said before, there are also many levels of the spirit world. And the difference between the lower and higher spirit levels is as different as that between your physical life on earth and a life in a lower spirit world.

It is also true that you do create your own reality in accordance with your expectations. If you expect to go to hell, for example, you will enter a corner of a lower spirit world that will reflect your concept of hell back upon you. That is one of my own major complaints about much of western traditional religion—the emphasis on punishment before redemption, and with no redemption for some, usually those with different belief systems. But that's karmic too. It is in your interest to go beyond these archaic and inaccurate representations of afterlife in order to avoid experiencing them, at least temporarily until greater wisdom is gained in the spirit world.

You ask about ultimate reality without quite knowing what you mean. At the same time you know what the answer to that question is. *Ultimate reality is God, by whatever name you care to use, and the ultimate objective of all beings is reunion with Him.* (I use the masculine only because it is easier and "It" has a wrong implication in your language. But of course God has no gender.) You know about Darwin's theory of evolution but you don't know that there is a spiritual form of evolution also. And the spiritual evolution is more important than the physical. The physical is just a way to set the stage (so to speak) for the spiritual.

If you can continue to keep your eye on the main ball, you will gain much progress. *Stay mindful of the fact that life on earth is short and its purpose is spiritual growth and not material aggrandizement.* If you stay mindful of these simple truths and guide your actions in this life accordingly, you can move to your spirit life at a higher level than would otherwise be the case and without some of the painful experiences that are encountered by many because of their belief systems.

You will notice that I am not telling you to totally discard your earlier belief systems, but only to temper them with what you yourselves intuitively and innately know to be true. And, to be blunt about it, we here don't care very much about your professed beliefs. As I've said many time before and will say many times again, what counts is what you do—how you live your lives on earth. Your actions reflect your true belief system, whether you are aware of it or not. The rest is just window-dressing—a hard statement but nonetheless true.

Personal question about your allergies and what you can do to overcome them. Let me think. I'm not a doctor, you know. At the same time you also know that physical ailments of all kinds are the result of psychic difficulties or shortcomings. So what to do? Meditate more often on your allergies and their psychic causes, not your cats. Eventually you will discover what is psychically bothering you and can then take steps to reverse the situation at its causal level. In the meantime, continue with a partially vegetarian diet—to the extent you can—and get out more for exercise. Walk more with your son and get back out on the tennis court. You don't have to be good in order for it to do you a great deal of good. Keep ego and vanity out of the picture.

W.G.: [The personal information above was left in because it might be helpful to others with allergies. Some additional personal information has been deleted here.]

Yes, this recent huge storm in the northeastern United States is not just a fluke, a once-in-a-one-hundred-year-matter. It is part of the earth changes that are beginning to happen and will continue for some time as the planet seeks to purify itself via Mother Nature. Remember, I am a Native American and we have always been very close to Mother Nature. You could see that she is beginning to clean house. It will be costly and painful for many but its ultimate result will be beneficial to this planet that you live on and therefore to those who come after you.

You ask about the Buddhist concept of Emptiness because of your son's interest. I cannot tell you much because I am not a scholar or a philosopher. To me, however, reunion with the Divine is the greatest fullness imaginable. Perhaps the term has a special meaning that I do not understand. If it means the emptying out of the human ego to make room for the divine spark to flourish, then I would certainly agree with that as a desirable course of action. But you must look elsewhere for scholarly treatment of this subject.

I am glad you came to visit today. I enjoy these conversations and I am pleased that you are sincerely seeking to know how to achieve spiritual growth. *Pass on hope to all because ultimately all mankind will achieve the desired growth.* Keep doing the best that you can.

The Historical Jesus

Session 12 - December 20, 1992

I know that your conscious mind urges you to reject my reality. That will be the case frequently but it will become less troublesome to you as we continue to get better acquainted and you learn from experience to believe me and trust me. I am not upset by your occasional skepticism about me so don't you worry about it.

✦ ✦ ✦ ✦

On a broader basis, you must recognize that people who seem less fortunate, in terms of the goods of this material world, may actually be making considerably more spiritual progress in this lifetime than many who are rich and successful. I don't mean to suggest that there is inherent virtue in poverty and suffering but they can often go a long way toward affording clear thinking to those who might otherwise be caught up in the trap of material success. Pain, grief and trouble can serve a constructive purpose if they are allowed to—that is, by causing you to refocus your attention on the enduring values rather than ephemeral and transient pleasures.

✦ ✦ ✦ ✦

You have just read about the historical Jesus and are interested in what is accurate about him. He was a real person and, as indicated in various writings, he spent time in the Orient during his lost years. His message was one of love and compassion, of forgiveness and sharing. He did sacrifice his life for those he loved—mankind as a whole. He did not claim to be divine, beyond the point that we all are divine. His message was so different from the conventional wisdom, especially in a small nation under the Roman heel, that he was regarded by many as a rebel and a threat. He would also be so regarded today if he were on earth now! Much of the theological trappings surrounding this wonderful person came later. Jesus readily understood that we are all brothers and his "I am the Way" meant, not that he be worshipped, but that his example be followed. The exclusivity and anathemas came later. Remember, Jesus was also a heretic in the Jewish tradition since that tradition is also one of exclusivity, like Christianity—insiders and outsiders. With Jesus there were no outsiders. In that respect he embodies the belief in universal love and brotherhood that you should all be seeking today throughout the world—but aren't.

What is the best way to try to get others to recognize your universal brotherhood? By living that way. I think it's fine to talk about it and maybe raise consciousness levels in some people—but you must also serve as an example of what you are professing. As you have already heard many times, and will continue to hear because it simply cannot be said too often, it's how you live that counts toward spiritual growth. Also, being an example to others is infinitely more impressive than just talking about it. Your being an example will have a much broader and deeper effect upon the people you come into contact with. Besides, in your society it's awkward to talk along these lines but you can always remain silent and let your actions witness to your beliefs.

W.G.: The following thought came after Seneca had finished, almost as an afterthought:

Explore various religious traditions and accept from each that which your heart, not your mind, tells you is true.

Spirituality in America

Session 13 - January 1, 1993

I am glad that you and your son went to the Moon Ceremony last Tuesday. You found it quite impressive and yet it is but a small indication of the riches of the Native American tradition. The respect for the earth and all its creatures is nothing new or surprising to you, but it was still moving. I hope your wife and Paula will go with you to the next one on February 24. They will find it inspirational and spiritually rewarding and you will all feel good at the end of the ceremony. It's too bad that people don't routinely use a ceremony such as this, or an alternative one, to rid themselves of the negativity that inevitably builds up over time in your material world. Don't forget to bring food and drink next time, and maybe your drum too. Also at some time your idea of reading, or better still telling, the story of Jumping Mouse to the group would be well received for it is a beautiful story with much spiritual content in it.

W. G.: Some personal advice has been deleted here, but Seneca then continued with this important thought:

...but don't lose sight of your primary objective in this life, which is not simply generosity, commendable though that be, but spiritual growth. Remember, you can do both.

I will not nag you about exercise because you know what you need to do but it is your choice to make, and your consequences to bear. I just don't want to lose you before we have completed a great deal more work. We can do it, you know; our connection is good and will get even better as time goes on and we become better acquainted with each other. Then the thoughts will flow so much faster than you can type them that I'm not sure how we will record them. But we'll find a way, you can be sure. In the meantime, please take care of your body. You don't have to become a vegetarian like your son but you do need to treat your body with greater respect—and by that I mean exercise. Go back to your tennis—you really enjoyed it and it will be good for you if done on a regular basis.

W.G.:[The above advice, though personal, was left in because there are probably many other readers who dislike exercise as much as I do and who might be helped by these thoughts.]

✧ ✧ ✧ ✧

What about spirituality in America? As we approach the year 2000 it will continue to grow. People all over the world, but especially in the U.S., are seeking spiritual roots, a spiritual foundation for their lives. In some respects the economic difficulties of the past few years have not been without their reward because they have helped transfer the focus of people's attention from the selfish material world to the more lasting and rewarding spiritual world.

Although the economy will improve, the seeds of spiritual growth have been sown much more widely than had previously been the case — and they will grow. With all their faults, and you have many, the American people as a whole are still the most generous and idealistic in the world.

How can you do the most in your remaining years here to help others grow spiritually? Your communications with me are a major part of your present mission. When the time is ripe, you will disseminate them more widely—and people who either would not have seen them or perhaps would have scoffed, will believe that there is infinitely more to life than this little cramped corner of the universe and this single learning experience over sixty, seventy or eighty years. *Your people are getting ready for the new era that commences with the year 2000 and you will see some surprising things happening very early in the next century. Good things, that is.* I am not talking here about any earth changes which, as Soaring Eagle expressed it at the Moon Ceremony, is merely Mother Earth purifying herself.

Predictions

W. G.: It is good to be with you again, my friend and mentor.

Seneca: Thank you. I have been waiting for you to visit again. You would like to talk about the Moon Ceremony you attended in Fort Myers?

W. G.: Not especially. This evening I am happy just being in your company and feeling your warmth and compassion and love. If there are any messages you would like to pass on to me, I will be happy to receive them but I am just seeking your nearness tonight.

Seneca: Good. I thank you and that desire on your part will strengthen our connection and make it easier for us to communicate in the future. The more we can get onto the same vibration pattern, the easier and speedier will be our communication. Eventually it will become faster than thought and you will have to pause to write it down. I too enjoy the pleasure of our connection. Even on this plane I find it soothing.

We don't have to talk every time. Let's just open ourselves up to each other and experience, at least temporarily, that wonderful feeling of unity—of at-one-ment, that you have read about and that all humanity seeks. It is a feeling of spiritual peace, rest, serenity and relaxation. It is accompanied by a knowledge of unconditional love. It is a kind of meditative state that you feel you could remain in for a very long time. And you could.

❄ ❄ ❄

Predictions are not ironclad, but really high probabilities based on a continuation of events along the same general path that they are on. But, thanks to free will, those probable results can be changed by a person's actions—for better or worse. *Always remember that you are the masters of your own fate, and not just victims.* I am pleased that you recognized the lesson inherent in my prediction because that same lesson applies across the board, to use an expression of yours.

The origin of creation? No, I'm not prepared to go into that information, at least at this time. That's more for the cosmologist or religious scholar, which you aren't, and it's not really important to what your task is on earth during this lifetime. Don't let your intellectual curiosity, of which you have a large supply, interfere with your prime mission—i.e., the achievement of spiritual development and, maybe, the communication to the outside world of some of my comments and recommendations on achieving such growth. Intellect is fine as far as it goes but it simply doesn't go far enough. The head is no substitute for the heart. To use the Native American tradition here, the head may be cold Wisdom from the North but the heart reflects the golden Illumination of the East. The East, the heart, has more power than the North, the head. Keep your intellect, which is after all a product of your conscious mind, in check as we go about our lessons and as you go about your daily life. It's important to you but give it only its proper place in your priority system.

❄ ❄ ❄ ❄

This was just a friendly visit this evening, rather than a meeting to receive a lecture or a sermon. We will have many, many opportunities for me to pass along my messages and observations to you, so don't worry about our having periodic personal and private get-togethers like tonight. We will always be in close touch but it is you who must initiate the contact with me, rather than vice versa.

࿇

Another Variety of Subject

Session 15 · February 2, 1993

I understand your periods of doubt but you must, and you will, learn that I will never lie to you about anything. Your explanation for my apparent error is correct. We here have no concept of time and therefore we have difficulty predicting events with accuracy. However, what I told you is still true.

✿ ✿ ✿ ✿

When I tell you something will happen, don't make the mistake again of assuming that it will happen in the time frame you want— or you will be subject to additional disappointments.

I'm glad you figured out for yourself the reasons for my apparent error—or your mistaken assumption—so that I did not have to enlighten you on something you already know. As we spend more time together, and I hope we will do that, you will come to know me better and trust me more. I was going to say "maybe even fully" but you still don't trust Jesus Christ *fully*—and you've known him a lot longer than me. Don't be upset or discouraged by these "lapses of faith" (if you will), especially with me. You must continue to search for verification of things I tell you and that is a healthy and commendable approach. So don't scold yourself for having doubted. All saints, or enlightened beings, have at some time in their lives on earth experienced doubt about whether they were on the right track. You're allowed to do that too, especially since you have a long way to go before reaching "sainthood." Yes, I do have a sense of humor, as you know, even though my appearance is that of a stern, severe high chief and elder to a young apprentice.

What would you like to talk about today? No, I don't want to talk about imminent earth changes because there are already enough alarmists around on that subject. When they happen, they will be severe but you should regard them as the earth mother purifying herself after a lengthy orgy.

I'm not terribly interested in your political conditions, either in the U.S. or the world at large, unless they have a bearing on spiritual growth and development. Everything of course has some bearing but I mean here a rather direct bearing. I am encouraged by the expectation that moral values and human rights considerations will play more of a role in the foreign policy of the U.S. than the *realpolitik* that has prevailed for the past twelve years. You like that fancy word *realpolitik*—well, it's really yours. No Native American ever used it!

I repeat again that much of the turmoil in the world today stems from ancient ethnic and religious hatreds that were suppressed under authoritarian governments and now are coming to the fore. Alas, that so many nations and groups can't handle freedom responsibly. But that has long-standing karmic roots that must be worked out. That doesn't lessen the tragedy you see all over the world, though, but it may help you to understand it and put it into a little better perspective.

❀ ❀ ❀ ❀

The Native American tradition that teaches "Walk as you talk" is a very pithy and catchy way of expressing what I have been saying about living your beliefs. It is a wisdom that my people have known for a long, long time—but they haven't always followed it either. Still it is gratifying to see the phrase reappear in today's world among young people.

Don't ask me about questions that even border on the theological because I won't get involved in them. As I have told you before, theologians in their intellectual arrogance and determination to understand that which man cannot have been a terribly divisive influence in the history of your world. These theologians have in many instances been men of honor and virtue themselves but their belief that they can understand the Mind of God represents an intellectual arrogance that is incomprehensible to me. So we will stick to what I would call practical guides to behavior on this earth during this lifetime. And the guides are really quite simple. You've heard them before and they form the common core of most great religious traditions. All you have to do is live them—that's the hard part. But if you work at it, you would be surprised at how much easier it becomes and also by the serenity of spirit that accompanies it. Try it and see for yourself.

The Spokes of a Wheel

Session 16 - February 17, 1993

Come sit on this bench with me and enjoy the beautiful day here in your secret garden. I am glad that you have not forgotten me in your busy daily life. That's not a complaint but only a kind of reminder—don't let the pressures of your daily life distract you from the things that are more important, the eternal truths that you are supposed to learn here and act upon here.

❉ ❉ ❉ ❉

Mr. Clinton's election as President will be a good thing for the nation and the world too. He *really* will try—and with considerable though not complete success—to face up to the economic problems that have plagued the U.S. for so many years. You still represent a set of divided special interests, each seeking its own well-being at the expense of the rest, but you must share in the hardships before you can solve your problems. You have all been stealing from your grandchildren because that is what these kinds of deficits mean. You have been living beyond your means as a nation for some time now and the time has come to begin to pay off some of the bills you have accumulated, rather than leaving them for your children and grandchildren. The people will participate in "shared sacrifice" as long as they perceive it to be fair—that the pain is fairly distributed—but not if everyone else is still attempting to feed at the public trough as before. Politicians, including the Clinton people, tend to underestimate the basic resilience, intelligence and strength of the American people.

Enough of that. I am pleased to see that you have started reading *The Phoenix Returns*, the book you bought in Sarasota. I steered you to it when you were there. You will find in it many of the same truths that I am trying to impart to you, about the unity of all religious traditions in leading to the same goal, although by different paths. I particularly like the "spokes of a wheel" analogy but I wish the various spokes could stay on their own path to the hub instead of trying to take over the entire wheel—thereby messing it up. The wheel also reflects the circle of eternity of the Native American tradition, the medicine wheel. I simply cannot understand the religious hatreds that permeate the world today when the various traditions have so much in common—so much more that unites them than divides them. I weep when I see so much of what is happening but then I remember that, ultimately, you all will transcend these limitations and will learn what you must to escape the cycle of rebirth here on earth.

❀ ❀ ❀

Walk your talk! That summarizes the way to spiritual advancement in a very simple fashion. If you actually live what you profess to believe, you will be fine. (I am of course assuming that you profess to believe in good things.) If you don't live what you profess to believe, then it follows that you don't truly believe them. Or you relegate them to some other aspect of your life, like Sunday morning if you're a Christian. And it follows still that you don't really believe what you are professing to believe. Be honest with yourselves! Otherwise you will continue to delude yourselves and will live on two inconsistent levels—the level of action and that of belief. And you will get nowhere in your spiritual quest. *Self-delusion stemming from ego interference is likely to be your greatest enemy—also your most subtle and sly one. So walk your talk or you are wasting the opportunities that this lifetime affords you for spiritual advancement.* Never forget—if you don't get it right, you have to keep coming back here until you do!

What about the coming millennium? Will there be major events associated with the arrival of the second millennium (approximately) after the birth of Jesus Christ? Yes, there will for it is true that this will be a time of transition. I can't say whether you are approaching the biblical "last days" but you are definitely approaching a time of transition. Though all periods of change are traumatic, particularly for those who fear change, be assured that the ultimate results of this period of transition will be good for mankind, though not without some grief and suffering. Purification, whether of man or nature, necessarily involves some "discomfort." With the earth it takes the form of earth changes, some of which will seem cataclysmic to people. In the case of people, it means some suffering and deprivation—but that can be turned into a positive force by allowing these material difficulties to focus your attention on the Eternal, instead of the ephemeral!

God

We actually started our conversation before you even sat down at the computer. It will continue to get easier to make the connection as you do it more often. You asked me to tell you about God and I replied that Yogananda is correct, that the best way to get to know God is meditate, meditate, meditate! So we can take it from there. I cannot tell you a great deal about God myself because, after all, I am not God, nor even a fully realized soul, but rather just a worker-bee helper.

W. G.: I think you're being unduly modest but I also think you're telling me that God cannot be described with anything remotely resembling accuracy—that He/She must be experienced in order to be truly known. I accept that.

Seneca: Good. Then you won't try to make me into a kind of theologian or religious scholar—which I'm not. They can fulfill a useful role but all too often they focus on the differences between religions rather than on their common bond.

I can see that you want me to talk about anything I want tonight. No mundane questions. Good. Your son has the right idea in thinking that it is practice that counts more than scholarship, although there is nothing wrong with scholarship per se. However, unless scholarship is accompanied by practice, there is a very serious risk that ego will find its way into the picture and the scholar will become so puffed up with all his so-called knowledge that he loses sight of the purpose of the whole effort.

I know you have started to read Yogananda's lectures on Man's Eternal Quest and *I have no hesitation in confirming that man's eternal quest is to find his way back to God, his Creator, and to reunion with Him.* (The Him/Her earlier was just my idea of a joke since Spirit is of course without gender.) *It includes recognition of our own share in that divinity and of our connectedness with all the rest of creation.* When we finally begin to appreciate and accept the reality of that connectedness, it makes an enormous difference in how we approach all our subsequent relationships, with people, animals, other living creatures and the earth itself. Spend time meditating on and marveling at this connectedness and it will change your life. For then, everything you say or think or do, you do to yourself.

⋘⋙

Good Friday and Easter

Session 19 - April 10, 1993

W. G.: I really am pleased about being able to make the connection with you much more easily now, without having to go through a prescribed meditation routine. I know you're here even before I sit down at the computer to type our conversation.

Seneca: As I told you, the connection will get easier and easier as you use it more frequently. Yes, I know that you want to ask about your dear friends, the Harpers, including why they are having such difficulties in their lives. It is of course karmic in nature and they are both doing a remarkable job of repairing past mistakes in previous lives. The Harpers' faith and trust will be rewarded, hopefully before too much longer. Think of the story of Job in the Bible—how he continued to love and trust God even while undergoing all kinds of afflictions as a test, and how he was ultimately rewarded manifold later. I think that is what will also happen here. Both Jim and Alice have persevered in the face of adversity and good people do get rewarded for such actions. I also think that when they emerge into the light at the end of the tunnel, Jim's health will also improve.

You said it well when you told Alice that there would be no Easter without a Good Friday first. I am not sure right now whether that was strictly an insight of yours or whether it resulted from guidance. In either case, I am pleased that you were able to make the connection between the two events and the human condition. I hate to disabuse you of it, though I think you already know, *but personal happiness is not the purpose of earthly existence.* If you can achieve it while still accomplishing your real purpose here on earth, fine! But that's not why you're here. Keep in mind that some of the greatest contributors to spiritual development and an awareness of God had short, difficult and personally unhappy lives here.

Oh, you have remembered that you should ask me where I come from—to be sure that I am really one of the "good guys." Fair enough. I do come from the holy realm of our lord and master, Jesus Christ. And, like Alice's Hindu guide, I have no difficulty saying that as a Native American. As he told Alice, there are many paths to God and they all lead to Him unless they become perverted on the way by ego or power or something equivalent that pulls them off the path. And Jesus Christ, who is known by other names elsewhere, is the chairman of the board or the president of the university, of which all the religious bodies are individual colleges. Don't worry so much about names. It doesn't really matter whether you talk about the Christ Consciousness or the Great Spirit so long as you follow the teachings.

Keep in mind also that legends do not simply appear out of the air. They may become embellished over the centuries but there is an element of reality underlying them. So it is with the legend of the Pale Prophet in *The Phoenix Returns*. Since God does not confine himself to this small planet when he has all of Creation to love and care for, how could you possibly think that He could confine Himself to a small, weak tribe in the middle of the deserts of the Middle East—i.e., Palestine. When you stand back and think about it without either human arrogance or religious chauvinism, you can readily appreciate how ridiculous the notion is.

From our vantage point here, we have much better perspective and you can gain it too. Listen to me, keep writing our conversations down, and when the time is ripe, I may ask you to add my comments to those of others who have already sent messages to the world through other channels. We all try to send the same basic message but it can get garbled somewhat both by our lack of complete clarity on this end and by our channels filtering it through their own consciousness and thought processes. You are trying to set down what I am telling you with as much accuracy as you can and, on the whole, you are doing a good job. Sometimes, however, ideas that I may try to convey are extremely difficult to translate into human language and to filter successfully though your human mind. But that is not intended as a criticism of you, just an acknowledgment of a limitation inherent in this kind of communication. But so far so good.

May you and your family have a Happy Easter tomorrow and celebrate the unconditional love and acceptance that God has for each and every one of his children—for every bit of His creation, as a matter of fact. You have briefly experienced that indescribable feeling on occasions, particularly when meditating. It is real and there is nothing else like it in the universe. And you all can experience it always and completely! Once you truly understand and believe this, and experience it, you have taken a major step toward what some call self-realization, others call reunion with our Father, and still others call returning home. I'm sure there are many other names that can and have been given to this wonderful experience but again it's the experience that counts, not the name someone may choose to give it.

Yes, major changes are coming. The world as a whole is also approaching its "Good Friday" as a prelude to its own "Easter" and you can see the signs amidst the hatreds and turmoil that exist all over, including your United States. Don't become complacent about your own country, which I know you love, because we see some of the same attitudes here, perhaps in miniature, that we see throughout the world. And you yourself, although you try, are not completely immune to some of these attitudes.

I am not a predictor of doom and gloom. On the contrary, I think the human race has a magnificent future in store for it—when it grows up and starts to realize its full potential. Humans talk about being God's children but they don't really believe it or act like it in most cases. When that message finally sinks in, quite literally, the changes in human behavior that will occur will amaze you. By then, however, you will be here with us and therefore very little that goes on with humanity will amaze you.

Morality

Session 20 - April 17, 1993

I know you worry about whether I really have a lot to tell you but I do, and I will. It is not only for your good but for the good of all human-kind—that is, if they pay any attention to what I pass on to you.

Today I would like to talk about what you would call morality. I know that humans think of it as dealing with certain categories of behavior, like sex outside of marriage or financial dishonesty. Well, those are far too limited a scope for what we call morality here. *Morality here encompasses the whole range of human behavior, including that toward all other beings as well as toward the physical planet Earth—what you would call the environment. It applies to everything you do or say or think.*

There isn't any written rule book that I know of that attempts to take each possible human act, word and thought and determine whether it is moral or not. Even if there were such a code, you would still need a room full of law books to interpret and apply it to the infinity of circum-stances that you must deal with. And morality is affected by the applicable circumstances. This is an important factor that you must take into account in attempting to categorize your own deeds, words and thoughts. I say it that way because each of you has the duty to so categorize each of his or her own deeds, words and thoughts—*but not anyone else's.*

Your purpose here does not include judging your fellow man, at least until you get summoned for jury duty and then you have a civil duty to do so. Otherwise, no. I grant you that it may seem to be "fun" to judge others and it can sometimes make you feel quite smug, but you do not gain spiritually by doing so. Certainly you want to help others achieve spiritual growth because of your universal connectedness but your role as judge should be limited to yourself. And I mean only yourself, not your parents, spouse or children either.

For those of you who like to go around feeling "holier than thou," this injunction will come as a bit of a blow to their self-esteem but that kind of practice is not really an example of healthy self-esteem but rather an exercise in ego, and therefore an obstacle to spiritual growth.

You are your own ultimate judge. You alone know what was in your heart (notice I say "heart," not "mind") when you did or said or thought something. You know what your intentions were—and that is how you will evaluate the morality of your deed/word/ thought. As you become more enlightened (I like that term because of its root in "light"), you will become increasingly more aware of the true scope of what morality means and what it encompasses. *It has little to do with what books you read and what movies you see. But it has everything to do with how you live your life on this earth, for everything you say, do or think is either moral or immoral, depending on the circumstances.* As a simple example, if you kill an animal for food, as my ancestors in the New World did, that is a moral act but if you kill an animal for sport, that is an immoral act. That one is easy but it gets much harder as the circumstances become more complex. And in the last analysis, you alone are the judge—of yourself, but only of yourself.

As in so many areas, the biggest obstacle to spiritual growth is ego, and one of the strongest ego drives is the drive for power over others. To be aware of this gives you a big leg up on avoiding this trap. The drive for power, and it takes many forms from the obvious to the very subtle, is a characteristic that is inherent in human ego so you can't simply ignore it and hope it will go away. You must be consciously aware of it so that you can deliberately suppress it. And, in the vernacular, "that ain't easy." But you must make a valiant effort to do so if you wish to make spiritual progress and eventually end the circle of mandatory reincarnation and find your true home.

On the subject of prayer, there is nothing I need to add to the beautiful words and thoughts of Paramahamsaji [Paramahamsa Yogananda] on this subject that you have just read. God your Father listens to you when you speak to him with sincerity and vigor as His son or daughter, and especially so when your prayer is for the benefit of others and untainted by ego. I also like the little phrase that I picked up from your own thoughts—that you read somewhere: "Work as if everything depended on you, and pray as if everything depended on God." You were also being guided several years ago when you got a message that told you that "prayer is the most powerful force in the universe." It was true then and of course it still is. You humans don't use it right—you don't use it enough and you don't use it for the right objectives. It's something for all of you to keep working on—you too, Bill.

Keep seeking, keep working, and eventually you will be able to experience at will that indescribable feeling of total and unconditional love and acceptance, and the warmth that accompanies it, that you have felt so far on only a few brief occasions. You were experiencing communion with God and there is no other experience in the universe that remotely resembles it. Having had such an experience, even if only for a moment, there is no possible way that you can ever again doubt God's love for you as a father for a son—much less his very existence or the eternal nature of your spirit. That knowledge—and it is *knowledge* and not just belief—can carry you easily though any trials and tribulations that you may encounter in an earthly life. It's a wonderful realization, isn't it? And you wondered whether I would have enough to pass along to you. Well, I've just started, so stay in touch.

Attending Church

Session 21 - April 18, 1993

You should not feel uncomfortable when you go to church. You are not being a hypocrite even though you no longer accept all the dogma that is taught by the Catholic Church. After all, you still recognize Jesus as the embodiment of the Christ Consciousness and the "president of the university" that I referred to before. As long as you derive spiritual uplift from attendance, continue to go; it gives you that much additional time to seek communion with God. And He is the same One for everybody regardless of what names we use in different parts of the world or in different houses of worship in any one part of the world. Since you understand this (and you always have), you can happily commune with God in any house of worship without feeling that you are being hypocritical because you do not accept the divisiveness of their various dogmatic teachings.

Those who are genuinely of God you will recognize, almost right away. And those who pretend to be of God but are in reality slaves to their own egos and lust for power you will also recognize, even though it might take a little longer to see through the facade. You are well served in the priests at St. Joseph Church. Father John and Father Richard are both men of genuine faith and compassion; their faith may be a bit narrow from a cosmic standpoint but they seek to do good for all people, not just baptized Roman Catholics. That is the true test—to have love and compassion for all humanity, not just those who are members of your "club."

Meditate more often, and not just by communicating with me. Meditation itself is greatly rewarding for it is the path to the knowledge of God. *It is in deep meditation that we experience God, as you have done for a few brief moments. But when you have done so, you are a different person. Never again will you doubt either His existence or His unconditional love for you as an individual soul.* Having experienced communion with Him, however briefly, you no longer have to have faith and believe. As I said to you yesterday, now you *KNOW*.

✿ ✿ ✿ ✿

At this stage of human history, the number of people who can be called seekers after God is much smaller than we here would wish. People are too preoccupied with the transient elements of life in this world, as if that were all there is, rather than just a temporary, passing fancy. But that will change in the not too distant future as popular culture in this country and elsewhere in the world turns back to the permanent and unchanging—namely, God.

I am glad that you were able to get your computer working so that we could have this meeting tonight. Did I give you the idea about changing back to System 7? No, I didn't. The idea was entirely yours. Don't assume that everything you do right or smart is "guided." You do have some good ideas entirely on your own—but continue to stay open to guidance because with it you can accomplish so much more than you can when acting completely on your own. That advice applies not only to your spiritual endeavors but also to your activities in the mundane world. I will try to provide guidance for you there as well.

I must admit that, while it is a joy to be free of the weight and confinement of a human body, I do occasionally miss some of the sensations that you still experience. For example, when you were drinking your root beer just now, I could almost taste it and I was sorry I couldn't. However, on balance, I have the better of the situation here than you do there. Before too long, you will see, when you join me on this side. I don't mean to scare you by implying that you are going to leave your earthly body very soon. I don't happen to know when that will be, I don't want to know, and if I did know, I wouldn't tell you anyhow. That knowledge would not be constructive for you to know—that's why God set it up that way.

≈≈

Death

Tonight I would like to talk about death. It is usually such a frightening topic for humans because they think all too often that their whole existence is wrapped up in this weak and temporary human body. But of course, as you know, that simply isn't so. In many respects, and for many people, death is actually a release from the burdens of life in the material world. And believe me, there are many heavy burdens that go with life in the material world. As a time of training and testing, you would not expect it to be easy. If it were, there would be no point in it.

Man has become so caught up in the attractions of the material world that he has forgotten his true and permanent home. He now must gradually (in most cases) make his way back—and that takes time (as you know it) and some learning experiences that may well be painful. *You must learn that your life on earth is a transient thing when measured against the immortality of your soul and that your purpose here is to learn to come closer to your Creator and Father, not to gain money, power and fame.* You would laugh if you truly appreciated how fleeting those "important" things of earth actually are. But you must learn to give them up willingly as you become more aware of their illusory nature. I don't for a moment suggest that it is easy to do so, especially when everyone around you is so preoccupied with achieving those things.

When you die bodily, you gain an enormous freedom from the burdens of the body. That includes health problems, both physical and mental, and the limitations of the human body—for example, you can't go from one place to another in the blink of an eye merely by thinking yourself there. It is true that you lose the physical sensations and you will sometimes miss them, as I did last night when I wished I could taste your root beer. On this side, you also become aware of whatever unfinished business you still have to deal with back on earth before you can finally end the cycle of rebirth. But when you are reborn, you forget why you chose the parents you did and you must learn that anew during your earthly lifetime in order to gain the spiritual advancement that you seek from it. Be encouraged, though; *everyone eventually makes it home. Some just take longer than others.* That should give you hope and encourage you to persist but don't let it become a vehicle for complacency or else you will condemn yourself to a long and painful process that is quite unnecessary.

Death is not something to be feared. It would be if that were the end of your existence but it is merely an interlude in which you can take stock of your situation, examine your progress and decide what you need to accomplish or correct in your next life on earth. You had come across a term that I like very much—you had heard death referred to as "God's other door." And that is exactly what it is—a door into another stage of consciousness but one in which your spirit or soul is vibrantly alive.

I need not tell you, however, that you do not do someone a favor by killing him or her. Every person must deal with his or her karma that has been generated here on earth and it must also be dealt with here. Therefore, if you cut short a person's life on earth, you may be forcing that person to return an additional time to complete the unfinished business that you prevented from happening. You yourself will thus acquire negative karma that you must later deal with. Be aware that, at some level of being, everyone determines the time of his or her death. *What you call chance is really the subtle interplay of causal forces too complex for human understanding. But understand that all events are purposeful, even those that are painful or horrendous.* You collectively have caused whatever it is, for this material world may have elements of an illusion about it but this material world is not a random happening. Your heavenly Father does a better job of creation than that!

If you ask me about what to do with terminally ill patients, I cannot give you categorical answers. I think that what you call "mercy killing," even with the best of intentions, deprives the other person of his God-given right to decide when to die—as we all do at some level of our being. By the same token, keeping a body alive through technology when there is no realistic hope of recovery does likewise—it traps the soul in a body from which it wishes to be free. That isn't a very clear-cut answer but it's the best I can do. The karmic consequences of your role in any of these activities will be determined by your intentions more than anything else, so keep that in mind if you are ever called upon to make any of these difficult decisions.

༄༅

The Environment and Levels of Consciousness

Session 23 - April 21, 1993

Welcome back. Tonight I would like to talk about wildlife and the ecosystem of which you are a part. After much too long a time you people have finally become at least mildly concerned about the ecosystem of which you are a part. You call it the environment but it is actually broader and more fundamental than that. But better late then never. It means that throughout the world, not just in the United States, people have a lot of work to clean up the mess made by generations of their forebears—actually not so many generations since the terrible pollution that I am talking about is the result of only a few generations of man, essentially since the industrial revolution. But the amount of damage done to your ecosystem is incalculable. No, it's not too late to fix it but it will require what amounts to heroic effort, and some sacrifice, in order to do so—and it will take a lot of time. However, if you want your progeny to be able to survive on this earth, or do better than merely survive, then you had better get started. The alternative is that the earth will purify herself—and by means that you will find ranging all the way from highly unpleasant to catastrophic, at least from your point of view.

From the standpoint of the Earth (now capitalized, you will notice), she has already been more than patient with you, treating you like naughty but lovable children and hoping that you will clean up your act—literally. But as I said, her patience is wearing thin and you can expect major repercussions if you continue to do little more than talk about cleaning up your environment.

I don't want to sound threatening because I know how humans of all times and places react negatively to threats. But I must, in good conscience, alert you to the dangers that you face if you continue along your present course unabated. After all, you wouldn't call it a threat if you shouted at a little child that was getting very close to the edge of a cliff, would you?

Enough on that subject. Now let's talk about some of the aspects of life, since we talked a little bit about death in our last conversation. *Life is lived by you on many levels, simultaneously.* I don't want to get caught up in nomenclature but there is a Christ Consciousness level, a spirit level, a superconscious level, a dream level, a material level and something approximating an animal needs level. They are like a TV set with numerous channels broadcasting at once. However, it is up to you to decide which channel you tune into at any given time. And some channels—the higher level ones—are much harder to tune into than others. You have to learn how to tune in to those; it doesn't just happen by itself, at least not in the usual case.

You already know that the material world is only a world of vibrations, temporary in nature, regardless of how solid everything looks and feels to you. You also know that your soul is eternal—dare I say "a chip off the old God-block?" So those levels of consciousness from the spirit level on up are real and permanent—they represent your true identity, not the various bodily personalities that you pass through on your path home. As for the superconscious level, it is a kind of bridge between the temporary and permanent; it gives you temporary access to the real and permanent but that access is brief and intermittent.

Train yourself to focus more heavily on the higher levels and forego the temptations of ego and worldly power. Each of us faces those same temptations that Jesus faced during his forty days in the wilderness— and successfully resisted. We can do likewise, but not easily or without some training to recognize what is truly important. Once you come to that realization, it becomes much easier to focus your attention and efforts where they count, although even then we occasionally backslide. If we didn't we wouldn't need to be here still. We would already have completed our cycle of lives on earth. So don't be too hard on yourselves for being less than perfect while at the same time striving toward that perfection.

You cannot imagine how patient and tolerant God is of our shortcomings. Always remember that each and every one of you is His child whom he loves unconditionally. That remains true even when we do stupid and hurtful things to ourselves and each other and all the rest of creation. *God does not sit in judgment on us; His love for us overflows too much for that. Each of us is his or her own judge.* We know what we have done or failed to do and what is in our hearts, even though we sometimes try to fool ourselves but can't. We evaluate our performance in each life against God's standards and we can then determine whether, in a given lifetime, we have made spiritual progress, stood still or retrogressed. We can then give ourselves marching orders for the next life in the material world—marching orders that we totally forget at the moment of birth, if not before.

So celebrate life and recognize that death is only an illusion. Make it joyful, make it holy, make it loving and make it compassionate toward all of creation. Then you will know that you are on the path toward your Father and that you are walking in the right direction.

Money

Session 24 - April 25, 1993

Today's lecture, students, will be on . . . money. I can see you thinking that's a surprising subject for me. But it represents an important obstacle, or hurdle, in your path back to your Father. I don't mean by that that money is in itself harmful or undesirable. What I mean is that the obsession with material wealth that afflicts too many humans diverts them from the right path and causes them to do things that result in levels of bad karma that can only be wiped out by numerous subsequent lives and sufferings. I can assure you that it just isn't worth it!

All too often money is only another name for power over others. And that desire is perhaps the most dangerous and insidious of all. *Power is the ultimate temptation, and the one that must be resisted at all costs.* It is a trap that is incredibly easy to fall into and nearly impossible to escape from later. Once again, I am not saying that exercising power over others is *per se* bad. It's not. There must be leaders in any society and to be one is not detrimental to one's spiritual growth. The dangerous elements are (1) a desire for power over others so that you can control and dominate what would otherwise be their free exercise of will and (2) the abuse of power that has come to you legitimately and properly. Unfortunately, there seems to be some inbred tendency in humans to want to dominate others. I don't know whether it might be a carry-over from the animal kingdom, with its dominant male leader of the pack, but it is something you must guard against at all times. You will also note that the best leaders in all ages were those whose followers trusted and respected them and followed them willingly.

If you acquire money, which is clearly a form of power though not the essence of power itself, it is important to your future development how you use that money. Perhaps it's really more important how you *don't* use that money. You can do a lot of good with it but if you use it to aggrandize your own ego, or to exercise abusive power over another, then you can wipe out all the good results from your affirmative use of money and wind up worse off, spiritually, than where you started. I hope that, when the right time comes, this small item of advice will be widely disseminated. It cannot be overemphasized.

One possible advantage to having money, if legitimately acquired and not abused, is the realization that all the material comforts and toys that you can buy will not fill the spiritual void in your heart. You will recognize, sooner than the poor man who may think his unhappiness is due to a lack of material resources, that the void can only be filled spiritually, by proceeding on the path back home to your Father. I use the term "father" because that is the common vernacular in the West—but I could just as easily have said "mother" because Spirit is without gender and because even all of us, who possess only a small spark of Divinity, have been both masculine and feminine in various different lifetimes on earth.

I would also add that there is no inherent virtue in poverty and suffering, any more than there is inherent vice in wealth. *The circumstances surrounding our lives are just that—circumstances. What is morally positive or negative is what we do with the particular set of circumstances that we are confronted with.* Circumstances themselves are morally neutral; our choices are what give them their moral content.

But remember, even when we backslide, we are always given another chance to make things right. There is great truth in the mythology of Pandora's box, when after all the terrible things flew out after the box was opened, the last being to emerge from the box was Hope. We are never without that, nor are we ever without the help and support of our guides and others in the spirit world—as long as we want that support. We also have a Father/Mother who loves us unconditionally and is waiting for our return home. With our own awareness of who and what we are, and with the help and support that is available to us, we can all make progress in every lifetime and overcome the seductive influences of the material world in which we must repeatedly find ourselves. And we will—you can bet on it!

The Spirit World

Session 25 - April 29, 1993

Tonight I would like to talk to you about the next world that you will visit when your life here is over. Right now I am not talking about a higher plane of existence but, rather, your temporary sojourn in the world of spirit while you wait for rebirth into a new earthly body. Much has been written about this world but I do not know how much of it is true. The spirit world reminds us of several key aspects of our being—namely, that our spirits are eternal and cannot be subject to death and that we can do so many things much more quickly and easily than we can when hampered by these clumsy, imperfect bodies that we are given during our stay on earth.

While we wait to go back, we are kept quite busy, and I don't mean learning how to play the harp. Depending on our level of advancement, some of us may become teachers and guides while others must go to school here because they still have so much yet to learn. One way or another, unless we are ourselves in school while in the spirit world, we are all busy trying to help our brothers on earth learn what they must do in order to find their way back home to God.

We all need each other. That much, I think, is clear from the extent of the interaction that takes place between beings in the material world and their spirit counterparts. *We are our brother's keeper, both in the life on earth and in the life in the spirit world.* That relationship continues. For example, when you pass from this body, I will still be with you as guide and friend, unless I have reincarnated for the purpose of dealing with my own karmic consequences.

When I talk about being our brother's keeper, I also want to make it clear that, in this context, our "brother" consists of the whole of God's creation. It is this duty that mandates that we all be ecologists and conservationists. For we have the duty to safeguard other beings (wildlife conservation) and the earth itself (ecology).

I do not suggest that souls that are waiting here for rebirth into the material world have become wise and enlightened souls just because they died bodily and entered this realm for temporary occupancy. That would be too much of a miracle to expect. However, while in this state here, at least some of the scales fall from the eyes of our inhabitants, making them much more aware of the purpose of earthly existence and, hopefully, giving them a head start for their next life on earth. The permanent residents here (and I really think I am one of those) represent souls that have advanced to a point where they can effectively serve as guides and counselors for humans. They haven't yet reached home but they are well on their way. Helping others may be all that it takes to breach any remaining barriers on the path home. In any event, one of my jobs here is to look after you, and that includes your spiritual development and your material needs as well as your bodily health and well-being.

Other Realms

Session 26 - April 29, 1993

I am glad that you and your wife enjoyed your plane ride today. And just think how much more exciting it would be to be able to do what you did today and not need the plane. You had some feel of what that was like when you took your shamanic journey on the back of your power animal, the eagle. Well, when you no longer have a clumsy material body to hamper you, you can do things far more exciting and impressive than that. I don't mean to suggest that we here spend our time soaring around the air like birds because we are much too busy—but the point is that we can. We would do that only for sheer enjoyment because we can go from place to place at the speed of thought and so we have no need for "mechanical" means of locomotion. Also, not everything is work or school for us here. We do have the opportunity to pursue our own personal interests to a reasonable extent. But for beings on the path toward enlightenment, helping our brothers and sisters is our most pressing interest as well as duty.

I really had not meant to go into that little speech about life on this plane but your airplane ride and what you experienced on it got me off on a little bit of a tangent. But that's OK. There is no reason why you should not know what I just told you. In fact, anything that helps to reduce the fear of bodily death that is so pervasive among humans is a positive contribution to your education.

What is our subject for tonight? How about other realms, though I'm not too sure I know enough to be able to handle a subject like that. Let's see. Well, we know that there is a material realm and a spiritual realm but I believe that there are actually a number of variations of each of those realms. In the material realm category, you surely don't think that humans represent the only intelligent life form in the universe. Of course not. While you are very special as God's children, it is also true that He has many other children elsewhere who are similarly trying to find their way back home too. Some of the others are further along than you here on earth while still others have not yet reached even your level of spiritual development and awareness. What I have just said is bound to shock you one way or the other. Either you will be shocked that you are not the most advanced and spiritual of God's children, if not the only ones. Or if you are troubled, as I am sure many of you are, by history's and today's lessons regarding man's inhumanity to man (never mind other living beings), you will be shocked to learn that God has other children even less advanced than you. As I say, one way or another, this information will create some shock waves.

In the spirit realm category, there are also gradations of progress. Those who are nearly back home again do not have a great deal of association with less advanced spirits except for the purpose of trying to raise their level of vibration by serving as guides and teachers, much as we do for those here on earth. Remember, as I told you, the mere fact that a spirit sheds a particular body does not automatically make that entity all-wise and all-good. If it were otherwise, we would not have to go through the lengthy and often painful process of achieving spiritual growth in a material world in order to incorporate it into our essence.

If we do not have the temptations of power and ego and lust to overcome, how can we know that we are spiritually ready to go home? If there are no temptations to be resisted, how can progress be made or ascertained? Muscle builders build their muscles by pressing against resistance, lifting weights and the like. If there is nothing to push against, muscles do not get built. Even though I'm not too impressed with this analogy, I think you understand the point I am trying to make. That is why I say to you, "Do not necessarily feel sorry for people who have had some tough times in their lives; they may be making more spiritual progress than those of you who have had a pretty easy time of it—that is, if they handle their tough times correctly." In other cases they may just be coming to terms with karma that they created for themselves in prior lives.

In this context, I need not remind you that personal happiness is not the purpose of your earthly existence, as I have already told you and will undoubtedly tell you many times more. I know that is a hard truth for you humans to swallow but, once you accept that fact—and it is a fact—you will be far better equipped to handle the circumstances that come your way, whether good or bad in human terms. I would also remind you that, if you are "fortunate" enough to have a rather pleasant and comfortable earthly life this time around, there is also a challenge there too. It is a more subtle one than that involved in handling difficult circumstances but no less challenging. The challenge, briefly stated, is avoiding complacency, patting yourselves on the back, arrogance, self-righteousness, the attitude of the Pharisees that Jesus found so offensive. Once you start thinking of yourself as better than anyone else, spiritually speaking, you are in danger of backsliding because you will have succumbed to ego again. I say "again" because we all do it but hopefully we learn over time and succumb less frequently. So be aware that, whatever your circumstances, the traps are out there; they just take different forms for different circumstances. Conscious awareness of this can be of great help to you in avoiding them . . . and their consequences.

I am amused that you are trying not to ask me about family matters because you know I prefer to focus on spiritual matters of concern to the entire human race. But it's OK. You have taken down my message tonight without any interruption to ask about personal things. So I really don't mind some non-spiritual questions as long as they don't involve lottery numbers.

Eternity

Good evening. I too have missed our conversations for the last couple of days. But I am glad you are back visiting me. Tonight I would like to talk about eternity. What does that really mean? It is a term that has meant many different things to different people. But what is it? Well, first, it is based on a misunderstanding because it presupposes the concept of linear time. And linear time is something that you already know does not exist in the realm of spirit. Therefore, a concept such as eternity is something that is necessarily associated with the material world because that is the world in which time exists. In that context, eternity means forever, both past and future.

We say our souls are eternal but that must mean that they have always existed and always will. That makes sense when we consider that our souls are a tiny spark of Divinity and we all acknowledge that Divinity—God—is eternal. But if a soul is, by definition, a natural occupant of the spirit realm, where time does not exist, it would seem that a concept of eternity would not have any meaningful content. So what is the point of all this deep philosophical discourse? All I am really trying to get across is that *fundamentally different thinking must be applied when we consider the material world and when we consider the spiritual world.* If we try to carry one over into the other, we will most assuredly create confusion. And we already have enough of that in the world—the material world, that is.

I think you already have a pretty good idea of the concepts that apply to the material world. For example, birth and death, sensation, pleasure and pain, the joys of the flesh and the sufferings of the encased spirit, and finally, the release of the spirit from its bodily schoolroom— or prison, if you prefer. Most of those attributes of the material world are fairly uniformly accepted by most, if not all, religious traditions. But what do we know of the ground rules applicable to the realm of spirit. Very little!

We know very little because those who have passed on to the spirit world do not usually communicate readily with those who are still functioning in the material world. In addition, some of the communication that does take place is suspect by those in the material world. And rightly so, for there are many who would mislead earth dwellers for money. Nevertheless, there continues to exist a substantial amount of communication between members of the spirit world and some humans—especially, holy men and women of all religious beliefs who sincerely seek to become closer to God and who live their lives accordingly. Communications to such people are very reliable but in many cases the communications are not publicly disseminated, or maybe they are not meant for public dissemination.

Then we have communication of the kind that is taking place between you and me. I don't put you in the category of the holy ones referred to above and I don't think you would assign yourself there either. Yet I find it desirable to have this kind of communication with you because I am your guide and because I know that you are a sincere seeker after truth and reunion with God. In addition, a good deal of what I intend to communicate to you is intended, eventually, for public dissemination. Those who will listen and heed what I say can benefit greatly from this information. Others who laugh at it or think it a hoax will continue on their earlier path and will miss out on a golden opportunity for spiritual growth. Their journey home will therefore require more lives on earth than would otherwise have been the case.

To the extent that you are persuasive in communicating my messages when the time comes to do so, you will be helping many people to search out a right path for themselves and you yourself will gain from it. I don't mind your sharing my messages with a selected group of friends whom you think would appreciate them before going public, but you certainly don't have enough material to interest any significant publisher yet. After we have worked together long enough, you will have enough material to go public with and I will tell you when I think the time is right to do so. I do not suggest that I am going to present startling new truths to you—truths that have not previously been presented by sages of many cultures. But you should not be surprised by this; after all, truth is truth and remains so.

The American public, in increasing measure, is becoming interested in matters of the spirit and this movement will continue as we approach the next millennium. The majority of people will still remain excessively attached to the material world and its enticements so you cannot expect anything but ridicule from them when you finally publish my little essays. However, where the seed falls on fertile ground, it will take root and you can feel pleased by that accomplishment.

Please take good care of your physical health. Not only because I love you but also for selfish reasons. I would hate to have to find someone else to communicate my messages after we have worked together so well. You may not know it but good channels are hard to find and, without wanting to give you a "swelled head," you are a good channel and will become an even better one with time and practice. So take good care of yourself and treat your body as the temple of the soul that it is.

Non-Human Beings

Session 29 - May 10, 1993

Do I have a topic I would like to talk about tonight? Well, let me see. Let's talk about the status of non-human beings. There have been many debates over the centuries on this subject, ranging from the position that other beings have no eternal selves to the so-called "group soul" for animals to the viewpoint that all living creatures possess some share in the Divine Creator's being—perhaps a smaller share than a human being but nonetheless some share. I don't have a definitive answer to this philosophical question but I myself subscribe to the latter viewpoint. That doesn't necessarily mean that I believe that a human entity who has fallen short in a given lifetime may reincarnate as an ant or a bird or a dog. But it does mean that all of God's living creation, and maybe even some of his inanimate creation, possesses a share in His divinity. After all, didn't He create everything ultimately out of Himself? How then can it be said that every bit of creation does not possess a divine spark of some level? I have said this rather clumsily or you have translated my thought in less than your usual articulate fashion but that may be because it is a difficult concept for you humans to accept. It is really a very simple one to comprehend—but a very difficult one for you to accept. That stems in large part from your western teachings that place mankind in a very special and superior place in the cosmos—with man as the *master* of creation and not merely its steward. But when you have time to reflect on the simple concept, you will gradually come to accept it. And that acceptance will also make a difference in how you live your life.

The affection that you feel for pets is an indication of the validity of this concept. Yes, they represent loyalty and companionship and sometimes protection but at a deeper level they also serve to remind us of our common heritage. It may be rather humbling to you arrogant humans who think you are just a little bit lower than the angels, but its recognition will make those of you who do recognize it better people. In a sense, your caring for your pets can also serve as a reminder that, to an even greater degree than with pets, you are your brothers' keeper. (Make brothers plural there.) When you have as a species evolved to that point, you will be far along the path to enlightenment, illumination, heaven, or whatever name you choose to apply to your reunion with God. Until you come to that realization, and live the kind of life that such a realization mandates, you will have to keep coming back to the troubled schoolroom of planet earth.

If people can start by loving and caring for pets, who are nonthreatening to them, they can gradually work up toward caring for and loving people and perceiving other people as nonthreatening to them. *The biggest obstacle to caring, compassionate human interaction is FEAR.* If you can get past the fear that your fellow man intends to do you harm if he can, or cheat you, or take advantage of you, etc. etc., then the rest of the way is relatively easy. Overcoming fear is your biggest challenge, for it is fear that brings about hatred and envy and hostility and all the negative emotions and behavior patterns. *When people learn to welcome and value diversity rather than fear it and seek to avoid it, or better yet exterminate it, then your species will be able to make rapid progress in spiritual growth.* As of right now, only a disappointingly small portion of the population of the world has been able to overcome those fears. But never forget, hope springs eternal and eventually everyone graduates; some just take a lot longer than others.

People

What subject for today? I think we will talk about people today, initiated by the events going on in what was once Yugoslavia. People, as you already know, are capable of the most enormous swings in attitudes and behavior patterns—almost literally from the sublime to the ridiculous, except that it is far worse than ridiculous what you can do to each other. Let us also remember that we are not just talking about some people "over there" whom you may consider, from your superior vantage point, to be less than fully civilized. The same ranges of attitude and action exist in all, or nearly all, of us. It is a part of the human condition and part of what you are striving to overcome while you are here on earth.

When you have reflected on the subject, you have recognized that, under some "appropriate" circumstances, you yourself would be capable of homicide. You have wondered about it and sometimes regretted it but you have been aware that the potential was there. Well, you are a relatively peace-loving individual, though by no means a candidate for sainthood, so you can just guess how close to the surface this tendency is in the great majority of people throughout the world, including these United States, where ethnic and religious heterogeneity has gone further and more peacefully than in most nations.

Ill-treatment of others who are different, which leads to the worst manifestations of genocide, springs from emotions such as hatred, envy and the like. They in turn spring from fear, which is itself a product of ego and a failure to recognize the essential unity and connectedness of all God's creation, especially among human beings who are supposed to have greater rational capabilities than other living beings. As I have told you before, once human beings become able to recognize their connectedness, the kinds of behavior among people that you deplore so strongly—and correctly so—will rapidly disappear. After all, you don't see many individuals cutting off their fingers because they look different from their toes. The analogy may seem a little extreme but I can assure you that it is not. The connection is merely more subtle and therefore not as obvious to finite and limited human minds.

It is a terrible thing to point out but it comes as no surprise to you that some people(s) can't handle freedom. We see that in many places in the world today. Remove the yoke of dictatorship and oppression from them and they readily revert to their old habits of hating and killing each other. This behavior extends not only to people who lived in peace reluctantly before because the heavy hand of authority kept them in line but also to people who lived in peace much more closely, as in parts of Yugoslavia before the ancient hatreds were stirred up again by false prophets. These are hatreds that have no part in a world that desperately needs spiritual development in order to avoid terrible destruction later—I don't mean by nuclear weapons but, rather, by "natural" disasters resulting from the earth purifying itself.

Compared to what the world may bring down upon itself if humans cannot get their act together, the abomination known as "ethnic cleansing" will seem like child's play. To put it in the vernacular, "You ain't seen nothing yet." There isn't a great deal you as an individual can do about events of this kind, other than to avoid being caught up in them. So, for you and those you love, keep trying to lead a life that focuses on spiritual growth as its main objective and stay away from the temptations of ego that you find all around you.

I am not trying to predict anything because the tremendous capacity for good that the human race possesses means that you can change at any time what would otherwise be the course of your planetary history. Whether you will in fact do so remains a mystery, at least to me.

Weather Conditions

What are you interested in tonight? Weather conditions? That's a rather unusual subject but I will try to talk about it. I am sure I can manage to turn even a weather report into a sermon. *Actually, weather conditions do reflect the results of the psychic energies of large numbers of people throughout the world.* After all, there are not many other conditions that represent such pure manifestations of energy as a weather system. It is perhaps the most concentrated form of energy that your material world is capable of. I believe that some people have made comparisons of the energy content of nuclear explosions and hurricanes or tornadoes. And it is clear that the energy content of one hurricane far exceeds that of the most powerful hydrogen bomb on earth.

You know enough about weather to respect its enormous power but you don't really know that the source of that power is the combined, albeit unknown, psychic power of a multitude of people. Remember, you create your own reality. That may seem strange to some but it is so. Also, if you follow the Buddhist view that life on earth is only a long dream with no actual reality, then it becomes easier to accept the proposition that we can control what we dream—that is, if we know how to go about it.

Regardless of whether you consider life on earth to be real or only a dream, you still create your own reality, primarily by your belief system. What you genuinely believe and expect to manifest will. So don't blame circumstances or others for the negative things that happen to you; they may be learning experiences, opportunities for spiritual growth or balancing the karmic books for your prior acts or omissions.

Again let me emphasize that life on earth is purposeful, even when it does not seem to be so from your particular vantage point or time frame. Without a belief in a purposeful universe, we would all be candidates for despair, that most numbing and dehumanizing of all emotions. But consider—does it make any sense to believe that a God with the power and wisdom to create this incredibly complex and harmonious cosmos would then abandon it, not to mention us and the rest of His creation, to the random workings of molecular interaction? To raise the question is to answer it. *Knowledge that there is meaning and purpose in all that occurs in your individual life gives us all hope,* that most wonderful being that emerged last from Pandora's box according to Greek mythology. It is something we all must have as we struggle along the path back to our eternal home. Nobody said it would be easy but, with hope, we know that it can be done.

You would like to learn more about lucid dreaming because of your interest in Namkhai Norbu's book. Well, if you can learn how to control your dreams and make them lucid, then you will have accomplished a great deal. Just think how much time we spend sleeping and how much could be accomplished if this time were put to constructive use, such as via lucid dreaming. The techniques involved are not familiar to me as a Native American but, as I see it, they are all manifestations of that level of concentration and focus that is characteristic of deep meditation. The techniques identified in the book are not necessary prerequisites to lucid dreaming but merely mechanisms to make the process easier than would otherwise seem to be the case. I would suggest that you give some of the simpler techniques a try. You might be surprised at the results you get.

It is all right to become involved with the matters you are presently involved in, such as [specific examples deleted]. However, make sure that you maintain your perspective of these events as nothing more than a dream, a passing event with no permanence, and conduct yourself accordingly. If you know it's a dream, you don't become too attached to the various subjects and you also don't feel anger or animosity toward others who may oppose the good things that you are trying to accomplish. Viewing these events in the manner of a dream, or a movie, helps you preserve your perspective and your compassion, caring and affection for the human race as a whole at the same time. That is spiritually valuable to you.

I am also glad that you are enjoying the fish tanks now that young Bill has cleaned them up very nicely. Your concern for these fish and invertebrates as living beings, a concern which you acquired from your son, is commendable and a good start on spiritual development. You are beginning to recognize and experience that connectedness of all God's creation that I have talked about earlier. Keep it up. Stay enthusiastic about your fish tanks. You can learn much from interaction with the fish in your tanks. And all the above is in addition to the beauty and harmony that these fish also represent.

∽∾

Economics

Session 32 - May 26, 1993

Tonight I would like to talk about economics. Sounds strange, doesn't it? But there is a great deal of interaction between economics and morality, most of it negative. The negativity is of course not inherent in economics but rather in the way that humans attempt to improve their own individual economic condition at the expense of each other. And in too many cases, without regard for the effects of what they do on future generations and on the planet earth itself. I am not really criticizing economics here—that was just the lead-in—what I am criticizing here is human greed. It is not wrong to want a better life for your family and yourself than was the lot of your ancestors. Actually that desire can spur innovation, hard work and ambition. What is wrong is to attempt to increase one's own wealth by taking it away from others. *Capitalism, with appropriate safeguards against unrestrained greed, still represents the most effective engine for directing human energy productively in the material world. But capitalism unrestrained by either government or morality simply invites greed, brings out the worst in its practitioners and sets them up for bad future karmic debts.* If you, or anyone else, has the opportunity to become a capitalist, keep this warning in mind and do not let yourself succumb to the temptation to acquire more material possessions while losing your spiritual edge. The latter you can take with you; the former you can't!

Since tonight's sermon started off with economics, let me continue with the same subject. Government has a role to play in preventing unrestrained greed and in enforcing some basic morality in this arena. But do not be deceived into thinking that more government is an inherently good thing. Beyond a certain point, it is clearly not a good thing. You have all seen the excesses perpetrated by government on people in Nazi Germany and Soviet Russia—and many other smaller countries that are less well-known to American audiences.

What is needed is to find the difficult balance between a government that affords its citizens reasonable protection against the injustices created by a system based on personal accumulation of wealth and a government that intrudes itself excessively into the private lives of its citizens, usually under the guise, or perhaps sincere belief, that it is protecting them from something worse. Sincere people may well differ on where this line should be drawn in any individual public policy issue, and that is all well and good. The very reminder that a balance needs to be struck should keep most men of good will from erring too far on one side of the line or the other.

You must also remember that a corollary of capitalism is that you must produce more in order to consume more—and still stay in balance. This corollary has, I am afraid, been forgotten by too many of our American people. As a nation, we have for too many years consumed more and produced less. We have done so using our national credit card, otherwise known as the government deficit. You are beginning to wake up to the fact that such a course of action cannot continue indefinitely— the chickens do ultimately come home to roost. To deal with this problem, Americans must again become a producing society, not primarily a consuming society. This may require some adjustment in the level of expectations of our citizens—a very difficult and painful undertaking.

I am also distressed at how many interest groups keep talking about the need for reduced expenditures and higher taxes, but when it comes down to specifics, each such interest group wants somebody else to bear the bulk of the burden. Probably many of the spokesmen for these various groups really believe that proposals that would inflict pain upon their group are unfair, but until there is enough sharing of pain to convince the American people that the proposed economic proposals, whether from President Clinton, conservative Democrats or Republicans, spread the pain in a reasonably fair way, no proposals will succeed in getting through Congress and the nation as a whole will suffer for it. You are all too selfish; you talk well about taking on a fair share of the pain but, all too often, when the details come out you all prefer to impose the pain on some other group than your own.

I did not mean to go into a tirade on this subject but I have been troubled about it for some time because selfishness gives the material world much more significance than it actually deserves. And it does so at the expense of spiritual growth and development, which is why we are all here. It becomes an obstacle to spiritual progress and sentences you to return to earth again and again until you can each overcome it. I hate to see that happen and, hopefully, my sermon will help those of you who listen and pay attention to it to avoid the pitfalls that are before you on your journey on earth this time around.

$\approx$ ∞

Healing

Session 33 - June 4, 1993

Tonight let's talk about healing. As you know, there are many kinds of healing. Your question pertained to healing of the physical body but I am more interested in talking about spiritual healing. That kind of healing lasts longer and does more good, even though it may not be as readily apparent in your material world.

Spiritual healing is designed to break down the barriers between each of you and God, your eternal Father/Mother. The barriers are of course of your making, not God's. They result from injustices committed in past lives, together with selfishness and greed and negative attitudes and behavior in your present life. We are all vulnerable to these negative behavior patterns (which includes attitudes, thoughts and ideas as well as actions) and we must be mindful of this vulnerability if we are to avoid the traps that result from it. I know I use the term "mindful" quite a bit but I consider it to be one of the most important paths to spiritual growth and development.

Being mindful helps keep us aware of what we think and do. As a result, we are less likely to think and act inadvertently in a negative way. Of course, if we do so after being mindful of what we are doing, then our negative karma is greatly increased. I remain optimistic about the benefits of mindfulness because I believe that most of our negativity occurs by our following mindless habit patterns that have become ingrained over time—and without our realizing what we are doing, both to ourselves and those others who are the subjects of our negativity. Intentional negativity is harder to eliminate because it stems from fear rather than inadvertence. Not until we can identify and come to terms with the underlying fear can we do away with intentional negativity.

But we were talking about healing, you will say. Yes, and this kind of spiritual healing is something we all desperately need. How to achieve it? *If you can accept the proposition, and truly believe it; namely, that all creation is an integral part of God, that we are all part of a single whole and that what I do to anyone else I do to myself, then we can overcome this spiritual negativity.* After all, do you get angry at your hand if it drops something? Perhaps momentarily, but you certainly wouldn't think of cutting it off just because it disappointed you or failed to live up to your expectations. So it should be in your relations with others, especially people.

As a result of our sojourn in the material world, we are all in need of healing. We all bear the scars of that sojourn, including previously acquired scars. One of the purposes of a life here on earth is to give us the opportunity to obtain a measure of healing for our scars. Here of course I am talking about spiritual scars, not physical ones. But you all should know that physical scars are manifestations of spiritual ones. The process starts with spirit and proceeds outward from there to the material world, including physical bodies.

Can physical problems be healed without also healing the underlying spiritual problems? Not entirely, of course, but some amelioration can be achieved even though the spiritual cause is not addressed. In all likelihood, the improvement will be temporary but that is still a big improvement to a person in physical pain. I am not going to spell out techniques and procedures for alleviating physical problems without dealing with the underlying spiritual ones. But you can do some experimenting and by trial and error come up with some methods that will work in some cases.

To do away with the symptom without addressing the cause can be dangerous to the patient. Let me use pain as an example. Physical pain is a signal that there is something wrong with the physical body. It can also be a survival element. You feel pain when you put your hand on a hot stove so you pull it away quickly. Therefore you minimize the injury. Without the pain to warn you, you would have suffered a far more serious injury, maybe even a fatal one.

If we extend the analogy to spiritual illnesses, then you will understand why I am hesitant to prescribe methods of alleviating physical problems only. At the same time I recognize that physical pain is not always a constructive way of bringing a situation that needs correcting to the attention of the affected individual. In such cases, the alleviation of the physical pain is a good thing. I believe that is the situation that applies in Paula's case at the moment. Your efforts to ease her pain were therefore constructive as well as successful. But keep in mind that, even when you learn to be more proficient in physical healing, you must always be mindful (there I go again!) of the fact that you do not usually know whether physical healing in a particular case is really in the spiritual best interest of the patient. If you get further into healing, you may find yourself forced to play God at times and, while that may seem exciting to your ego, I can assure you that it is a heavy burden.

I think I have said enough about healing for one evening. You have done successful healing in past lives and you can also do so in this life with additional practice. At this stage of your life, I think you could accomplish healing without the dangers of an inflated ego that might have been the case earlier in your life. You now recognize that you are but an instrument of a higher power when you accomplish a successful healing. Just see where it takes you but don't worry about it and don't let it distract you from our joint task. That is your primary remaining mission in this lifetime.

Forgiveness

Session 34 - June 1, 1993

Thank you for coming to see me before you go, old friend. You know I wanted to talk with you at least once more before you went on your trip to New Mexico. I did not want to push too hard but I know I made my presence and my wish known to you over the past several days. Tonight's subject is forgiveness. (Unlike some other occasions, you knew that would be the subject for some time now.) *Forgiveness is at the heart of spiritual growth.* It means that you recognize that someone who has done you wrong is nevertheless a participant in God's divine creation even though he may at the time appear to be misled, deluded, or something worse. It represents mindfulness by you of the fact that that person possesses the same divine spark that you possess and that you are each a part of one another. From that standpoint, forgiving a person who has done you wrong is equivalent to forgiving yourself.

That last statement brings up another important truth, namely, forgiving yourself. Just as you cannot esteem and respect others unless you already esteem and respect yourself, so you cannot forgive others until you have first forgiven yourself for your own transgressions against others. Of course, when forgiving yourself, you cannot get by with merely giving lip service to forgiveness as some kind of abstraction; you must also resolve to work at preventing yourself from repeating your transgressions against others. You may not always succeed but a sincere intention to try hard is a necessary prerequisite to self-forgiveness.

While it is important that you forgive those who have wronged you in some way or other, you don't necessarily have to like the wrongdoer or wish to associate with him or her further. Do not assume that if you forgive someone, you must thereafter be a friend to that person. That would be too much to require from entities that are still on the material plane and struggling with all the many lessons to which they are being exposed. Besides, when I speak of the importance of forgiveness by you, I want to emphasize that its objective is *your* spiritual growth; it benefits *you* even though it may not particularly benefit the person being forgiven. Never forget that you are the real beneficiary of a sincere act of forgiveness by you.

Forgiveness ennobles the forgiver, even when the recipient of that forgiveness may not be deserving. If the recipient is somehow made aware that he has been forgiven his wrongdoing, that knowledge may in some cases lead him into his own path of spiritual growth and under those circumstances he may also benefit from that act of forgiveness.

❋ ❋ ❋ ❋

Remember, the more time we spend conversing with each other (although most of the time I talk and you listen), the easier our communication will get and the better our results can be. As you know, I communicate with you by thought primarily and you translate my thoughts into your words using your own vocabulary. So don't be at all reluctant to visit me while you are in New Mexico, even though my thoughts and comments will not be reduced to writing. If I conclude that something said in New Mexico (or anywhere else when you are not sitting at your computer) is important enough that it deserves much wider dissemination when the right time comes, I will repeat it to you while you are at your computer.

Challenge and Impudence

Session 35 - June 28, 1993

Welcome home. I am glad you had a good trip. I did not provide any guidance on this trip as there was no need. You saw and learned what you needed to on your own.

You are correct that I wanted to talk next about challenge and impudence. I came through to you briefly on your trip to remind you of that. Do not hesitate or be afraid to challenge statements, especially dogmatic ones, that may come to you from any source, including me. As I have told you before, I am not God and I am not infallible. I have certain insights available to me that you don't have, but I still can make mistakes. So don't be so disappointed if something I tell you will happen turns out to be wrong. Also, for the same reason, feel free to question. I am not offended by questions. God gave you a mind to think with and you are not supposed to put your intelligence into neutral just because you happen to be talking with a discarnate entity. That is not impudence but, rather, good sense. As you know, many people receive all kinds of information via channeling, automatic writing, etc. Not all spirits providing that information are high-level spirits who are out to help mankind—nor is their information always accurate—in some cases. It may be intentionally inaccurate for any number of reasons that you can figure out for yourself.

Truth is not found by the blind acceptance of other people's views. You find it for yourself by studying, exploring, inquiring, selecting . . . and eventually you end up with a strong internal intuitive conviction that you have found a genuine piece of Truth. There are a multitude of paths to Truth and *how* you find it is not very important. You now know enough to recognize the fallacy in those religious views that hold that only by following their particular path will you find Truth, or salvation for that matter. Keep an open mind about Truth and when you finally find a piece of it, you will feel it in your heart and in the pit of your stomach. That may sound like a strange place to identify Truth but it is nonetheless the case.

Impudence is the other facet of the search for Truth that I wanted to mention briefly. Impudence implies disrespect and is a proper description for insincere questioning of information furnished. To question or challenge as part of a sincere search for Truth can never be impudent. But to question or challenge to show how smart you are or as an intellectual exercise is impudent because it is really nothing more than a manifestation of ego. So always feel free to ask me or anyone else you may encounter, in either the material or spirit worlds, but always be mindful of your motivation when asking.

I had also indicated to you during your trip that I wanted to talk about the subject of power. *Power is the greatest and most insidious temptation of the ego.* There is nothing wrong with the possession of power or its exercise—inherently, that is. Someone has to exercise power in any society. *The key elements affecting its morality are whether one seeks power and, if obtained, whether one abuses it.* To seek or desire power over others is a grave moral wrong for you would thereby interfere with another human being's God-given gift of free will. It can be a heady sensation, which is what makes it so tempting, but it is a highly dangerous one from the standpoint of the spiritual development of the person involved.

Similarly, if one finds himself in a position of power, how that power is exercised will determine its impact on the spiritual condition of the exerciser. The exercise of power for the good of the society is morally commendable, especially because the task is so difficult and the temptation toward self-aggrandizement is so great. But the abuse of power, even in petty ways, will result in the accumulation of bad karma for which the actor must one day pay. Again, as in so many areas, mindfulness comes to the rescue. By being mindful of the temptations and risks associated with both the desire for power and the susceptibility to abuse of actual power, an individual can successfully avoid these great temptations. In our own small way, these temptations are akin to those which the Christian scriptures say Jesus was tempted with in the desert by the devil. There is much we can learn from an enlightened reading of the holy literature of all religious traditions. But it requires an inquiring and open-minded approach on our part. In so doing, we are more likely to find the nuggets of commonality that are present in different religious traditions throughout the world. Maybe Westerners can then overcome the exclusivity that their own individual religious traditions tend to impose on them.

Habits

Session 36 - July 1, 1993

As I had already told you, I would like to talk tonight about habits. The idea came to me when I told you that you should try to get into the habit of talking to me at least three or four times a week.

What is a habit? A regularly repeated course of conduct that ends up becoming semiautomatic, almost as if the regular repetition had carved a groove in your mind. As humans, we do many things every day without consciously thinking about them—for example, brushing our teeth each morning and night. Well, we can acquire good or bad habits in much the same way; namely, by regular repetition of the conduct involved. If that repetition reflects a good or constructive action, then we are acquiring a good habit. If it is something negative or destructive, then we are acquiring a bad habit.

Once the grooves have been carved in our minds, they become very difficult to erase. Perhaps the only real way to erase the groove of a bad habit is to carve an even deeper groove for a good habit to replace that bad one. And even then, the bad habit groove will still come back occasionally to haunt us. We will still on occasion act out the bad habit without consciously and intentionally thinking to do so.

Obviously the best approach is to start generating good habits early in life and to continue to observe them throughout your life. But that is the exception to the rule. By the time most of us have achieved a level of mindfulness so that we are even aware of our habits, we will already have accumulated our share of bad habits, and hopefully at least a few good ones.

So what are we to do under these circumstances? By focusing our attention on what we are trying to become; i.e., spiritually developed beings, we can escape from the unconscious grasp of habits and can again become the intentional and mindful masters of our fate. By directing ourselves toward the objectives of kindness, caring and compassion, we can see to it that we behave accordingly toward all God's creatures. After behaving that way for a time, we will begin to reconcile our thought patterns with our external actions. And then we will totally cease to be prisoners of our habits. I don't want to knock good habits but until these become an ingrained part of your personality, I find more virtue in consciously and intentionally doing good things than I find in doing good things out of habit without even thinking of them at all. That is a personal position and one that is open to considerable argument on the other side.

In spite of my sounding like such a purist, I remind you, as well as myself, that the bottom line is determined by what we ultimately do, rather than by how we get around to doing what we do. Therefore, it can certainly be argued that doing good deeds, as a result of having acquired good habits somewhere along the line, contributes as much to spiritual growth as doing good deeds mindfully and intentionally. I do not intend to try to resolve this debate by some kind of decree of mine. However, I would again remind all of you in the material world that what really counts is the motive behind the good deeds. I think you can take it from there and come to your own conclusions on this question, although I am afraid I made the discussion quite convoluted. Anyhow, this may well be a conversation that you will have to edit at a later date in order to make it reasonably comprehensible to your readers.

I don't think I need to add a lot about motive being the determining factor in evaluating the spiritual significance of what we do, or even think. We can get a number of different combinations: good motive for good actions, good motive for bad actions, bad motive for good actions and bad motive for bad actions. The first and last categories are easy to evaluate but what about the middle two, recognizing that they are necessarily oversimplifications? Which is spiritually more acceptable—a bad act with a good motive? Or a good act with a bad motive?

Because I personally believe that motive is the overwhelming touchstone to the moral or spiritual evaluation of actions, my own conclusion is that a bad act with a good motive is superior to a good act with a bad motive. Of course, there will always be a multitude of shades of gray, both with respect to the act and with respect to the motive, but if you agree with me on this question, my touchstone will help guide you in matters of this kind. You will appreciate that only a good act with a good motive truly qualifies for an A-rating and everything short of that is incomplete or worse. But I sincerely believe that the person who performs a bad act with a good motive earns a lesser amount of negative karma than his counterpart of the good act with bad motive.

❧❧

Punishment

Hello. I've already indicated to you what I would like to talk about to-day—punishment. Although I have told you this before, some reminders are useful. *God does not punish; He teaches. Punishment as such is a human concept, not a divine one.* In some cases it may really result from a misunderstanding of the law of karma, cause and effect. To say that we reap what we sow may to a human mind imply punishment for evil deeds and rewards for good ones. But it is actually more in the nature of Newton's law that every action has an equal and opposite reaction. The law of karma is not a matter of reward and punishment but more in the nature of a law of mathematics or physics.

It is important that you realize that God does not punish but, instead, He teaches and, hopefully, we learn from our mistakes, albeit sometimes painfully. To speak of punishment in connection with God is to attribute to Him some of our human failings and thereby to belittle Him.

God's love for each and every one of us, His children in spirit, is unlimited and His acceptance of us, warts and all, is unconditional. If we are honest with ourselves, we have a pretty good idea of our short-comings and spiritual failings. Knowing these, we may find it hard to believe that God can love and accept us as we are, without qualification. But that merely reflects our pitiful attempts to create God in *our* image rather than to appreciate that He has made us in *His* image. When you come to realize that God loves and accepts us all unconditionally as we are, regardless of our failings, that is major progress toward spiritual development. But when you have actually experienced this unconditional love and acceptance, then your life will never thereafter be the same.

You will have had a religious experience, maybe only for a moment in time, that religious mystics of all traditions spend their lives trying to achieve and then sustain. Of course you still have to live in this material world until you have achieved all you can from that particular lifetime— obviously I'm talking here about achieving spiritual growth, not material wealth or power. But when you reflect upon your experience(s) of true communion with God, you cannot help but be more kind, caring and compassionate than you were before you had such an experience.

Knowing intellectually what I have just been talking about is progress. But knowing it in your heart is even greater progress. And actually experiencing it yourself can represent a kind of spiritual rebirth. No, it doesn't make you a "born-again Christian" but it can make you a "born-again child of God."

Punishment in your material world is, at its best, an attempt to introduce a karmic cause-and-effect cycle into a single lifetime, since karma does not necessarily reflect itself within a single lifetime. Another possible way of putting it is that punishment in the material world attempts to introduce a measure of fairness in relationships between people. If I am allowed to commit a crime and apparently get away with it in this lifetime, that appears to be unfair to the victim and to those members of society who do not simply take what they want from others who may be weaker or less wise than they. Punishment in your material world is also used as a deterrent and as necessary glue to preserve the social order among men since they cannot be trusted to behave as they should without laws, customs, rules and punishments for violation.

In the world of spirit, at least when one reaches a certain level of enlightenment, the kinds of controls that are, regrettably, necessary in your material world have no place here. We don't need them.

At its worst, punishment in the material world is simply a matter of vengeance. It reflects the worst in us and we must all admit that such flaws are an inherent part of our common humanity. Our big challenge is to transcend the relatively coarse vibrations of our material existence in favor of the higher and finer vibrations of our spiritual existence. What kind of challenge would it be if it were easy and didn't take many lifetimes to achieve? How many lifetimes will of course vary with the individual and I won't go into averages because I don't want to discourage you.

You want me to talk about the death penalty issue here in the United States? Well, I know it is a highly controversial topic among people of good will in this country. I also know what your own view is but I won't say it here. What is my view? If you agree that life, even in the material world (which is all you have experience of while in it), is sacred, then you will ultimately find yourself opting against a death penalty, even for the most horrendous crimes and most depraved killers. It may be hard to swallow now but you must remember that such a person must still deal with the law of karma, either in this life or another, and he must learn of the pain he has caused and experience it himself in his own life. Again, not as punishment but as learning.

I also know your views on the sensitive abortion issue. While I am inclined to agree that the civil law should stay out of matters pertaining to a woman's control over her own body, at least for the most part, I must still say to you again that, if life is sacred, then it is morally wrong to take life except under the most compelling circumstances. This conclusion on my part applies not just to human abortion or death penalties but also to more socially acceptable areas such as hunting when not required for food, and the putting to death of thousands of unwanted puppies and kittens every year. You may conclude that you have to do it but there is a moral blemish associated with such conduct. It is also true that God forgives all the transgressions of a sincere human heart.

So once again I find myself back on the subject of motives as perhaps the single greatest determinant of the moral status of any individual thought or action. Consider it well.

Respect for Different Points of View

Session 38 - July 6, 1993

You can pick up my thoughts more quickly now and without going into as deep an initial meditation as you had to before. That's good because it will make us more efficient.

You already know that today I want to talk about respect for different points of view, especially with regard to religion but also with regard to matters in general, such as politics. You use the term "tolerance" in the United States but I don't like that term. To tolerate something means to me to give it space, albeit grudgingly. I am talking about something that goes much further and is much more productive, and that is a genuine respect for views that may differ from our own. This is particularly necessary in the field of religion where so many views are taken on faith and where so many proponents of their particular viewpoint are convinced—sincerely at that—that they have found The Truth and that they have gained a monopoly on it. Rational discussion of diverse and opposing points of view comes more readily in other arenas, even politics, than it does in the religious one and yet it is in the religious arena that such an attitude of respect is most important.

Respect for a different religious belief or tradition does not require that you forego or dilute in any way your own belief system. It merely recognizes that there may be others which will lead their adherents to the same God that you worship. *If you can stifle your human arrogance, you can more readily accept the proposition that there are many spokes to the wheel but they all lead to the same hub.* Jesus said it well when he said: "My father's house has many mansions." Do we have the effrontery to consider our knowledge superior to his?

Along with a respect for different religious traditions comes the realization that many religious traditions share common ground, either by virtue of common roots or by virtue of common commandments regarding human behavior. The more we focus on the common grounds of our various belief systems, rather than just the differences, the easier it becomes to respect those other systems. We all succeed in snatching a little piece of Truth with our various views but it is the utmost in human arrogance that causes us to insist that our own view reflects Truth in its entirety. We do not—any of us—have the knowledge and wisdom of God even though He has permitted us to share to a degree in His divinity.

This same kind of human arrogance is what leads so many of us to believe that humankind is the only intelligent life form in the universe. Sure, we send out radio signals and we look for signs of contact with extraterrestrials but too many of us think we are exclusive. Well, face it, we're not. We may be precious to God because we are His children, all too often rowdy ones, but we are not exclusive. The universe is much too big, as is God's plan for it, to be satisfied with this one tiny enclave on a small planet of an insignificant sun. It should take no more than a brief reflection on the size and grandeur of the cosmos to restore a healthy humility to you about your place in the grand scheme of things.

While I am trying to encourage humility because humans badly need a large dose of it, I don't want to ignore the other side of the coin, which is that you are uniquely God's children and are infinitely precious to Him and lovingly accepted by Him as you are. I am sure that He would like to see major improvements in all of us but it does not change the nature and extent of His love and acceptance of us. Try keeping both of these concepts in balance and you should then have a healthy relationship with both God and your fellow human beings.

I've given you quite a mouthful to reflect on. But I think you can handle it. When you eventually publish this material, this message, if heeded, can become a great source of comfort to many. We are all pilgrims—seekers after reunion with our spiritual Father/Mother from which we originated. Most of us have still a long way to go and many lives in which to learn what we must learn. But we can have confidence that eventually we will reach our objective of reunion. What that means in terms of chronological time in the material world is unimportant. What is important is that we constantly strive to improve our thoughts and actions while in the material world so that we may gain the spiritual growth necessary to enable us to transcend that world. It all starts with Spirit and it all ends with Spirit. Simple, eh?

Prayer, Love and Unity

Session 39 - July 7, 1993

Good afternoon. Today I would like to talk about some aspects of Prayer, Love and Unity. That should keep me busy for a while. Several years ago, in a meditation you came up with a very clear insight to the effect that Prayer was the most powerful force in the universe. It came as such a surprise to you that you never forgot it. Also, you remembered it because you knew that was a real message from another entity and not just your subconscious talking, because you had never had anything resembling that viewpoint about the power of prayer.

Well, I am glad to confirm the validity of that insight. But it then leads to the question of exactly what is prayer. We have a tendency to think of prayer as communication with God, which it is, but also as a kind of communication in which we try to wheedle things out of an indulgent parent. All too often when we pray, we want something, sometimes for others but more often for ourselves. I call that a kind of selfish prayer and am not surprised when it is not answered in any form that we can recognize. Why? All too often such prayers—like winning the lottery, maybe?—are not answered because God has concluded that it would not be in our spiritual best interests to grant the thing requested. Prayers for spiritual benefits and prayers for others are more likely to be granted because they are more unselfish and because they bind us less to the limitations of the material world, from which we are all ultimately trying to escape.

I like to think of prayer as communication between ourselves and God—two-way communication rather than one-way with us in the role of supplicant. Do we really have to beg a loving parent for assistance in achieving spiritual growth? Of course not. God is delighted to help us move in that direction because we are then getting closer to home. But prayer as a two-way communication also carries with it the need to *listen*, not just talk. When we truly listen in prayer, our inner being, even if not always our conscious mind, will hear what we should be doing to advance along the path of spiritual growth. It may not even be translatable into human language but it's there and it's real and you will know it at the deepest level of your being. If the advice is for you, you will resonate with it or perhaps I should say that it will resonate within you and you will thus know its validity and applicability to you.

Try talking to God more often. You don't have to be asking for anything or even seeking His advice. Maintaining the communication and remaining mindful of your relationship is itself highly beneficial to you. Such contact will also help smooth your way through the difficulties of life on the material plane.

I said that I would also talk about Love today. Or at least some aspect of it because there is so much to say about love that I don't know where to start. This is a new thought to me but I think maybe prayer leads to love—love of all God's creation, including your fellow human beings, who are sometimes the most difficult parts of God's creation to love. Prayer can help you to recognize not only your own relationship to God but also that your fellow human beings have exactly the same relationship to God as you do. That includes people that you may consider most undeserving—something of a blow to your ego and self-esteem if you consider yourself to be a fairly virtuous person. But when you come to accept this little truth, it becomes much easier to love your fellow human beings, even with all their faults, which you of course don't have. I must gently chide all you out there who may some day read this material so that you do not fall into the trap of thinking yourselves more virtuous than some of your more unattractive neighbors and therefore closer to God. Remember the Pharisees!

When I started out this chat, I wasn't sure how the three elements that I mentioned—Prayer, Love and Unity—were going to fit together. But I think I see the connection now. *Prayer leads to love which in turn leads to unity.* Tinker to Evers to Chance, just like baseball. In this instance the unity I am talking about is the knowledge that all creation partakes of the divine and that we are inextricably bound to each other, whether we like it or not. When we really understand it, we will like it. But like it or not at the outset, that is the case.

It's not a new thought; it's as old as time. But it has become so attenuated by the separation fostered by the I/Other line of thinking that it has become almost lost. Illusion has almost overcome reality, at least for a time in the material world. That is an ever-present danger that you must avoid. When tempted to give too much credence to your role in the material world, remind yourself that any given lifetime is only a dream, a passing momentary thought. What is eternal is what lies behind the dream.

It seems to me that when we are able to progress to this level of unity—and I don't mean just intellectually but in our inner being, where we live—then we are getting close to the point where enlightenment will free us from the necessity for coming back to school on earth for another lifetime in the material world.

Popularity

Session 40 - July 9, 1993

No advance hints tonight about my subject because I am still thinking about what it should be. For some unknown reason, the word "popularity" popped into my mind just now so maybe that is what I should talk about. Although I don't see a very direct connection between it and spirituality.

Maybe that's the point! Popularity is something that all humans desire as part of their life in the material world, unless they have psychological problems and enjoy being loners. But there is no connection between popularity and spirituality and it is important for you all to remember which is the important objective in your lives.

There is nothing inherently wrong with popularity just as there is nothing inherently wrong with wealth or power. But a strong desire for popularity can make people, while on the earth plane, behave in ways that undermine their spiritual progress. Sometimes you have to take positions on moral issues that reflect your inmost values, regardless of whether those values happen to be in vogue at the time. And when you take unpopular positions on such issues, you can expect your popularity with your friends and neighbors to be jeopardized. Or at least you are afraid that will be the case.

Don't be afraid to stand up for what you sincerely believe in, even if it does not happen to conform to the mood of the time. These moods are passing fancies that often last only a short time and then disappear. To try to stay current with moral fashions in your world is no more durable and satisfying that to try to stay current with the latest designer fashions in women's clothing. And at least equally short-lived and unsatisfying.

Intelligent people of good will will like and respect you far more if you speak up for your own values and beliefs, especially if you do it in a reasonable manner that acknowledges that other, differing points of view may also have merit. This is not to say that any point of view is just as good as any other—of course it's not—but it is also important to avoid the human arrogance that insists that your particular point of view or value system or moral anchor is "right" and everyone else's is wrong. That is the kind of absolutism that I have so often criticized before about traditional western religions and their exclusive view of God, Truth and Morality—all with capital letters.

There need not be any kind of conflict between popularity and spirituality. I happen to think that the best way to achieve popularity in the material world without any sacrifice of spiritual beliefs and values is by the simple expedient of dealing with all persons with whom you come in contact with kindness, caring and compassion. We all need that kind of treatment because it helps to remind us, at some level of our being, of our common unity with each other. It also inspires comparable behavior on the part of the recipient of your kindness, caring and compassion—at least in most instances. Another way of putting it is that your own conduct is reflected back to you. Remember Sandy's story about the negative personality who was encapsulated in a blue bubble so that his own negativity was reflected back at him rather than coming into contact with others. You could almost call it a kind of instant karmic response, or "instant replay" in today's terminology.

Do not be afraid to be different. After all, those who have made the greatest contributions to the material world in your history, whether in art, science or other fields, were usually considered "different" during their lifetimes. They did not live routine, conventional lives and have the same views as their neighbors. And how much more so is this the case with the founders and leaders of the great religious traditions of your material world! It would be hard to imagine people whose lives were further from the then-beaten path than these spiritual leaders. Also, as you well know, you don't have to wear a hair shirt and live in a cave to seek—and find—spiritual growth, development and, ultimately, enlightenment.

Follow your own course and don't be surprised if your own course is vastly different from others who also seek spiritual growth. Each must follow his or her own river wherever it leads and my river, or path, is not necessarily yours. So take joy in your diversity and be mindful of the spokes-and-hub analogy to help you when you are troubled by doubts about your own particular path.

This little talk started with the subject of popularity. As we proceeded, we found that, as in the case of wealth and power, there is nothing inherently good or bad in any of these things. Our actions with respect to the gaining of these things and our motives for doing so and the uses to which we put them when we have achieved them are the considerations which determine the effect of any or all of these items on our spiritual development. As you know, this fits with other previous comments that I have made to you.

For example, there is no inherent virtue in poverty—humility perhaps, but that's an entirely different story. And you had better define humility first before you endow it with inherent virtue. In my dictionary, at least, it does not mean fawning or self-abasement; that to me is "mock" or "false" humility and probably worse than no humility at all from the standpoint of its impact on your spiritual growth. *Genuine humility carries with it a sense of self-worth together with an absence of either moral or intellectual arrogance.* That definition of humility is something that I think it would be helpful for all men and women to strive for.

Gifts

Yes, today we're going to talk about gifts. I don't mean the kind you get for Christmas or your birthday but, more important, the kind that you get for life. I'm really talking about what Paul called "gifts of the Spirit."

We all have them and it is quite obvious that they are all very different. That is one of the wonders of creation—the almost infinite diversity of human beings that we see all around us. That same diversity, though perhaps not as widespread, is also applicable to God's creation generally. If you think about it even a little, you readily recognize it in your own household pets. Your dogs have all had very individual and different personalities. And the same is true of your cats. You can even see it in the tropical fish in your tanks.

Well, it's equally true where you can't see it—in the wild and throughout nature. You don't interact with them enough to know but each of the multitude of little lizards that you see in your yard is different from every other one. This magnificent diversity among and within God's creatures is in its own way a "gift" to mankind—in this instance, not a gift of the Spirit but by the Spirit.

Getting back to humans, this diversity is and should be a great source of strength to you. It acknowledges the absolute uniqueness of every single individual in the world and therefore the separate value of every such individual. It also is supposed to enable you to avoid behaving like clones of each other, the way mobs do.

But you have succeeded in turning this strength into a weakness. You have allowed fear to overcome what should be joy and have managed to reject your God-given diversity and seek a mind-numbing similarity. You have learned to fear people who are different from you, whether in color, appearance, language, or any one of a multitude of other ways, instead of embracing them as a source of enrichment in your own lives. As long as this kind of fear dominates, you will continue to have racial, religious and ethnic strife throughout your material world. And this same fear will prevent you from recognizing your common humanity.

You yourself have recognized that it may take the appearance on earth of little green men with large heads and a single great eye for you to appreciate that your own differences of race, ethnicity, etc. are indeed insignificant. Until you can get beyond your fear of "differentness" you will remain stuck at your current level of world development spiritually—and I need not add that it's not a very high level of development at that.

To return to the subject of gifts of the Spirit, there you also have many differences among people. *If you can learn to respect and value the gifts that were passed out to others, that will help to bring you closer to your brothers and sisters—the rest of humanity.* None of us has all these gifts, or we would no longer need to be here, so it should be easy to recognize the fact that all of us here have imperfections and should therefore avoid the temptation to be arrogant about those gifts we do have. For example, one person has been given the gift of intelligence while another has been given the gift of patience. Both of these are valuable gifts but they are not listed in any order of priority or pecking order. Neither is superior to the other although one may be more helpful to the individual at different times of his life or under different circumstances.

In terms of intellectual problem-solving on a day-to-day basis, the person with intelligence will undoubtedly have an advantage. But for coping with adversity and the difficulties that afflict every life somewhere along the line, the person with patience will undoubtedly have an advantage. So let's get away from trying to establish an order of importance for the various gifts of the Spirit to each of us. We need to stay away from even thinking of ourselves and others in terms of superior or inferior people but, instead, to appreciate and rejoice in our simultaneous diversity and unity. You don't need to understand this apparently inconsistent concept; just follow it without a whole lot of intellectualizing and you will all be the better for it.

The knowledge that you, the eternal entity and not the material body that you happen to inhabit this time around, are utterly unique throughout the universe should make it easier for you to accept and believe that God, your Creator, loves and accepts you unconditionally just as you are. Sometimes in periods of difficulty and discouragement, we may wonder whether this is true and think of ourselves as just part of an undifferentiated mass of people. Those kinds of doubts are quite commonplace in times of adversity. But it is then that you need to remember the absolute Truth that you are unique in the universe and that God loves and accepts you just as you are. With that knowledge—and I call it knowledge and not just belief because I experience it and you have too—you can cope with any tests and trials that may occur in your earthly life. The support network is there—use it! And at the same time, always remember that what is true of you is also true of every other human being on the face of the earth, including those who are the "bad guys" in human terms—even Saddam Hussein and Moammar Kaddafi.

Pain

Session 42 ·July 12, 1993

Tonight I would like to talk about the subject of pain. It may mean different things to different people, and there have been many books and articles written about it. We need to consider both physical and mental pain—and any other kind we can think of, such as spiritual pain.

Is pain simply the absence of pleasure, or is it something in its own right? You could also ask the same question about pleasure. Actually, both are affirmative items and not merely the absence of something else. I may have surprised you when I said that pain was an affirmative element because we tend to think of it as a negative thing, something to be avoided if at all possible. Of course, it's not possible to avoid it altogether in an earthly life and it really is an affirmative part of your existence in the material world. That is, if you make it so.

In order to make constructive use of pain, we must get past all the conditioning and stereotypes regarding pain. First, in the physical realm, pain is an indicator that something is wrong with your body. It may therefore be an essential contributor to your physical survival. An obvious example is if you put your hand on a hot stove, you feel immediate pain so you quickly pull your hand away. Without the pain you could easily have left your hand there and done irreversible damage to it. None of this means, of course, that you should seek out pain as an objective in life—you don't need to because you will experience some during every lifetime anyhow. What it does mean is that you should not be as fearful of pain as you are—and you should learn how to make constructive use of it.

Mental or psychological pain is another category to be dealt with. It is also a form of pain that we are all subject to at various times in our lives—longer and more intense for some than for others. But mental pain can also have healing capabilities. Facing it, identifying its causes and coming to terms with it are important prerequisites to sound mental health—or physical health for that matter.

Pain of any kind should focus your attention on the nature, intensity and duration of the pain, what its causes are and then how to relieve the pain permanently by eliminating the causes. If we don't do that, we are merely treating the symptoms and any results will only be temporary. Blocking the nerve impulses to the brain through medication helps to relieve the symptoms and may often be necessary or useful. But it does not eliminate the pain itself. Until that is accomplished, if the pain is physical, there is still something significantly wrong with your body. You are not expected to enjoy your pain but you must realize that you can't run away from it either.

You may be able to run away from physical pain for a while when you are asleep or drugged, but you can't even really do that when your pain is mental. Part of your mind is never asleep and therefore, in the case of mental pain, you never escape from it, even though your conscious mind may for a while. Only by facing it and dealing with it constructively can you totally eliminate a particular source of pain. And believe me, we have plenty of such sources of pain in our lives, both physical and mental.

Let me talk for a moment about spiritual pain, because that is something that is likely to be new to many, if not most, of you. You may not even recognize it as pain when you are experiencing it. That is because it occurs at such a deep level of your being that your conscious mind will often not recognize it. Because it occurs at such a deep level of your being and is so hard to recognize and identify, it is also the hardest form of pain to deal with. But the underlying message is still the same. If you are able to identify the fact that you are experiencing spiritual pain at a particular time in your life, the message being conveyed is that something is wrong with your spiritual condition. Exactly what that is may well be more difficult to identify and deal with than in the case of physical or mental pain—but the message is basically the same.

If something is wrong with your body, mind or spirit, don't you want to know it so that you can try to do something about it? Well, that's what pain does—it enables you to know that something is wrong in that aspect of your being. Then it's up to you to identify the problem and its causes and do something about it. But unless you first know that there is a problem, you won't know that there is something that needs to be done to correct it.

I also think that there is another aspect to pain that may help make it at least more endurable, if not more affirmative. And that is the old analogy of the two-sided coin. Stated briefly, the proposition is, at least for humans: "How can one comprehend and appreciate the heights of joy if one has not also experienced the depths of sorrow?" You can pick whatever opposite you wish for pain, whether pleasure, joy or almost any favorable emotion, but the two-sided coin analogy still works. Again, I don't mean to suggest that pain is something that should be sought out by any of you. You don't need to worry about that, it will seek you out all by itself, because that is the nature of the life experience on earth. It's also how we learn here, though not of course the only way. I am saying what I am so that you will, in the future, regard pain with a better perspective than most of you now do, and so that you can make it a more affirmative and constructive experience for you than will otherwise be the case.

There is much more than can be said about human pain and suffering so I may come back to that subject at some future time.

Strength

Session 43 - July 13, 1993

Tonight I would like to talk about strength, or fortitude. I'm not talking about physical strength, of course, but rather about moral and spiritual strength. Moral or spiritual strength, I believe, amounts to the same thing since moral strength is necessarily derived from the spirit.

First, we need to define what we mean by moral strength. In my opinion, moral strength involves standing up for what you deeply believe to be "right" when that position may not be the popular or prevailing one. When I use the term "right" here, I am not talking about factual or intellectual matters; I am talking about moral viewpoints and judgments. Your view as to what is "right" in a given situation is not the result of a rational, intellectual analysis but is what filters up to you intuitively from some deep level of your being. You may have trouble explaining it or defending it in debate, but you nevertheless know that it correctly reflects a firm conviction of yours.

In order to become aware of what your moral convictions are, you must first learn to listen to that still, small voice deep within you that speaks to you in the quiet of your soul. You can call it conscience if you like, but names don't matter. That voice speaks softly and can easily be drowned out by all the noise going on around you in your daily life in the material world. So you must listen carefully if you really want to hear it and not allow yourself to be distracted by the multitudinous experiences and sensations being offered to you at the same time.

Listening to the small voice within you is necessary but not sufficient in itself. You must also have the moral strength or fortitude to speak up for what you know in your heart to be "right." That is where strength enters the picture. It takes great fortitude to buck the tide of opinion among your friends and neighbors and in your community. After all, we all have an unquenchable desire to be loved, and we are afraid that we will lose that love if we differ with those around us. It's entirely natural to think that way in the material world but to act in accordance with that thinking is a manifestation of weakness, not strength, of moral cowardice rather than fortitude.

Take the chance and stand up for what you deeply believe. You don't have to be confrontational or obnoxious about it and you will be surprised how many people will respect you for having the courage of your convictions. You may also be surprised to find that many who appeared to be going with the tide will agree with you, but were afraid to do so when they thought they were alone.

You have long since learned that you can be good friends with people and still have strong differences of opinion on any subject under the sun, including those most controversial ones like politics and religion. You know that if you liked only people who agreed with you, you would learn very little in your life and your friendship horizons would be frighteningly limited. The same basic proposition applies to moral issues as well. The key, I believe, to combining friendship with disagreement on issues lies in mutual respect. Of course you will continue to believe that your viewpoint is correct but you must also be able to acknowledge those elements of the differing positions that may have merit. Fanatics rarely have friends; they may have followers if they are charismatic enough but they don't have friends.

If you also recognize that all God's creation, including humans, is inextricably joined together in an unbreakable unity, it may help you to appreciate that the other person also has access to deep levels of truth. It can help keep you from the arrogance of believing that your moral viewpoint is the only acceptable one. I say these things to help you gain perspective on these matters. I do not suggest that you should change your viewpoint if it has in fact filtered intuitively up to you from some deep level of your being. Under these circumstances, your viewpoint on the particular issue is "right" for you and is deserving of your implementation and defense. It may not necessarily be equally "right" for everyone else on earth under the same circumstances.

This latter statement is a very hard one to accept, or even understand. The complexities of human moral behavior do not lend themselves to the kind of simplistic absolutes that we might all like to have. Even earthly laws that sound clear and simple often turn out to be complex in their application. How much more is this the case in dealing with moral laws!

You recall the law enacted by some ancient king that proclaimed: "He who sheds blood in the streets of the city shall be put to death." It sounds simple and straightforward, but only at the outset. Almost immediately, questions of application arise. Does it apply to a case where a person sheds blood in the streets of the city while defending himself against an unwarranted attack? While defending his family? While attempting to apprehend an alleged criminal? What about the person who accidentally cuts his finger in the streets of the city? What about the person who intentionally slashes his wrists? I could go on and on with this simplistic little example to show you that one must be careful about literally applying the language of man-made laws. I think that cautionary note applies even more strongly when trying to apply what we consider to be divine-made moral law, especially when we perceive that law in this world through a dark cloud and not very clearly.

The end result of all this conversation is as follows: Listen to the small, still voice within you that intuitively filters up to you from deep within your soul. Have the strength to stand up for what it tells you. But do so with respect for what is meritorious in other points of view and without personal acrimony. And avoid like the plague the arrogance of thinking that your viewpoint is the only "right" viewpoint on the issue, not only for you but also for everyone else in the world.

Enough for tonight. Good-bye for now and God's peace and love to you all. By the way, whether the reader is Christian or not, I am especially fond of the introductory greeting in the Catholic Mass that begins: "The grace of our Lord Jesus Christ, the love of God and the fellowship of the Holy Spirit be with you always." Now there is something for you to reflect upon until next time!

Pity

You're getting my advance signals pretty well now. Yes, pity is what I would like to talk about today. There are at least two kinds of pity that exist in your world, and you must be sure that any pity you feel is the right kind. What do I mean by that cryptic statement? I'll tell you. *Real pity is a feeling of genuine compassion for others who are living under difficult conditions or encountering serious problems of a financial, emotional or spiritual nature.* It can also include such feelings for animals as well as people. To feel this way you must empathize with them and try to put yourself, to some degree at least, in their shoes so that you vicariously experience their pain. Genuine pity and compassion are virtually synonymous terms.

But there is another phony kind of pity. It isn't really pity — it merely masquerades as such. This kind of pity is an egotistical manifestation of superiority over those who are supposedly being pitied. It is hypocritical and Pharisaic and will not gain any spiritual merit for its practitioners but, rather, bad karma that will have to be worked out at some future time. Remember the story of the Pharisee and the humble sinner in the Bible. To paraphrase it briefly, the sinner prayed to the Lord: "Forgive me, Lord, a humble sinner." But the Pharisee prayed: "Thank you, Lord, for not making me a sinner like him." Well, to complete that picture, all you would have needed to add, in modern terms: "Thank God I'm not like that poor pitiful guy." No genuine pity there; no compassion for a tormented fellow human being and no spiritual merit either.

We all have to be very careful in evaluating our emotional reactions to events of this kind. We must be certain that we are reacting with genuine pity, real compassion, not the false variety. If you feel real compassion for, say, the flood victims in the Midwest, there is nothing wrong with also being grateful that you are not one of them. The key word here is "also." First, you must feel the genuine pity then you may be grateful that you are not being subjected to the same test.

I am sure there are other feelings that sound as though they meet our little recipe of "kind, caring and compassionate" that you have heard before, but are really selfish feelings or feelings of superiority — ego-driven, of course — masquerading as spiritually desirable feelings. Let me see if I can think of some at the moment. For instance, a fellow employee has just lost his job. You say that you feel sorry for him but you really are glad because it now gives you an opportunity for promotion. In a situation like that, you may fool others, but you are not fooling yourself, even at the conscious level, because you yourself know what your real feelings are.

The tricky situations occur when, like the Pharisee, you really think, at the conscious level, that what you are feeling is pity, when it is in fact superiority. Then you are fooling yourself—and that's when it gets to be dangerous to your spiritual health. The masquerades can be very subtle and you must be on the alert so that you are not taken in by them.

Whenever you are inclined to feel superiority toward another person, always remember that such feelings are merely reflections of ego. And ego is simply that part of you which is bedazzled by the illusions of the material world and has forgotten that you are eternally a spiritual entity who is passing through here as part of your journey home where you belong; i.e., with God. If you remain mindful of that key fact—and I tell you it is a fact, not just a belief—you can manage to avoid both the ego traps and the temptations/illusions of the material world.

Retaining that mindfulness is something I will repeat to you again and again in our conversations because it is so important. If you were to regard ego traps and material world illusions as insects, then this mindfulness is like a very effective insect repellent.

To retain this mindfulness, it is helpful to regularly set aside some time to meditate and reflect upon your fundamental nature as a spiritual being. A brief period of reflection every day would be ideal, but if you attend a church and use some of that time for such reflection, that is much better than nothing. If you never stop to reflect on your true and eternal nature, I can just about guarantee that you will succumb to the ego traps and illusions of the material world. At least until you approach the time for shedding this body. It is never too late, of course, but by then you will probably have generated a considerable amount of bad karma which you will have to work out in a later life, and possibly with considerable difficulty.

How much better to have become aware of your fundamental spiritual nature earlier in this sojourn and then to conduct your life accordingly, and undoubtedly differently. However, if you acquire this mindfulness even late in this life, it will carry over to your next life in some vague subliminal form and will hopefully influence your conduct there even though you may not be consciously aware of it. Never forget—there is always hope! It's really much more than just hope because, as I have told you before and will repeat again, ultimately we all reach our destination. The journey just takes longer for some than for others—in some cases, a lot longer.

I am trying to come up with a snappy set of alliterative nouns beginning with "c" to summarize the desirable behavior in this world of a truly "mindful" person. I want to start with "kindness" but that of course doesn't begin with a "c." I know, I'll use the alliterative sound "k" or hard "c." Now I have kindness, caring, compassion (the three I started with) and will add courage and courtesy now. Maybe I will come up with more as we go along. But these can be simple mnemonics to help you recall some of the attributes of the mindful person.

Opportunity

Session 45 - July 19, 1993

Today I would like to talk about opportunity, as I indicated to you earlier. What do I mean by opportunity? *By opportunity I mean the chance to take control of our own lives here on earth.* Opportunities surround us constantly throughout our lifetimes although we usually are unaware of them. And we are unaware of them because we don't look around us with an eye to them. *In my definition another word for opportunity is choice.* Unless you are locked up in a prison or are in a situation where you literally have no choice, you always do have choices you can make. As you well know, deciding to do nothing about those choices that come your way is also a choice you have made.

Many people fear opportunity or choice because very often it means change. And while some people welcome and embrace change, many more are afraid of it. They would rather live dull, boring and secure lives rather than take a chance on the changes that often accompany making choices or seizing opportunities. I do not criticize people with these tendencies—after all, we all are what we are. However, I can safely predict that these people will take longer to achieve spiritual growth and development. The reason is simple. *Spiritual growth involves a great deal of change from the conventional material value system which worships power and possessions. Spiritual growth involves considerable risk-taking.* Right now you are taking a risk in believing that I am a separate, independent entity speaking to you, and not merely a figment of your imagination in overdrive.

Opportunity of any kind involves elements of risk. Intelligent risk-taking requires that you evaluate the extent of the risks involved, as well as the risk/return ratio, before deciding whether or not to take the risk. I am not encouraging foolish risks. But we should not forget that all of us do make foolish, ill-considered choices at various times in our lives.

While I have said before that the purpose of life on earth is spiritual growth, or coming closer to God, I do not suggest that life must be dull or painful or otherwise negative in order to permit spiritual growth. *Life can be very exciting and still lead to spiritual growth.* Misery on the earth plane is not something to be sought after. You do not grow spiritually by flogging yourself, either physically, mentally or emotionally. Success, prosperity and the enjoyment of your life on earth are completely compatible with spiritual growth—there is no correlation either way.

In any event, I can assure you that every human lifetime will have its share of pain and suffering. The amounts are not evenly divided but all share in pain while in the material world. *While none of us seek pain— nor should we—we should remember that painful experiences usually teach us the most memorable and important lessons.* If we did not have some pain in our lives, I am afraid that our rate of learning and spiritual development would be far slower than it now is, and some of us might not learn much of anything at all from an earth sojourn.

So don't be afraid to say "yes" to opportunities that confront you. There will often be hard knocks in the process—which you may later look back on as having been ultimately beneficial, though they certainly didn't seem so at the time. Always remember, though, while enduring the hard knocks, that God's creation is essentially a benign universe even though you "see" hurricanes, volcanoes, tornadoes and all kinds of natural disasters around you, not to mention man's inhumanity to man. Those events are only part of the dream that constitutes a lifetime in the material world.

104

Never let yourself forget that you and every other part of God's creation partake of the Divine—the real you is eternal—and that God loves each and every one of us unconditionally and unqualifiedly just as we are, even while He/She seeks to help us rise to a higher level of spirituality. If you can accept this, you will never be afraid of anything again. Fear is the biggest obstacle in the way of loving your neighbor. And separateness as a manifestation of ego is the other big obstacle to spiritual growth among human beings.

When you can remember who and what you truly are, then fear will be overcome by love and separateness fostered by ego will be overcome by Unity—by the knowledge that we are all part of One—that is, God—and that what we do to others we are doing to ourselves.

I did want to say a word about bigotry before I finish, since I mentioned the word to you briefly before. Bigotry is one of the uglier manifestations of fear. I have called it a manifestation of "frozen" fear—a level of fear that is so strong and visible that it is as ice is to water or steam.

You are indeed fortunate to be part of such a loving, close-knit family unit, especially in these difficult times. Be grateful for it (I know you are, but this comment is for others who are equally fortunate but don't appreciate that fact).

❧

Love

Session 46 - August 25, 1994

What shall we talk about today? *How about love? It is a subject that deserves the greatest attention because, as I have told you before, it is the second most powerful force in the universe—second only to prayer.* So it's definitely worth talking about a lot. I am of course talking about the kind of selfless love and nonsexual love that the ancient Christians referred to as agape. This is perhaps the noblest kind of human love because it seeks what is best for the loved one rather than for oneself. It is unselfish and may be exemplified by the love of a parent for a child. It is protective but with ample allowance for exercise of free will by the loved one.

A love of this kind will usually be accompanied by a feeling of good will toward others in the general vicinity and, if one has progressed far enough, it may even be accompanied by feelings of good will toward the remainder of humankind. Ultimately, it may even extend to kindness, caring and compassion toward all of God's creation. When we can genuinely achieve that level of selfless love, we have arrived at a major plateau in our journey toward spiritual growth and development.

Love does not mean being a doormat for the selfish desires of others. People who say that they do things which they know to be harmful to another—but say they are doing it out of love for that person, because it is what he or she wants—are merely deluding themselves. That is not love. It is more like indulgence, including self-indulgence.

Love may sometimes require a person to say no to another as a means of making that other person take charge of his life and do what is necessary to fulfill his potentialities. That is the situation as I see it with Alice's friend Nancy. Nancy is not really being helped by being allowed to take advantage of the Harper family. She can probably be helped more by being told that she must take charge of her life and make her choices, including living with the consequences of those choices. However, the important thing is that, for any of this to be effective, it must be presented calmly and firmly, but without rancor. If done in anger, it loses all effectiveness and even generates some negative karma for the person making the statement.

Love is strong. Never forget that—love is a manifestation of strength, not weakness. It takes much more strength of character to love than it does to hate. Love overlooks flaws and shortcomings in others because we know that each of us possesses his or her own collection of flaws. It recognizes our common humanity—and the conclusion that goes with being human—namely, that we still have a great deal to learn before we are ready to graduate from the school of earth.

Because love has these kinds of characteristics, it also encourages a healthy humility—something that most of us need and some of us need very badly. *A healthy humility, which means a genuine humility, is a great virtue and a key prerequisite to spiritual advancement.* Note that I said a "genuine" humility because there are many manifestations of false humility that occur every day in this material plane. False humility is in reality nothing more than another manifestation of ego, which is perhaps the biggest obstacle to spiritual development.

Getting back to love—if you can achieve the highest levels of unself-ish human love, then you are ready to attempt the much harder task of achieving divine love. Let me make it very clear that I am not talking here about God's love for you but about your love for God. As regards God's love for each and every one of you, you already know that God loves and accepts you unconditionally just as you are, warts and all. But when we say that we "love" God, that presents a much more difficult series of questions.

What do we think we mean by that? And how do we manifest that alleged love of God? Clearly it means much more than going to church on Sunday for an hour and reciting a prearranged set of prayers. That may be all right as an introduction, but it is only the merest introduc-tion. How do we truly show that we love God when we can't see Him, touch Him, taste Him, etc. The answer seems pretty obvious when we think about it. *We show our love for God by loving that which we can see, taste, and touch—i.e., God's creation.* And it shouldn't be too hard to tell by our actions with respect to God's creation what our true atti-tude is toward God. That's the proof of the pudding; the rest are merely words that are devoid of content.

We will have much more to say about love in future conversations, but I think I have given you a good deal to reflect on already so I will end this discussion for today.

જીજી

Part II

Michael

The Appearance of Michael

Session 47 -August 29, 1994

[Note: This session marks the first appearance of the being who allowed me to call him Michael. Michael does virtually all the talking from now on, though Seneca is always present.]

W. G.: Seneca, who is this being that you have brought with you today? I see a blinding light shimmering around a human figure beside you.

Seneca: It is a good friend who has come with me to also help guide you. He/She is far more advanced than I and has no name that is pronounceable to humans.

W. G.: I don't know what to say—but I am grateful to you for this manifestation of your love for me and your concern for me.

Seneca: You don't have to say anything. Just listen.

Entity: I am here to help and to reinforce what Seneca has already told you. I will command you to publish these and more talks by him and me when the time is right. In the meantime, I will also provide guidance for you as well as answers to questions.

The name Oneida stuck in your mind a few minutes ago and you thought that Seneca was answering your question about *his* tribe, but instead, it was *your* tribe in a past life. You were a chief and a medicine man in that life and you led your people in paths of peace, for which you have since been rewarded by good karma. You were never a great warrior or hunter in that lifetime. Your contribution was greater as a leader for peace and as a role model for the young men. You lived to a very old age because you had much to teach the young men of your tribe, so your work was not finished early.

You also have much to communicate in this life, but its sources are Seneca and myself. I can answer questions that Seneca cannot but that will depend on when I believe you are ready to receive such answers. Seneca is a warm and loving friend to you and he has indeed been watching over you from birth. I, on the other hand, while more advanced— further up the food chain as your friends would put it—am more of a teacher and disciplinarian for you. But do not be upset or afraid because I am not a spirit without humor. I, too, consider humor to be a survival requirement for the human race.

I want you to be a clear and major channel for the communication of our views and warnings to the world before it is too late and the world must suffer severely from the purification of Mother Earth via the earth changes that have already begun. That means you have duties to follow and those duties include regular communication with Seneca and/or me, regular meditation unrelated to our communication, and care of your physical body. Today you walked for about a mile—that is good, but you must exercise regularly. That is a necessary prerequisite to your mission, not just a helpful comment to you. So do it! The same is true of the other elements namely, regular communication and regular meditation.

You have an important mission to perform in the remainder of your earthly life this time and you can gain greatly by performing it well. You can also be of great help to your fellow human beings for we find you to be a clear and articulate channel for what we are trying to pass on.

This comes as something of a shock to you, so we will terminate this discussion and give you time to reflect upon what I have told you.

Getting Acquainted With Michael

Session 48 -August 30, 1993

W. G.: Thank you both for coming to see me this evening. Am I correct that I have your permission to call you Michael, though I understand that is not your real name?

Michael: Yes, you do. And some day, when you are ready, I may reveal my real name to you. But you already know that names are not important. I am pleased that you are taking my instructions of last night to heart. You have started to improve your body through simple exercise and I am confident that you will keep it up. Yes, it is true what Paula told you—that you must get your physical body in suitable condition to receive my higher vibration. You communicated very well with Seneca but I need a higher vibration for my communications. So I thank you for beginning to fulfill your mission responsibly. Keep it up. The same is true for meditation. I know you have done a little today while lying in bed. That is not the best place but it is at least a start and shows that you are serious about following my instructions. Tonight's communication is another good example, although I recognize that you were curious whether I would appear tonight, either alone or with Seneca.

Seneca is and will continue to be your principal guide for the rest of this lifetime. I would never think to push him aside—we don't work that way here. But I can appear with him and supplement his statements with additional insights of my own or I can know things that Seneca may not yet know.

You still have to get used to me just as you now feel comfortable with Seneca. That may take a little time but it won't be long. As I told you last evening, I am at a higher spirit level than Seneca and I manifest as light around a human figure without gender. Don't take what I said as a put-down of Seneca because, as you well know, he is far up in the food chain and he is a caring, loving, compassionate "person" with a gentle sense of humor. Seneca has been preparing the way for me to communicate directly with you and we have now reached a point in your development where I can talk to you directly.

I am pleased by the reading you are doing of a spiritual nature. For example, the book *Rolling Thunder* is both informative and moving. It reminds us that the American Indian, or Native American if you prefer, knows many of the secrets of nature and, most important, he knows how to live in harmony with the earth. There is much that you can learn from him about the uses of plants, herbs, and what you would call weeds in healing a wide variety of illnesses.

Your friend, Alice—and, as you thought, she was a sister in a prior life as an Oneida—was a wise medicine woman who in that life was one of the most respected elders of the tribe. Self-confidence in her abilities is what she needs [now], and you correctly told her that she must overcome her doubts and give proper honor to her talents. The more you communicate with Seneca and me, the stronger and more accurate will your psychic capabilities become. You are already learning to trust what you call "intuition," but it is, of course, your psychic powers that are being strengthened. Listening to your intuitive self gives you the sensation of "instant knowing" without all the difficulties and roadblocks involved in the rational, analytical process.

❈❈❈❈

This evening is not the right time to begin a spiritual odyssey for you and me. That will come in due course; we have plenty of time. Tonight gives us a chance to get better acquainted and to deal with the serious problems of a member of your extended family. It therefore helps us to grow closer together, and I will continue to hold up my end of the relationship as you will hold up yours.

Please know that I am not preempting Seneca. He too will speak whenever he wishes. But tonight was our get-acquainted night.

Spirit Guides

Session 49 - September 1, 1993

Michael: Good evening, Bill. Both of us are here again. We were pleased with your efforts yesterday to help your good friend, Jim. As you could tell from time to time during your conversation, you were guided. That was particularly true with regard to the affirmation you suggested to him. If he will continue to affirm what it says and come to believe it at the deepest level of his being, the rest will follow and he will again be like the feisty old Jim that you knew a few years ago. Well done. Your time was better spent in giving this help than if you had been walking, so don't feel bad because you didn't walk yesterday. Your perspective on what is really important is pretty good and you were right to give helping Jim the higher priority than following my instructions to the letter.

You too are in for a time of renewal, as is your wife. In fact, I see this happening to your entire family, including your extended family. Listen to what your heart tells you and pay attention to the so-called intuitive voice within you. That's where a good deal of our guidance comes from.

You have indicated some curiosity about whether I, Michael, have been with you since birth and watching over you like Seneca. The answer is no. That is because only recently have you reached a vibrational level where I could communicate with you directly. In fact, until fairly recently Seneca could not communicate directly with you, even though he has been watching over you throughout this lifetime.

No, you don't have the same guide in your different lifetimes. You get a new one each time. After all, your guide in a particular lifetime may have other assignments to fulfill when you begin a later lifetime. *But all of us have the same ultimate mission—to help you learn what you must and encourage you to live on earth as you must in order to find your way back to union with your Creator.* In other words, to help you reach the level where you merge your divine fire with God's and become a co-creator with Him. Everything else we do here is subsidiary to that job assignment.

As you can appreciate, if I—Michael, and Seneca—can communicate through you our views and insights regarding what mankind must do in order to advance spiritually, then we have accomplished a great deal more than we can by a number of one-on-one conversations. That is why I am hopeful that, when the time is right (and I will tell you when it is), you will disclose to the world the substance of our conversations, editing out the personal parts that are not applicable to humanity as a whole. Those who are ready to listen will and those who do not listen will have to go through the more difficult times associated with Earth's purification of herself.

While interest in matters of spirit is growing by leaps and bounds throughout the world, and in the United States as well, there are still far too few of you who even come close to living the kind of life that advances your spirituality. I feel deep sadness and sorrow that this is the case, but I cannot avoid the conclusion that an enormous amount remains to be done to raise the consciousness of humankind before we can abandon earth as a schoolhouse because you all have successfully graduated.

We here can only do what we can to help and the same is true of you. So in addition to being a clear and articulate channel for Seneca and me, and maybe others later, remember to live your life in the material world in accordance with the teachings you have received, and will receive, from us and you will benefit greatly. I don't want to leave you with the mistaken impression that you are approaching the end of the need for incarnations but you will certainly shorten the process by doing a good job now.

Your interest in the American Indian tradition is commendable and should bring about some useful insights into the basic relationships between Earth and its inhabitants—including every kind of living being, and even nonliving matter. This leads me into consideration of the conversations that Alice and Enid [my wife] have been having about herbs and a business venture. As you know, your wife would love to get into a fun-type of business with Alice and whether or not it succeeded financially, you would all learn a great deal more about natural processes of healing. You have been told by Joe that you were once a healer in a past life and it is correct. So was Enid. So that old knowledge is there, stored somewhere in your psyche.

I don't exercise control over lottery ticket results, as you know, and I doubt that that will be your way of getting rich materially. I said "materially" because you are already richer than King Croesus in terms of love and friendship. Never let yourself forget that and keep the attractions of the material world in sound perspective. I don't worry greatly that, if you became rich monetarily, you would abandon your spiritual odyssey. I know you too well for that and I believe that you could use any such funds to good advantage. So just wait and see, huh.

Thanks for calling on us this evening and keep coming back regularly as I have requested. Right now is still a part of your orientation with me, Michael, which is why I am talking about you, your family and friends rather than about more universally applicable spiritual matters. That will come when you are ready and I think that will be rather soon.

Further Orientation

Session 50 - September 5, 1993

Michael: Good evening and thank you for resuming our discussions. As you know, we do not intrude into your consciousness under normal circumstances unless you initiate the contact.

I am pleased that you are continuing to walk fairly regularly. Also I want you to communicate with Seneca and me at least three times a week. It is different when you are away or something like that but under normal conditions that is a minimum requirement. It would be better yet if you did it on a daily basis but I don't want to push you too hard.

We are getting close to the end of our orientation period and I will soon be able to pass on to you some of the more spiritual and universally applicable messages that I want you to convey to mankind when the time is right. They are similar to the messages that you have been getting from Seneca before I appeared on the scene. However, my messages may cover more details that Seneca is not familiar with, and they may also cover more obscure or esoteric subjects that are not yet within Seneca's sphere of knowledge, because, as I have said, I am somewhat further along than he is and therefore have access to information that he is not yet privy to. When you get such information, you will know it.

Energy

I am sorry that your friends are leaving because you generate good energy as a group. The whole is greater than the sum of the parts.

That gives me a subject for tonight's conversation—namely, energy. It is a large subject and I will touch on only a small piece of it now, with more to come later. *I have already told you something important about energy by saying that the whole is greater than the sum of its parts.* When you have a group of sincere people gathered together for a common purpose, the total amount of energy generated far exceeds the sum of their individual energies. Though not literally correct, you might say that the total amount of energy thus generated is the exponent of the number of people participating. That is why groups are valuable for all kinds of psychic and spiritual activities, from prayer to healing to many other kinds of events.

Like physical energy, spiritual energy can also be used for good or evil. Those who use it for unworthy purposes build up a sizable karmic debt quickly, which they must then work off with difficulty, often over a number of lives. The culprit is usually ego and so long as you remain mindful of the insidious influences of ego, you are much less likely to fall into that trap.

The story you just read about the encounter between Rolling Thunder and the young sorcerer illustrates the point. The young sorcerer had received instruction in the use of psychic powers but without the self-discipline and ego control that are also required. He wanted fame and importance and he abused his powers in an effort to attain them. He will pay for his adventure, not as punishment, but in order that he may learn to use the powers of nature for worthy purposes—and only for such purposes. Rolling Thunder actually did the young man a great favor by depriving him of his powers, otherwise his price would have become heavier and heavier over time.

Psychic energy follows its own set of natural laws, just as physical energy does. At this stage of human development, you just don't know what those laws are and how to make use of them. When your race reaches a high enough stage of spiritual development, then you will be allowed to learn those laws. Until then, only a few highly spiritual and selfless members of the human race will be allowed to understand these laws, and even then only partially. Some others will learn how to use them without necessarily understanding them, as in the case of Rolling Thunder and others who are able to accomplish things that appear to violate the laws of nature as you know them. As you already know, you don't have to understand something to be able to make use of it. You yourself know little or nothing about automobile mechanics but you are still able to drive a car and make use of the application of laws that you do not pretend to understand. So it also is in the case of nonphysical laws.

Everything starts with energy. Even your eternal spirit is a kind of condensed, coalescent energy. As its vibrational rate lowers, energy transforms itself into matter and then becomes part of the material world. While you accept Einstein's theory of $E=mc^2$, and have demonstrated it in the field of nuclear energy, you should note that you have only demonstrated the equation in one direction, that is, you have successfully transformed a small quantity of matter into energy. But you are a long way from ever doing the reverse, or transforming energy into matter. You don't have the foggiest idea of how to go about doing it. And yet, spiritual people have been able to do this for centuries—you call them materializations. They are able to do it without also knowing how or why it works.

Well, the day will come when you will be taught how to do it and how it works. When I say "you," understand that I don't mean you personally—I mean humankind. But that kind of awesome and dangerous power cannot even be considered for transfer to you until you have reached a stage of spiritual development where we can have confidence that you will not abuse your powers. I don't see that happening in the very near future.

The life force that keeps you alive and functioning throughout your lifetime is also a form of energy. Again, it is a nonphysical form of energy, but don't ever lose sight of the fact that spiritual energy is energy also—and very powerful energy at that. When that energy is diverted or attenuated, illness results on the physical plane, and if that energy is interrupted, physical death results. Of course, your eternal spirit and the energy comprising it are not affected by physical death of the body.

I like the description that you were given about your dog as "the little person in the dog suit." It is a good metaphor for you to use in your dealings with other people. You all happen to be people in people suits, but the external configuration is nothing more than just a suit, and a temporary one at that. Instead of being influenced excessively by the suit, take the time and effort to look at the person inside the suit and see what the real person is like. It will give you a much more valid picture of who that other person is. It may also show you how you can help that person to improve his or her spiritual development by penetrating beyond the superficialities of the external suit. Use of this technique should also help you to become a more compassionate person yourself, because you will see more clearly the essential personhood of the other and will not be put off by some of the ego posturing that many people use to hide their own feelings of inadequacy. Try it and tell your family and friends to try it. They will all benefit from the use of this technique.

I will talk more about various kinds of energy at a later time. For now you have enough to reflect upon for a while.

Sincerity

Session 52 - September 7, 1993

Today I would like to talk about sincerity. *Sincerity is a great virtue because it is so closely tied into motive. And as you been told before, motive is the key factor in determining the moral value of a thought, word or deed.* Sincerity also includes within it an element of concern for the other person with whom one is interacting. It carries with it a measure of respect too. All these elements make sincerity such a highly prized virtue. But it is one that can, with practice, be cultivated fairly easily even under the conditions that prevail in your material world.

Do not make the mistake of equating sincerity with lack of tact in dealing with your fellow humans. It certainly does not mean being abrupt or abrasive under the guise of being sincere. That kind of false sincerity is nothing more than another manifestation of that sneaky and omnipresent fellow—ego. If a friend of yours asks you how you like her new, expensive dress and you think it is horrible, it is not an act of sincerity to tell her so. That would be a put-down and those do not lead to spiritual development, at least not without pain. At the same time, you are not required to say that it looks magnificent on her. You could get by with the statement that "Yes, it certainly looks expensive" or maybe "I don't think it would look too good on me" or something of that sort.

You must always remember that, while sincerity is a virtue to be cultivated, your first rule is to do no harm to others—and that includes psychic harm. So even if you sometimes have to indulge in a little white lie to avoid hurting someone, the noble motive will far outweigh the negative effects of the little white lie. For a lifetime on earth, you must live in the material world and fulfill its demands, and you know that courtesy and civility are essential lubricants that enable you to live together in communities without killing each other off over trivia. Of course, as communities get larger, that benefit tends to disappear and you manage to do quite a bit of killing each other off over trivia.

You would apparently like me to talk somewhat about spirit. All right. *Spirit is something in the nature of energy personified—endowed with an individual essence that is eternal because it is of God.* Spirits exist at all levels of development and some that have lost their way misuse their spiritual powers and cause trouble until they learn better. But while they are in that bad condition, they can work a great deal of mischief and are best avoided. They are usually spirits that were not very highly evolved when they acquired human bodies and they learned little or nothing by way of spiritual growth or progress during their lifetime(s) on earth. When they shed their bodies and go back into spirit, they don't really remember where they are, what they incarnated to do and how good or poor a job they did. They are temporarily like strangers in a strange land and it brings out their worst characteristics. But our message is always one of hope and eventually these lost spirits do find their way home, even though the journey may be a long and painful one for them. As Seneca has said to you before, God does not punish—He teaches. Most of the actual punishment we experience is self-inflicted.

Let me say a word about the apparent dilemma you were talking about last night about the relative power of prayer and love. Prayer is stronger because, while it is a manifestation of love, it is love for God. And that transcends human love or even love for God's creation as a whole. Prayer is a way in which we express our love for God, our desire to do His will and our hope for reunion with Him when we are ready for it. Prayer is also the form in which we communicate our human needs to God and ask for His help. And we get that help when it is in our long-term best interests. We *think* we know what our best interests are but we are driven by a sense of immediacy, so we know only what we think are our best interests *now*. And we can even be far wrong on those as well. That is why there is much wisdom in the joke: "Be careful what you pray for because you may get it!" Much human wisdom may be found camouflaged in humor.

The term "grace" just popped into your head. I don't think I put it there. What is it? Well, I am not about to get into theological discussions because I share Seneca's views on that subject, but give me a moment and I will try to think of a short working definition for your practical use. *God is always open to our love; He gives us His and He seeks ours. In my definition, when I have recognized and accepted God's unqualified love for me as an individual, just as I am, at the very core of my being, then I would say that I have been a recipient of the grace of God.* There may well be other definitions, but that is my favorite and the one most likely to happen to each of you as you go through your life in the material world. I know it has already happened to you, Bill, and it has made a major difference in your whole attitude toward life and people, even though that change may not be entirely visible to the outside world. I might add that the receipt of grace has the same effect on everyone who is fortunate enough to receive it.

Have I given you enough to think about for a while? I think maybe so because what I am giving you are short bursts of some very heavy material.

Justice

Session 53 · September 14, 1993

What shall we talk about tonight? The term "justice" popped into your mind just now so let's make that our starting point. In a very real way, justice is not much more than a synonym for karma. The term "karma" does not itself carry with it moral connotations but sounds similar to a law of nature — the law of cause and effect. On the other hand, the term "justice" does carry with it moral connotations. It includes the element of fairness too. But when you apply the law of karma to a person's conduct, don't you find that you come up with justice as a result?

Let me use an example. A person commits a terrible crime against another. That person is found out, tried, convicted and sentenced to a term of imprisonment, or perhaps even death if the crime was heinous enough. That would seem like an instantaneous example of the law of karma, but wouldn't you also call it justice? Wouldn't it also be considered to be fair?

The application of karma in subsequent lives is usually much more subtle because the person involved has no memory of what he did in past lives that he may be paying for now. In that case, let's assume that the person who committed the terrible crime got away with it, at least as far as the civil authorities were concerned. He died as a wealthy and respected citizen of his community. But in a later life, he may choose to be a victim of an equally terrible crime as a way of learning the full impact of what he did and compensating for it. He won't know why he is now living the life of a victim unless he has an appreciation of the law of karma, and realizes that he must have done something terrible in a past life and has not previously come to grips with that action. But isn't that also fair and just? Keep in mind that, while the bodies involved in the two lifetimes are different, the spirit that inhabits them is the same one and it is the spirit that is engaged in the learning process and the spiritual journey.

How much do we really know about that virtuous concept that we call justice? We give it moral connotations, and that is all right, but we also define it all too often in terms of our own very limited human concepts and therefore apply it only to the framework of a single lifetime. Unless we understand the simple operation of the law of karma over many lifetimes, we are unable to understand that bad things that are happening to an apparently good person may merely be his way of making peace with his past.

Karma is in principle no different than a system of double entry bookkeeping. Both sides have to balance. It is also beautifully expressed in the biblical phrase: "As you sow, so shall you reap." The biblical phrase, however, at least as it has come down to you, implies that the books will balance when we are judged at the end of one life. But that is a corruption of the true meaning of the phrase. Power and ego got in the way and powerful leaders took it upon themselves to ban the fact of reincarnation because it would, they thought, weaken their control over their followers. They were wrong, and it is an unfortunate failing of the institutional Christian church that they illogically make a person's eternal future depend on his conduct in one lifetime, a mere blink of an eye in time.

Since we don't know what recompense is being made for past actions when, say, a person falls ill, we seek to cure him and even pray for divine intervention to help with the cure. We really don't know whether we are doing that person a service or, instead, are preventing him from balancing the books regarding some past conduct. Our motives are good and therefore we improve our own karmic condition somewhat. But God knows what the underlying causes of that person's illness are and whether a cure would or would not be in the best interests of his soul's spiritual development. So while it's fine for us to pray for that person, we must also remember that God knows far better than we do what is truly in the best interests of that spirit.

You would like to know how one can tell whether he is getting close to the end of mandatory reincarnations. When is graduation? *When you have overcome your ego traps, have genuine love and compassion for your fellow beings and realize at the very core of your being that you are indeed connected indissolubly with every other part of God's creation—animal, vegetable or mineral—then you may be ready for graduation exercises.* You should all have a pretty good idea of when you start coming close to meeting these criteria—or to state it differently, start coming close to passing your final exams. In the meantime, keep at it on a continual basis because, as you struggle to become that kind of person while in the material world, and it is a struggle, you will not only achieve spiritual growth in the process but you will also enrich your lives immeasurably.

What I am encouraging is an offshoot of a previous message to the effect that God loves and accepts each and every one of us totally and unqualifiedly just as we are, with all our faults and imperfections, because He knows that we all bear a piece of His divine flame within us. Our job here is to try to emulate, to the maximum extent we can (after all, we aren't God), these same qualities toward our fellow humans. When we can achieve this, the rest will fall into place, I am sure.

And it will happen! It may take longer than we would wish and there may be considerable pain in the process, as with the Earth purifying herself from what we have done to her, *but never forget that the message is always one of hope. Eventually we all graduate, even the slow learners. So don't ever give up; don't ever consider yourself as outside God's loving care, no matter how unworthy you may feel about yourself.* That is tonight's message.

Pride

Session 54 - September 16, 1993

Hello again. Yes, you got the message very quickly that tonight we will talk about pride. You see, it gets easier as we do it more often. Also, your intuitive powers are growing by leaps and bounds, largely due to our connection.

Pride is described in religious terms as one of the seven deadly sins. That's quite true, when pride is properly defined, but pride is nothing more than another manifestation of ego. The kind of pride that is criticized here and in the bible is not pride in a job well done, or in helping someone out, but the kind of pride that looks down its nose at others. It is accompanied by feelings of superiority to others and, at its worst, it can consider other living beings as mere things. It is at its most egregious, with equivalent karmic consequences, when it is applied to other humans.

This wrong kind of pride focuses on what separates you from each other and from the rest of God's creation, rather on what unites you. This emphasis on "separateness" is a direct result of ego. Your ego in this lifetime makes you want to believe that you are unique, special, different from everybody else, and superior as well—whether in intelligence, physical ability, beauty, money, or whatever. Well, each of you *is* unique, special and different, but that is true of your eternal souls, not just their temporary housings. But are you superior? Absolutely not. The ironic thing is that, at the spirit level, we tend to have a kind of reverse hierarchy—those who are most advanced and closest to God are the most humble, while those who are least advanced are likely to think of themselves as far more advanced than they really are. So you see, we do have some of the same problems here that you do in the material world, but not to as severe an extent.

Another thing that ego does is that it tries to convince you that the life you are presently leading is the one and only life you will ever have. Since you usually cannot remember past lives, and since church teachings support this proposition of only one life to a customer, ego tries to convince you that this one life is everything. No second or third or fourth chances to make up for past injustices—or to be rewarded for good things you may have done in the past. There is just now, that terrible sense of immediacy and urgency. But those who can see through the ego trap and recognize the eternal nature of their spirit and their lengthy journey along the path back home are better able to put the events of this lifetime into better perspective.

If negative things happen to them, they are able to conclude that maybe they are working out issues from past lives, rather than blaming some mysterious concept called "luck" or deciding that they are innocent victims of some kind of conspiracy. Or they may appreciate that there are important lessons to be learned by them from unfortunate events—lessons being taught by a loving Father, not an avenging angel. Throughout it all, knowing who and what they are, they can continue to keep their eye on the right ball and not be diverted from their long-term path by either good or bad events in their lives. That is what we mean by perspective.

As more and more people in the western world come to accept the fact of reincarnation, with everything that goes with it, this perspective will become more widespread and will eventually overcome the shortsighted individual egos that so many in the west must contend with now. It is our hope and expectation that this process will lead to a greater sense of awareness of our fundamental and inescapable unity, something we should rejoice in once we finally come to realize it. When that happens, the kinds of horror stories that are so abundant now will cease to exist. How can anyone do something terrible to someone else when he knows that he is in fact doing it to himself? It may seem like a far-fetched analogy but I'll use it anyway. People don't cut off their own hand because they accidentally dropped a coffee cup or hit their own thumb with a hammer.

I am pleased that you are making use of the "person in the person-suit" metaphor as you come into contact with other people. It enables you to see what the real person is like that is occupying the particular person-suit. When you see a frightened, insecure child inside the facade of a big tough suit, you are able to feel a greater degree of understanding—and, yes, compassion as well—toward that person in spite of the obnoxious bravado emerging from the suit. You don't necessarily have to like the person in the suit, or even associate with him, but you will have a much better perspective regarding who the real person is that is hiding in the particular person-suit. The reference to Mitzi [our family Schnauzer] as "the little person in the dog suit" was really a very fortuitous one when Jim and Alice were visiting you. It brought that kind of viewpoint into your conscious mind.

❋ ❋ ❋ ❋

As you know, both you and Enid have been healers in past lives, and you should understand that healing by listening and with words can in many cases be as effective as the use of medicinal herbs or the laying on of hands. Listening particularly, and then responding from the heart, seems to be your healing technique for this lifetime, so make good use of them. They really do work.

Honor

Session 55 - September 20, 1993

Welcome back. Today we will start off by talking a little bit about honor. Like so many of your terms, it requires definition before it can be discussed meaningfully. *In my view, honor can be best and most simply defined as the recognition of a sense of personal worth that requires the person to act fairly, civilly and considerately toward all others with whom he comes in contact.*

It is not the kind of characteristic that one fights duels over, as was once the situation in your world. Those so-called "affairs of honor" were really nothing more than ego trips for their perpetrators or, at worst, a device for killing or injuring someone you didn't like without being punished for it.

On the other hand, to call someone "an honorable person" in the true sense of the term is a compliment of the highest order. *In addition to the characteristics I mentioned earlier, an honorable person will be guided in his speech and actions by his own honest perception of what is the right thing to do in a given situation.* He will stand up against wrongdoing and injustice, even when that is not the popular course of action. Without knowing that much about them, I can be reasonably sure that the persons described in John F. Kennedy's book *Profiles in Courage* were honorable men, at least with respect to the action that won them their place in the book.

I don't know whether you are ready for it, but the earth changes of which we have spoken before are occurring faster than anticipated. I think they will become more and more severe as we approach the end of this millennium. The united prayers of sincere people can help stave them off a little, and by stretching them out, make them somewhat less severe. *But they will come;* they *have* to since the earth must purify itself from the rape and pollution that mankind has inflicted upon it. That cannot be avoided, only eased a little.

Do you therefore go rushing to the mountains because of what I have said? Not at all. If that should become a necessary thing for you to do, I will let you know. But since nothing happens without a purpose and a reason, if you are killed in the course of earth changes, it merely means that you have completed your assignment on earth in this lifetime as fully as you are able and you are now ready to move on to the next challenge. You don't really have to worry greatly about this, however, because I still have a lot of work left for you to accomplish before you depart this life.

✦✦✦✦

Note that the path back to God need not be through membership in institutional churches. It can be, of course, if the teachings emphasize love, compassion, respect for diversity, and an awareness of our common humanity, and if the members choose to follow those teachings. On the other hand, an individual can find his or her way to God without being affiliated with any organized religion if he or she lives in accordance with God's plan. *Thus, every human being on earth can find a path to God, whether on his own or together with others.* It helps and is easier to do it with others because the trail has already been blazed, at least partially. Nevertheless, that prescribed institutional path may also be obstructed by doctrinal disputes, internal power struggles or other excess baggage that contributes nothing to the spiritual journey. You and Enid went to church yesterday and you were much impressed by the homily and some of the other prayers. Good. Much of what you will hear in church will help you on your spiritual journey, once you are able to overcome the exclusivity and implied superiority of one set of doctrines over another. One major advantage that sincere churchgoers do have over the solitary individual is numbers. *As you know, the prayers of a group have an energy level that is closer to exponential than to merely additive. Therefore, group prayer makes a much greater impact than the separate, solitary prayers of the same number of people.*

Communication

Session 56 - September 21, 1993

Hello again. We are glad to see you back so soon. Yes, Michael is here even though you are having difficulty seeing his illumination. That was done earlier for your benefit so that you would know there was someone else with me, Seneca. Now it doesn't matter whether you see him or not; he's here with us and will talk to you the same as he has been doing.

What to talk about tonight? Your conversation with your son last night was interesting to me because of the difficulties you discussed in translating concepts from one language into another. He talked about what is translated as "suffering" or in some cases "unsatisfactoriness" and you talked about translating the Greek term "arete" into "virtue" in English. It is an important step forward in intercultural relations when one can appreciate the shortcomings of translation to express the concepts contained in the language of another culture. As I say, that is a good start. But you must also remember that *all languages fall short of expressing—much less translating—complex or subtle concepts.* Your human languages just aren't up to it.

That is why telepathic communication will ultimately be the method of the future. Then you can communicate on a mind-to-mind basis without the necessity of words. And concepts come through much more clearly that way. In the meantime, we must do the best with what we have. Even if we could—and to some extent we do—talk to you, Bill, on a mental basis, you still have to try to translate our thoughts, as best you understand them, into words so that you can communicate them to your fellow humans when I tell you to do so.

Communication—something that is sorely lacking in your world today, in spite of all the technical devices you have developed in order to make it more widespread and immediate. When Seneca and I talk about communication, we mean *real* communication, not the never-ceasing barrage of noise that you are enveloped in here in the United States and many other parts of the world. That kind of noise is more of an obstacle to communication than the realization of it.

Real communication includes both listening and compassionate understanding of the other person. Listening has become almost a lost art in your country. Everyone wants to talk but the talk is meaningless if no one listens. It is perhaps worse if people listen, as they do sometimes, and what they hear is demagoguery. When I say "listen," I mean to listen with both the mind and the heart, rather than the emotions.

Emotions are often too susceptible to manipulation by rabble-rousers and they are the kind of people that appeal to the worst in us. They are the ones who spread hatred of others and create lynch mobs. In this country you think you have progressed beyond the lynch mob, but if you have, it's still a close call. Even you, who are a relatively peaceful man, are aware of the potential for violence that lies within you under the correct circumstances—and I can assure you that the same potential lies within the entire human race, with the possible exception of a few saints who are presently living on earth. And for many of your fellow humans, that potential for violence is a good deal closer to the surface than it is in your case.

Again I come back to mindfulness. While in your material body, you are what you are, although your spirit is in ultimate control. Being mindful of your human weaknesses goes a long way toward enabling your God-given spirit to exercise control over your antisocial inclinations. So mindfulness again becomes a key characteristic of spiritual growth. It also helps put ego in its proper place. *While in the material world, you need an ego in order to survive in it. But you must keep your ego very much under control so that you do not become its prisoner.* Mindfulness of your human shortcomings—and you all have them or you would have already graduated from this schoolhouse called Earth—also helps keep you properly humble during this lifetime and helps you to remember the big picture behind your very temporary visit to this small planet for a given lifetime. I will continue to come back to it from time to time, because I cannot stress too heavily the importance of mindfulness in accomplishing our spiritual journey with a minimum of distractions and blind alleys.

You would like still more tonight? Good. Maybe we can accelerate your education if you can make the connection longer.

W. G.: While I do get tired after a length of time, I also find the connection so stimulating that I look forward to our visits and hope that I will be able to extend the duration of them as we proceed.

Seneca: We will match your pace since we don't get tired. However, we don't want you to do more than you can handle at one sitting. We have plenty of time to accomplish what we are setting out to do and we don't want to wear you out by trying to do too much too soon.

Though I am tempted to stop now, I will continue for a few more minutes at your request. Your daughter, Sue, was asking about the origin of the Bible myths. Well, as with all mythologies, the early Bible myths were produced under inspiration from the spirit world and were described in terms that were understandable to the levels of culture and sophistication that existed at the time they were written (or orally created) and in the country in which they were written.

But you should note that, while there are wide variations in, say, creation mythology among various cultures, there is a great deal of similarity among them regarding how people should live with each other, this planet Earth and our universal Creator. That shouldn't be too surprising to you since, after all, inspiration ultimately comes from the One Source, even though in some instances it may be funneled through helpers like us. Given what you have already learned about the interconnectedness of all God's creation, shouldn't it surprise you more if it were otherwise? You see, once you accept that fact—I almost said "proposition" but it isn't just a proposition, it's a FACT— it changes your entire perspective on a whole host of things, maybe even everything, doesn't it?

Cleanliness

Session 57 - September 22, 1993 the ages.

Tonight I would like to begin by talking about cleanliness. That may seem a little strange, but of course I am not just talking about physical cleanliness. For you in America with all your physical resources and advertising, it is easy to stay physically clean. I am talking about the much more difficult and important task of becoming, and remaining, morally and spiritually clean. Moral cleanliness is of course something entirely different from physical cleanliness, and cleanliness of spirit is a step beyond even moral cleanliness. It is the goal of our work here in this material world, and even in the spirit world. *Complete cleanliness of spirit is what is required to enable us to achieve reunion with our Divine Source. That's why it is so difficult and takes so long.*

Let's talk a little about moral cleanliness. Some might think that it is limited to refraining from sexual misconduct or dishonesty. But that is just the tip of the iceberg. It is really much more demanding because it extends to your thoughts and words as well as your actions. It also covers attitudes and behavior that are not dealt with by society's laws. It therefore represents much more of a challenge than most people believe it to be.

Moral cleanliness really consists of a way of life—it is a constant part of one's life, rather than something that we may reflect upon from time to time if we are feeling introspective. I don't mean that one spends every waking moment thinking about how to remain morally clean rather, the elements that comprise it ultimately become second nature to the individual struggling to achieve it. And I can assure you that it is a struggle. Don't be discouraged by that statement because we all have to go through the struggle in order to emerge as better beings. Yes, that applies to Seneca and me as well. We too were once human so we know something about the trials and tribulations that are an inevitable part of the struggle. But remember that most worthwhile things in life, even in your material world, don't just fall into your lap—you have to work hard for them. So it is with moral cleanliness.

One of the predominant elements of moral cleanliness is love—love for one's fellow humans and also love for all God's creatures. Also love for the living Earth that sustains us. That love manifest itself in a kind of natural exuberance and an optimism about the future, even when things may look bleak. Strengthened by love, a person does not want to take advantage of his fellow human beings or of living creatures generally.

He or she will also be an environmentalist who understands that Mother Earth sustains us and we must not abuse her gifts or pollute her to the point where she must respond. I am not talking about environmental extremists who are motivated by ego and self-importance but, rather, about those sincere believers who respect what our relationship to the Earth—should be namely, that man is a steward, not a master. And as a side note, I might add that even a master, if only slightly intelligent, would not wantonly destroy what is his!

I have said that spiritual cleanliness is a step still higher than moral cleanliness. But I am finding it hard to explain the distinction in words that can be understood by you and other humans. Let me think for a minute and see if I can. Morality pertains to your conduct while in the flesh. Though your conduct is ultimately governed by spirit, it is nonetheless greatly influenced by the circumstances of your life in the material world. It is therefore by its very nature imperfect. But spiritual cleanliness, or purity as I am now calling it, pertains to your eternal essence. It is not influenced by earthly considerations and it is capable of achieving perfection. It has to be in order to be capable of reunion with God and we know that such reunions happen. Maybe that is the principal distinction between moral purity and spiritual purity—one is necessarily imperfect in light of the circumstances within which it functions, while the other is capable of achieving perfection. At least for now, that's the best I can do in trying to explain this distinction.

I think I was not quite accurate when I said that your eternal essence is not influenced by earthly considerations. While it is not *surrounded* by them in the way that you are during an earthly life, as is your moral attitude, your eternal essence is *affected* by the experiences of your earthly lives. If that were not the case, what would be the point of living earthly lives? But the effect is far more attenuated than when you are actually living a life in the material world. I think it is important that I not leave an erroneous impression so please modify my earlier statement accordingly.

I need not tell you that there is no correlation whatever between physical cleanliness and moral or spiritual cleanliness. Jesus made that quite clear when he used the "whited sepulcher" metaphor in referring to the contrast between the outer and inner cleanliness of the Pharisees. The converse is of course also true all over the world, and especially in materially poor countries. You were amazed and impressed, when you read the book *City of Joy*, to read about people who were living in abject poverty and yet who shared and laughed and loved their neighbors. The contrast between their external living conditions and their inner serenity moved you greatly. Well, there are many examples throughout the world and throughout the ages.

Generosity

Session 58 · September 23, 1993

Good evening. I am pleased that you are beginning to feel more comfortable with me. I am really not as frightening a person as I might first have seemed to be. However, that image may have helped you decide to follow my instructions about exercise and communication more faithfully than would otherwise have been the case. If so, then it was good. But it is no longer necessary, I think. You understand that you have a mission to perform and you are undertaking to do it willingly, even gladly. You will gain good karma from doing a good job of it, for your mission can be of great help to many, if they will listen. If not, then at least you and Seneca and I will have tried.

Was I too philosophical last night? I want to try to keep these conversations as simple as possible and focused on how you should live in this material world in order to grow spiritually, rather than on intellectual pursuits. The latter may be very interesting (and I know you have a good deal of intellectual curiosity) but what counts is not what we *know* but what we *do*. Therefore, I prefer to stay away from that kind of subject matter, except when it has a definite bearing on how we should live. Maybe the distinction that I talked about last night between moral and spiritual purity was getting a little off the track but it may also have been of some help to you on the question of how you should live your lives on earth.

Tonight I would like to talk about something simpler—generosity. As with so many other terms we have talked about, this one also has many meanings and levels. The first, and most obvious, is material generosity toward others in the world who may not be as fortunate in terms of their material possessions or economic status. Generous donations to help the less fortunate certainly constitutes behavior that is deserving of commendation. Properly motivated, it carries good karma with it. But don't forget, it must be properly motivated. As I have told you before, motive is the touchstone to be applied to all thoughts, words and acts in order to determine their moral value. I will keep repeating this from time to time so that none of you who read this material will ever forget that fact.

Another level of generosity, and I consider this to be a higher one, might be called generosity of heart. What does that mean? It applies to people who may not make large material donations but who give of themselves for the less fortunate. This kind of generosity usually takes the form of personal service, rather than financial contribution—and while both are worthy, this ranks higher in the spirit world. Your wife is a good example of this. She gives of her time and talent to help others and reflects what I have called generosity of heart. Many others in your American society also do all kinds of volunteer work, and in most cases it is motivated by the highest considerations. *Generosity of heart is a manifestation of compassion, which is one of the greatest virtues humans can possess.* As you can readily appreciate, people with genuine compassion are almost incapable of hurting their fellow humans—or animals for that matter. I think they also possess what I would call a reverence for life, recognizing that life is God's greatest gift to His creation.

Is there also a distinction between generosity of heart and generosity of spirit? Maybe so, but it is a rather small one. Because we are only human while on earth (at least nearly all of us), even generosity of heart is not totally free from some element of ego or self-interest while generosity of spirit, unencumbered by any of these constraints, can be truly and totally selfless and pure. Thus, there is still a distinction between the two but it is not one that should concern you. It has no effect on how you should live your lives on earth.

Another subject—free will. That is a subject that I will come back to many times because it is of enormous scope and importance. Free will goes with the divine spark that all of us were given by our Creator. The two go hand in hand. Free will gives us the choice as to how we conduct ourselves while in the material world. Some call it the choice between good and evil. I prefer to call it the choice between spirit and ego. It is ours to do with as we see fit. I like to think it means that God, in giving us this incredible power that we take largely for granted, has chosen to trust us to conduct ourselves in accordance with the teachings of spirit, rather than those of ego. *Spirit teaches unity, while ego teaches separateness. Unity carries with it a sense of sharing, of our all being in the same boat and needing to work and live together; separateness teaches individual isolation, selfishness and fear of others who are not just like us.*

God has given us this choice by giving us free will and we have a long way to go before the great majority of people in the world choose to follow the teachings of spirit rather than those of ego. But always remember, God is patient, infinitely patient, and eventually we will all come to follow the teachings of spirit. The trend is growing though it may not be highly visible, but as I said there is still a long way to go. As always, however, the message remains one of hope because it will ultimately come to pass. Some people are just slower learners than others, that's all.

You would like still more tonight? Let me see what I can come up with that is brief. I hardly need to say it but I will remind you that *a concomitant element of free will is choice and with choice goes responsibility for the consequences of the choices that you make.* That should be pretty self-evident to you, but not everybody recognizes that inevitable sequence of events. Remind people of it. It is nothing more than another variation of the law of karma or cause and effect. Choices made (causes) necessarily give rise to consequences (effects) and we must be prepared to assume responsibility for the choices we make. We may not always like the consequences but we must understand that they flow from our choices and we must therefore accept them. Hopefully, we learn from unpleasant consequences that accompany certain choices and therefore decide not to make similar choices in the future.

Doubt

Session 59 · September 25, 1993

Good evening. You really don't have to try to think of topics for me. I know you have some trouble coming up with them and I appreciate your efforts but I can come up with them myself. Tonight's subject is doubt. It occurred to me to be appropriate because you seemed to be having some doubt about whether you could keep coming up with subjects for our discussions. But *you* aren't doing that. *I* am and I assure you again that I still have a lot to talk about.

Doubt is a very understandable phenomenon in communication with spirits. It is still hard for you, and others similarly situated, to believe totally and unequivocally that you are really communicating on a mind-to-mind basis with a non-earthly being—by which I mean someone who is no longer living in the material world. That is your cultural and rational background resisting what your heart knows is true. I am not the voice of your subconscious or superconscious or any other part of you that you may care to name. I am a totally separate entity, as is Seneca. At the core of your being, you know that to be the case. It is just that, from time to time, you just can't help wondering a little . . . .

That's a rather simple definition of doubt—wondering a little whether something you believe is indeed true. If the doubt becomes great enough and deep-seated enough, it can effectively destroy whatever it was that you had believed in.

Doubt is by no means negative, at least not entirely. Doubt is a way of checking the validity of information or advice that you may be getting, especially if it comes from a source that some would say doesn't even exist and others would say does exist but certainly doesn't communicate with mere mortals. Since psychic matters do not lend themselves to laboratory analysis, at least not with the tools that are available to you today, there are all too many frauds out in the world preying on the gullibility or hope or wishful thinking of people everywhere. A healthy doubt can help keep you from being victimized by these frauds.

In general, though, doubt is not a positive characteristic. Along with it goes hesitation and uncertainty. Doubt in the context that I am talking about represents a lack of self-confidence, either in your facts, your judgment or your intuition. I am here using the term "intuition" to refer to your psychic capabilities. Unfortunately, in your material world at this stage of its evolution, it is all right to have good "intuitions" about many things but it is much less acceptable to have "psychic capabilities." The situation in this regard has been improving in recent years and it will continue to improve as people throughout the world, but particularly in the western world, become more spiritually aware.

I assure you that neither Seneca nor I is upset if you have occasional moments of doubt about whether we exist. That is both natural and understandable in light of your background and training. However, that momentary doubt washes away very quickly when we are having our conversations. Your intuition, which is becoming quite good since we have made contact, tells you in a great loud voice that Seneca and Michael are real and that they are in fact communicating with you in an effort to help humanity ameliorate some of the unfortunate events that lie in store.

You also know, through use of your rational resources, which are considerable, that you are not listening to yourself—you have not been thinking the kind of thoughts that you have been receiving. So if they don't come from you, then where? You can be quite confident that you are not hallucinating; you are a pretty stable personality, a Taurus, and rather well-grounded even though you would like to soar with the eagles. Well, my friend, that is exactly what you are doing now!

Another reason you know we are real and are communicating with you is the warmth you feel during our discussions. You can feel the love that we are sending to you and your family and we feel it being returned. That can only happen between two or more entities one cannot do it all by himself. Also, as an offshoot of our interaction, you have been privileged to experience what I described as the grace of God. Yes, it was brief—it lasted only a few moments—but you will never forget it. Well, if you can interact with God Himself, why can you not interact with some of His helpers? The answer is that you can—and you do.

To come back to the subject of doubt, I should tell you (and I am sure it will come as no surprise) *that the most unfortunate example of doubt in the world today is doubt as to the existence of God.* Although I think it is becoming much less so, it used to be fashionable among scientists in your world to question the existence of God as Creator of the universe and to claim that random chance over a long enough period of time could have produced this amazing universe that we live in. That's nonsense and I can tell you that worship of science—and that's what it amounts to—is just another form of idolatry, maybe a little more sophisticated than the golden calf or the almighty dollar but idolatry just the same.

The second most unfortunate doubt is to doubt God's love for each and every one of us. We have portrayed God as stern judge as well as loving father—punisher of our transgressions and consignor to hell of His children who stray. We endow Him with some of our own worst characteristics—God, whose love and kindness and support are beyond our poor ability to begin to comprehend. If we can get past this god of fear that we have created, perhaps we will then be able to treat each other the way we know we should.

Sex

Session 60 - September 26, 1993

Hello. Glad you made it back so soon. Today I would like to start off talking about sex. As you know by now, when I start with a topic, that often turns out to be just a lead-in to other subjects. However, sex sounds like a subject that would be of interest to people in the material world since so many are preoccupied by it.

Sex is not only inherently good but also necessary. It is obviously the means by which a species is perpetuated, whether humans or other species. With some limited exceptions, some form of sexual action is required in order to reproduce. For animals, nature establishes periods when the female is ready to mate—what you call being "in heat." Males have sensors that tell them when that is the case and, since the sex act is pleasurable, they are happy to perform it. Again with limited exceptions, animals who have mated do not remain together to protect and bring up their young. The males leave and the females remain as the caregivers and nurturers until the young have grown up to the point where they can fend for themselves.

Why the speech about animal habits? Well, since you humans have evolved from animal origins (though some of you don't like to admit it), you still retain within your psyches some of these tendencies and it is important that you know it. Because you as humans have been blessed with reasoning power, free will and some moral sense, you have learned, to some extent at least, to control your animal urges including the sex urge. So for humans—whom I like to think of as spirits made in the image of God and containing an ember of the divine fire while attending school on earth—what is sex supposed to be all about? Obviously procreation, as in the animal kingdom, but also much more. It is a means of expressing love and comfort between a man and a woman—or it should be. It is also a way of expressing a sense of unity between two persons— a unity that, on a spiritual basis, is what we are seeking to foster among humankind as a whole.

Viewed in this manner, sex in the lives of men and women can be a kind of bridge between the natural urges toward procreation, which is of the animals, and the sense of unity of all persons, which is of the spirit. It represents a kind of way-station on your spiritual journey. We who are here in spirit do not experience any physical sensations, including sex. We may remember it fondly if our experiences were good on earth, but we don't experience it here, and I regret to inform you, we don't need it here. Actually, you find on earth that, as people get older the sex drive becomes less important, while other qualities become more important in a spouse. I have to admit that it may be due as much to declining human capability, at least in men, as it is to spiritual progress.

As in so many other areas, sex also can have its dark side. That takes the form of abuse, not necessarily physical abuse but abuse just the same. Use of sex as a means to other objectives is a form of abuse. Use of sex as a means of control over others is another form of abuse. Because sex is such a very powerful instinct in humans, it can be used— really abused—as a source of power over others. Use of sex solely for its pleasurable features, devoid of caring or tenderness, is abuse. The sexual athlete, who seeks to number his so-called conquests in the highest numbers he can achieve, is an abuser. Don't misunderstand me. Being only human, there will be times in your lives when each of you, both male and female, will have abused your sexual gifts. The important thing is to recognize its genuine purpose and not to abuse it on a regular or extended basis. As in so many other areas of human conduct, mindfulness will stand you in good stead in avoiding abuse of this gift.

ॐॐ

Loneliness

Session 61 - September 28, 1993

Good morning. Today I would like to start by talking about loneliness. It is a feeling that accompanies the rampant individualism represented by your ego. This excessive individualism separates you from everybody and everything else in the world. Thus, surrounded by the rest of God's creation, you still feel alone, isolated, separate. That is the price that must be paid for the kind of excessive individualism that your ego demands of you.

Look at the opposite. Of course you are still an individual but you are a part of something far greater than merely yourself. You have a link with everybody and everything that is alive on earth. You are also, by virtue of your divine spark, a part of God Himself. Under these circumstances, it is impossible for a person to be lonely. The term simply does not exist for people who understand and accept their place in the universe.

When you have God or one of His helpers available for consultation and advice at any hour of the day or night, how can anyone suffer from loneliness? While most ailments are in fact self-inflicted, loneliness is one of the most obvious of these self-inflicted ailments.

The truth is that you are never alone, unless you choose to be. You can choose to be alone, as an exercise of your free will, but unless you so choose, you always have one or more spirit beings watching over you and ready to offer advice and comfort if you only ask for them. The often-used term "guardian angel" is generally correct, at least as far as the name "guardian" goes. But we aren't angels, that is for sure. We are spirits at various levels of growth and development who are trying to help people on earth. We think we have learned something from our own journey in the material world, and we want to protect you from having to learn those same things the hard way. In another, more spiritual sense, we are trying to keep you from reinventing the wheel over and over again. If you can learn from our experiences, you will make much faster progress in your spiritual development while on the earth plane.

The person who feels lonely with any frequency has allowed his ego to shut him off from the rest of the world—people, animals, things.

Once you have gained control over your ego, you need never feel lonely again. Then you realize that you are, while still an individual entity, connected to the rest of creation and to God Himself.

Oh, you would like me to say something about anger? Well, I can tell you flatly that it is not a constructive state of mind. Anger itself is an unhealthy emotion. However, a sense of moral outrage at wrongdoing is something quite different. The person experiencing the latter is more likely to do something about the item that gave rise to the feeling of moral outrage than the person who merely gets angry. Anger will usually require a human object against whom the anger is to be directed. Moral outrage, on the other hand, will usually be directed at the act in question, and not necessarily the people involved in it.

Anger may also be a vehicle for the assessment of blame. And blame will usually also have a finite and definite person to be blamed. Since you are all still human, at least while going to school here on earth, you will all at various times experience anger and express it, either as blame or otherwise. But anger is a negative feeling and is inconsistent with the positive emotions of love, compassion and concern for others—positive emotions that are prerequisites to spiritual development. So I encourage all who may some day see this manuscript to appreciate the negativity of certain emotions, such as anger, and to steer clear of them to the maximum possible extent. Again, mindfulness will help you to be aware of negative emotions when they first show signs of manifesting themselves; then you are better able to reject them and the trap they represent.

For some reason, you are not up to a longer session right now. Maybe later today you can return for some more. In the meantime, our love and peace to you all.

Welcome back. I am glad that you are able to continue our discussion this evening. My topic for now is silence. I always seem to pick topics that have multiple meanings, but then those are the most interesting ones. Silence exists at a number of levels. The first and most obvious, meaning is lack of speech. Even there you will encounter many different kinds of silence. These include the companionable silence that often occurs between husbands and wives who are comfortable with each other, the hostile silence between adversaries when in a group with others, or the intimidated silence of subordinates in the presence of a domineering boss. These we are all familiar with.

Another entirely different level of silence can best be described as an interior silence. It is when the mind is still and the soul is listening—listening for advice or guidance from the Divine. It is a silence that comes with going within and searching there for truth—often truths to live by but sometimes truth about man's relationship to God or other deeply philosophical and profound questions. It is in this realm of silence that one hears the small, still voice that is so often drowned out by the noise and turmoil of the material world. It is this same voice, which we sometimes call conscience and sometimes God or His helpers, that reminds us of who and what we really are, and that this material world is merely a temporary way-station on a far greater and more important journey.

It is in silences of all kinds that we learn things, both spiritual and otherwise. You are well acquainted with the wise saying: "I learn more when I'm listening than when I'm talking." That piece of advice is all too true, though also very obvious. You can only learn when you are listening but you can't listen and talk at the same time. So once again, silence brings about good results. As I said, it also helps you in your progress toward spiritual growth. Right now, for example, you are listening to me, Michael. I could not communicate with you unless you were willing to listen; neither could Seneca or any of us here in the realm of spirit. By listening and taking down our thoughts, and ultimately disseminating them, you are contributing to your spiritual growth—not just by listening, but also by paying attention to the messages that are being given to you for the people as a whole. That is a right use of silence.

I will have more to say on this and related subjects later, but I am glad that we could finish our earlier conversation today.

Forgetfulness

Session 62 - September 29, 1993

This evening I would like to talk about forgetfulness. Given our human limitations while in the earth plane, we all suffer from forgetfulness to a greater or lesser degree. Most of the time the things we forget are not of great significance, either to our earthly activities or to our spiritual life. However, there are some things that we cannot afford to forget without running the risk of serious consequences. This applies in both the material and spiritual worlds. For example, in the material world, if you forgot an important appointment with a major client or customer, the consequences could be serious for your job or your business. In the spiritual world as well, there are things that must not be forgotten.

At least in the spiritual world, the opposite of forgetfulness is mindfulness and you have heard both Seneca and me speak repeatedly about the importance of mindfulness. If we forget who and what we really are, we are much more likely to be caught up by the lures of the material world and conclude that that is all there is, instead of appreciating that it is only a very small and temporary part of our total existence. If we forget why we are here on earth, we are subject to the same danger. We emphasize mindfulness as the positive alternative to forgetfulness.

Forgetfulness can also take the form of indifference to the plight of others who are not as fortunate as we are. That includes the less fortunate both in this country and in the rest of the world. Forgetfulness can also blur our memories of events showing man's inhumanity to man in the material world. Obvious examples are the rise of Hitler and the Japanese warlords resulting in World War II and the Holocaust, and more recent horror stories such as current events in Bosnia and Somalia. People have forgotten the interrelationship among all of us—how we are irreversibly connected—and that what we do to others we are doing to ourselves.

Forgetfulness is the lazy man's course, while mindfulness takes work and effort. Also, forgetfulness does not result in demands for action, at least with regard to one's self, whereas mindfulness does. Being mindful means that we must conduct ourselves with the awareness of who and what we are and why we are here. It therefore has a profound effect on how we live our lives and what kind of example we set for those around us. *There is no preaching that is anywhere near as effective as a concrete example.* People understand and respond to what we *do* though they may be highly skeptical about what we *say*. That is why we can have more influence on the behavior of others when we set an example by how we conduct ourselves.

As individual souls, we cannot change the behavior of others; they have free will and therefore the ability to use or abuse their power. But while we can't make others behave (even laws are less than fully effective in doing so), we can accomplish more than we realize by quietly setting a good example. A good case in point is Mother Teresa, who worked for many years among the poorest and most neglected before she received any public notice. That kind of example of love and compassion has a much broader influence than we can estimate because it helps to remind us of who and what we really are.

Without belaboring the subject, each of you in this world interacts with a multitude of other people. If your conduct reflects the messages that Seneca and I have been giving you, you have had a constructive influence on all that you have come in contact with. That influence may not be measurable, and it may not be enough to translate their forgetfulness into mindfulness, but it has had some influence.

When you finally disseminate these messages from Seneca and me, you will be making a substantial contribution to the mindfulness of people in America—and maybe elsewhere as well. How widespread that influence will be will depend on the number of people that read this material, and more important, the number of people that change their behavior to conform to the content of these messages. At least the material will be there for one and all to see. Who will choose to accept its validity and live accordingly will be a matter of each individual's free choice. The most we can do is make the material available. Beyond that, it is up to each individual to decide upon his or her own course of action.

It is our hope that those who heed these messages will thereby ameliorate some of the difficulties resulting from the earth changes that are upon us already. Sincere prayer may also help ease some of the pain that will necessarily accompany those changes. We see the beginnings already with natural disasters like Hurricane Andrew and the Mississippi floods. You may call them "natural disasters" but we call them examples of Mother Earth purifying herself. And this is just the beginning.

Even more severe natural disasters are in store although I cannot say when precisely they will occur or what forms they will take. But I believe you and other like-minded individuals will recognize them when they occur. Their impact can only be eased but not avoided because you humans have already gone too far in your desecration of Mother Earth, not to mention what you continue to do to her and to each other. Pray, preferably in groups, that the purification will not last too long or be too painful; that is about all you can do at this stage of events.

My final word tonight is to reemphasize mindfulness and be aware of the dangers of forgetfulness, at least where forgetfulness affects important spiritual matters. *Let mindfulness govern your conduct toward each other and all God's creation, and you can't go wrong!* It's that simple.

Responsibilities

Session 63 · September 30, 1993

Good evening and thank you for your prompt return to talk with us. The terrible earthquake that you just heard about this morning in India is another example of the earth changes that are occurring—and with what appears to be increasing frequency. Just imagine what the extent of the deaths and destruction that would have followed if it had occurred in a heavily populated area. As I told you last night, there is little you can do, other than prayer, to ease the pain of these changes. They cannot be prevented from occurring and you are well aware of the incredible power that Mother Earth has when she exerts herself.

Your conversation at lunch today is another illustration of how you people in the United States, the richest and most blessed country in the world, at least materially, have failed your children. *Your society focuses on the rights that people have and those rights are important elements of a civilized nation. However, your society has tended to ignore the opposite side of the coin—namely, responsibilities.* With rights, as with free will, go *responsibilities.* And your society has left children in the hands of incompetent or uncaring biological parents who do not impart either family stability or moral values to them. Is it surprising then that so much of the crime epidemic that afflicts your country is created by

146

youths—youths who have been given no role models or guidelines or values to live by? To them the world is a jungle and survival is the prime objective, followed by material goods to compensate for the lack of enduring values.

While the intentions of the people who structured this nearly idolatrous worship of rights without regard to responsibilities may have been good for the most part, the result has been a self-perpetuating monster. If you think the health care system is badly in need of reform, just take a look at the other elements of your society that produce these results and ask yourself if they are not also badly in need of reform. Perhaps it is a political impossibility, but at the same time it is a moral imperative to change a system that is so hopelessly dysfunctional.

I had not intended to get on a soapbox, but how can one communicate the messages we are trying to communicate if we are speaking to people who know only the tooth-and-claw law of the jungle. And even that isn't a fair analogy because nature at its harshest does not involve random violence and pointless killing and maiming. The earth changes alone will not get the attention of those young people who have been brought up on the streets without role models or guidelines. The earth changes are more likely to get the attention of the more affluent and educated among you who have lost their perspective and succumbed to the lures of this material world. But to these others, it will be meaningless because they have no frame of reference within which to evaluate the significance of these events.

It is neither my province nor my intention to attempt to provide solutions to the social problems you have created, especially in this country. *You* created them and *you* have to find your own solutions. All I can do is point out that what you are doing now is totally unsuccessful in bringing up good citizens with sound values for your next generation. Obviously I am not talking about your entire population of young people; if I were, your country would already be in a state of chaos. However, I am talking about much too large a percentage of your young people, and especially the poor and disadvantaged minorities.

If I sound impatient, as I do now, it is because I sometimes find it hard to believe the extent to which you humans have fouled this magnificent place that God created for your schoolhouse. To continue the analogy, you have killed and beaten up other students in the school for no reason other than that they were different from you. You have vandalized the school facilities and have covered the walls with obscene graffiti. From my vantage point in the spirit world, you have turned your schoolhouse into a garbage dump, with the students out of control, learning little or nothing in too many instances, and terrorizing or ignoring those who seek to teach.

What a mess! You have to clean it up, you know. Nobody else is going to do it for you. But you can't begin to clean up the mess—and I don't just mean the environmental mess—until you acknowledge that the mess exists and that you are ready and willing to address it, rather than paper the problem over. Maybe the impact of the earth changes will induce the leaders among you to address these problems, but I cannot say that I am optimistic about seeing this in the near future. Maybe later.

I didn't announce a topic for tonight's conversation, or should I say tirade, but I guess you could call the topic "responsibility." What we do or fail to do comes back to us one way or another and either in this life or another. That is a simple statement of the law of karma. But it also is a statement of responsibility because we must accept responsibility for our acts and omissions. Actually, it doesn't matter if we refuse to do so consciously because the law of karma sees to it that we suffer the consequences when our acts or omissions are negative, and we reap the rewards when our acts or omissions are positive. Since there is no escape from the consequences, the watchword for you people on earth is: "Take charge of your lives, because even if you don't, the cosmic bookkeeper is adding up the debits and credits anyhow." Therefore, be proactive rather then merely reactive or even just passive.

I think that is enough for one night. As you can guess, your conversations at lunch struck a strong responsive chord with me and produced this unusually emotional lecture, which as you know is not my usual style.

Patience

Session 64 · October 2, 1993

Good afternoon. Today I would like to start off by talking about patience. Patience is a virtue that all humans would do well to learn. That is especially true of Americans. You are always in so much of a hurry that all too often you don't stop to think through the ramifications of what you are about to do or say. If you had stopped to think about it, you would have decided not to do or say some of the things that you did or said. As a result, you would have avoided the negative karma that goes with some of the thoughtless deeds and statements that you all are guilty of.

Patience will also help you be more sympathetic to the shortcomings of others. If the shortcoming is viewed by you as intellectual, then perhaps a little more detailed and simplified explanation of what you are saying will make the communication meaningful. If the shortcoming is perceived by you as a personality defect, then a patient vision of the scared little child in the tough person-suit will enable you to perceive that person with a little more compassion than would otherwise be the case.

Patience can also help you to accept the unattractive experiences that you encounter with greater equanimity and look for lessons to be learned from those experiences. If you are too busy complaining about those experiences or feeling sorry for yourself, you are not very likely to learn much of anything useful or spiritually productive from the experience.

Patience helps give you a much better perspective on life in the material world than you can have without it. And that perspective can help you greatly toward recognizing who and what you are here and what you are trying to accomplish in the cosmic sense. It gives you a nearly overall perspective that could be described as a little bit like God's.

While patience is a very important virtue in terms of your spiritual growth, its influence on your material progress should not be underestimated. An example that comes to mind is the American propensity to focus on the next quarter's earnings in evaluating investment opportunities. Contrast this with the Japanese approach toward long-range goals and a willingness to sacrifice short-term goals for much more substantial long-term goals. I do not suggest that the Japanese system of doing business is at all better than yours in the U.S., because I don't believe that on the whole it is. However, patience is practiced to a much greater extent in business there.

Even within the fast-moving American business world, patience can still be an important virtue in progressing satisfactorily to higher levels within the organization. By patience in this context I don't by any means have in mind the time-server or the embodiment of the bureaucratic mentality. I mean the patient entrepreneur who can nurture a project through to successful completion, like your friend Steve. How long have you two been working on this project? And how long was he working on the subject matter even before you became involved? Every important long-term project requires patience on the part of the participants. By their very nature, there are no instant solutions to long-term projects.

I think that patience includes an ability and willingness to listen to others, whether it be creative ideas, politics, investment strategies, or what's going on locally. You humans don't do anywhere near enough listening, especially in your American culture. And I mean more by listening than just not talking. I mean paying attention to what is being said, and as may be appropriate, offering brief comments on what is being said. As you already know, listening—truly listening with your heart as well as your ears—is and has always been a form of healing. It's really the same kind of thing that psychologists or psychiatrists do routinely but it doesn't require lying on a couch in an office and paying fifty dollars or more per hour. If you want to, you can all do it; just listen and pay attention when someone else is talking. First, you may well learn something and second, you will undoubtedly acquire a reputation as a scintillating conversationalist, welcome at anyone's party.

Listening to other people in a constructive way is also good practice for listening to us if and when a spirit being should see fit to initiate conversations with you such as these with Bill. Our voices are not loud and do not intrude on your conscious mind unless you so choose. By spending time and effort listening to other people and perhaps helping them by so doing, you can get some good practice that will be helpful to you in communications with your guides.

There is another sense in which the term "listen" may have meaning. I believe that it also can mean: "Listen to what I am saying and then go do it!" When parents use the phrase "listen to me" with their children, they mean a lot more than just listening; they mean in addition that the child is to follow the advice or instruction given. Certainly that makes sense until children have reached the age of discretion (which varies from child to child); afterward, when children are expected to conduct themselves like responsible adults, the expression can properly revert to an advisory, rather than a directive, one.

I think I will stop for now. *If those who read these messages can successfully achieve true patience and genuine listening, those two virtues will greatly help to propel them on the path toward spiritual growth and development.* It's certainly something that is worth thinking about, eh?

Intuition

Session 65 - October 3, 1993

Good evening. Yes, I already gave you the subject for tonight—intuition. Since you already have a pretty good idea of what intuition really is, I expect to have some fun with this topic tonight. I see two rather different kinds of intuition at work in your world. One may be referred to as rational intuition but it isn't really "intuition" at all. This kind occurs when you suddenly know the answer to a question that is answerable by a process of reasoning. What happens is that your mind goes through the various reasoning processes so fast that it appears to jump right from the question to the correct answer. This type of mental short-cut is impressive and is a welcome addition to your array of tools with which to survive in your world—but it isn't intuition.

The second kind of intuition that comes to mind is when the question under consideration does not lend itself to being solved by purely rational means, such as where judgments are involved, or maybe choices, or where you don't have all the necessary information and must act on what you have. In situations such as these, where the answer to the question comes to you suddenly, as if in a flash of inspiration, and you later confirm that it was the correct answer, that is truly intuition. That is the kind of intuition that I am talking about tonight.

You already know that what you have chosen to call "intuition" is nothing more than a manifestation of psychic capabilities that you all possess but that too many of you are afraid to use. I can only repeat in a loud voice, to try to overcome your earlier conditioning, that *there is nothing abnormal about psychic abilities. You all have them but most of you have been conditioned by your American culture to regard these abilities as something sinister or evil.* Or you have been conditioned to believe that events that you may see with your own eyes don't really exist—that they are only hallucinations. So in your idolatrous worship of physical science you relegate any phenomena that don't fit the mold of your present very limited knowledge to the rubbish can. Either it's fraud, hallucination, mass hypnosis or some other form of trickery.

And yet in your world you tend to rely rather heavily on what you call intuition, especially on the part of women. It seems that women in general are more receptive to right-brain usage and are more responsive to the prompting of their inner selves via the process known as intuition.

I find it somewhat amusing (but not really) that a given experience is socially acceptable if you attribute it to intuition, whereas it is quite unacceptable in many circles—especially so-called scientific circles— if you attribute it to the use of psychic capabilities. It shows you some of the lengths to which people will go to avoid acknowledging the existence of anything to do with spirit, other than maybe some vague acknowledgment that humans have eternal souls, whatever that means. But nothing about interaction between humans and spirits now. Well, these conversations that I am having with Bill serve to refute that nonsense, although I recognize that the skeptics will call these messages either a sham on Bill's part, or self-hypnosis, or something else that denies our reality and ability to communicate with humans while they are on earth.

I don't really care what you call it—intuition or psychic ability or something else—so long as you pay attention to that still, small voice that you hear from time to time (your conscience or your guides) or that feeling in the pit of your stomach that tells you what the right answer or course of action is. *The more frequently you pay heed to your intuition and discover that it is correct, the stronger will your intuition become because you will have developed and strengthened it like a muscle.* Eventually you will come to understand that your intuition really represents the influence of your guides upon you and the workings of your own psychic capabilities. When that happens, you will come to trust your intuition completely because you will know by then what it really is.

In your own individual case, Bill, you are developing a better intuitive awareness of the various people with whom you come in contact on a day-to-day basis. Seeing them intuitively also helps to give you a much clearer picture of the inner person behind the facade of the outer person and thus will usually enable you to be more compassionate toward others than you might otherwise be.

To those of you who read these messages, don't let anyone talk you out of following your intuitive sense once you have tested it and found it to be accurate and reliable. There will be scoffers, but there will always be people who scoff at what they do not understand. Keep your own counsel, if necessary, about your psychic capabilities, develop them like any other skill and use them constructively and they will ease your path through this material world and its many snares.

Seneca and I have both referred to this earth as a schoolhouse for humans. But it also has many of the characteristics of a "fun house" at a carnival as well—except that the consequences can be much more severe. As in a "fun house," you must watch out for the pitfalls, trapdoors and other snares that you will encounter on your way through the house. Properly developed intuition can be of great assistance to you in this respect.

Punishment

Session 66 - October 5, 1993

What to talk about tonight? I don't recall whether I already talked about punishment before, but if so, this will be repetitious and you can exclude it from what you ultimately disseminate to the world.

Punishment is a human-created concept; it does not really exist in the spirit world. Punishment carries within its meaning the concept of externally imposed negative consequences for conduct that the social order has determined to be unlawful. That covers quite a broad range of activities, or omissions, in the material world. Experts on the subject in your world give a variety of justifications for punishment, such as deterrence, revenge, protection of the public, and perhaps a few others. But as I have said already, punishment is a human concept, not a divine or spiritual one.

Let me talk for a moment about karma in the context of punishment. *Karma, or the natural law of cause and effect, may sometimes seem to embody the concept of punishment but it really doesn't.* The law of karma does not attempt to embody human views of morality, the violation of which leads to punishment by society; karma is more analogous to mathematical or physical laws where specified causes produce predictable effects and do so on a consistent basis. There is no morality as such in mathematical or physical laws, nor is there in the law of karma. It is therefore something quite different and separate from punishment although it may sometimes superficially seem to be the same thing.

Another thing I have noticed about the subject of punishment is that the most severe punishments inflicted on an individual are usually self-inflicted. I am not talking here about punishments imposed by the law for crimes against society but, rather, about the smaller moral transgressions of which we are all guilty at one time or another. *Even as you strive to advance on the spiritual path, it is important to appreciate that, as humans, you have limitations and shortcomings and that part of your purpose here on earth is to work toward overcoming them. If you didn't have those limitations and shortcomings, you would no longer need to be here.* So don't be discouraged by that fact but also let it keep you from becoming complacent about the state of your spiritual progress. A healthy balance is what you should be looking for.

I know Seneca has previously made the very clear statement that "God does not punish; He teaches." I am sure that this has come as a shock to those of you who follow a tradition that portrays God as a stern judge, rather than a loving and merciful Father. I am also sure that some of the teachings that we are compelled to learn as a result of our conduct may be rather painful and may therefore seem very much like punishment. But God does not intentionally inflict pain, although pain is sometimes a necessary prerequisite to getting a message across to those who will not otherwise hear it or heed it. But that does not make it punishment.

Loving parents on the earth plane do not "punish" their children for bad behavior. Rather, they try to teach them that their conduct has consequences and that bad conduct has bad consequences. To drive the lesson home (no pun intended), the parents may deprive the youngster of the use of the family car for a specified period of time. But I emphasize that in my examples the purpose is to *teach*, not to deter, protect society, or exact vengeance. Can we expect less from a loving God and Father?

I am disturbed by the biblical information that has come down to us through the ages about the character and personality of God. We must always remain mindful that God's ways are not man's ways and that our limited human minds are incapable of comprehending even a corner of God's grand design for His universe. So let us especially avoid the tendency to create *Him* in *our* image, complete with those human behavior patterns and emotions that God transcends to an infinite degree.

Don't go around blaming God for punishing you, and don't threaten someone with burning in Hell for eternity as divine punishment for his misconduct. Instead, adopt the message of hope that tells us that no matter what our shortcomings may be, we all will ultimately make our way back to reunion with our Divine Creator so our individual bits of divine fire can be merged with His. Nobody goes to Hell for eternity, although some who think in terms of brimstone and hellfire may indeed create such a condition for themselves temporarily. But not eternally. That isn't the plan!

Naturally, the shorter the journey, the sooner we get back home to our Father. Therefore, it is definitely in our interest to live our lives on earth in such a way that we can graduate from this schoolhouse in the shortest possible time, and with the least pain. However, if we continue to make the same mistakes, lifetime after lifetime and fail to learn from our prior experiences (which we don't remember when in a later life), then we have to keep repeating similar kinds of lives until we get it right.

Listen to what your heart tells you and follow it; you will rarely go wrong. But if you listen to your ego, then you are extremely likely to fall into the snares and lures of the material world to your spiritual detriment. Always be mindful of who and what you really are and why you are here and you will find it very difficult to stray from the path of spiritual growth and development. That's the bottom line for all of you.

Possessions

Session 67 · October 8, 1993

Tonight we will start off talking about possessions and see where that leads us. When you think of possessions, you think of material possessions usually. But there are other important, nonmaterial possessions that each of you has, even in your material world—your reputation, for example. And beyond these, there are also spiritual possessions which you seldom think about, unless you are meditating, praying or having a conversation like this one.

I don't have to describe material possessions for you; you are all quite familiar with what that term encompasses. And, I hasten to add, there is nothing inherently wrong with having material possessions. They not only make life much more comfortable for you in the material world but they can also give you the wherewithal to help other, less fortunate souls and thereby gain some good karma—provided, of course, that the motivation for helping others is pure and not ego-driven. What you are willing to do and how far you are willing to go in your dealings with other people and with God's creation, in order to acquire material possessions, is the key criterion in determining the karmic consequences. So be advised.

Your nonmaterial possessions are also highly valued by you in the material world. Nearly everyone wants to have a good reputation and be respected by his peers. That is important to you, whether your peers, as you perceive them, are community leaders, members of your bowling club, street gangs or drug pushers. To a great degree, our self-esteem is greatly influenced by the esteem in which we are held, or think we are held, by those we regard as our peers. For some, the loss of these non-material possessions can be more traumatic than the loss of money itself.

But what if your "peers" happen to be people who are regarded by society as outcasts? Then the easy course of action, and the one that most of you take, is to regard society as wrong or irrelevant or even hostile and to dismiss its rejection of you and your peers. Perhaps the most obvious example of this is the street gang, or the violence-oriented cult, such as that led by David Koresh. While society's standards may not always be right (look at Hitler's Germany or Stalin's Russia), you should at least examine them to see whether perhaps your peer group is the one that is in the morally indefensible position before dismissing society's evaluation. If you can be honest in your own examination, you may then find the strength to escape from the peer group that is leading you to destruction in the material world and negative karma in the spiritual one.

What do we mean when we talk about "spiritual" possessions? What are they and how do we go about acquiring them? *Spiritual possessions are attitudes and states of mind leading to actions that reflect God's plan for His universe.* I know that's quite a mouthful and it's also rather cryptic but I have trouble making it clearer and still keeping the definition down to a reasonably short and comprehensible one.

"How do we know what actions reflect God's plan that you so blithely talk about?" Yes, I recognize the question in your minds—and it is a perfectly legitimate one too. I think the best answer I can give you is this: *If your attitudes and states of mind are those of love, caring and compassion for your fellow humans and for all other creatures as well as the earth itself, then your actions cannot be contrary to God's plan.* With the attitudes and states of mind that lead to spiritual growth and development present and active within you, you are incapable of conducting yourself in a manner contrary to God's plan.

Oh sure, I know very well that you all fall short of this ideal because you are only human and therefore less than perfect. Don't forget, I too was once human and know the difficulties that go with that condition. So I don't expect you to be always kind, loving and compassionate toward everybody and everything you come in contact with. But if you remain mindful of these teachings—I told you I would reiterate the importance of mindfulness again and again in these messages—then you will manifest spiritual attitudes and states of mind most of the time and will therefore conduct yourself in a manner that is consistent with God's plan most of the time. When you finally reach the level where you can do it *all* the time, then you can graduate from this school and move on to better things.

I will take a private moment to commend you for your handling of your fish tank flood. After the first shock, your first concern was for the survival of the fish in the rapidly emptying tank, rather than for the damage to your material possessions. You managed to save them all and both you and Enid felt very good about that, even though your living room was something of a shambles. Congratulations on having your priorities right. I am encouraged to think that you are paying attention to these messages from Seneca and me and are making healthy spiritual progress as a result. The same comments also apply to your efforts at caring for the fish that jumped out of the tank and was stranded on the floor. You looked after him to the best of your ability, as you would with any sick animal, and he is now functioning satisfactorily in the tank with his companions. Good work.

I don't think I need to point it out, but just in case some of your readers may need to have our views made very explicit, I will say that *the most important of your possessions are your spiritual ones, because they accompany you from life to life. Next are your nonmaterial ones because they reflect your character in a given life and nobody can take them away from you. Last in line are material possessions which may be here today and gone tomorrow.*

Earth Changes

Session 68 - October 11, 1993

Tonight you would like to hear about the situation regarding earth changes in the context of the dream that Enid told you about—the dream about New York City experienced simultaneously by Shirley and her sister. Was this some sort of precognitive dream about a disaster that is yet to occur there, or is this merely an example of telepathic communication between two sisters at the dream level? I think it is more than just telepathic and does indicate future events. But exactly when this event will occur and what form it will take were not revealed in the dream.

To say "soon" is not very informative because it means too many different things to different people. And to us in the spirit world, time means nothing, and for God time does not exist. Since these ladies are not like Nostradamus who made prophecies far into the future, it seems to me that the event will occur before the end of this millennium, which means within the next seven years. What form it will take and how great the devastation will be are questions that are still unresolved. Remember, I have told you that, while the earth changes cannot be avoided, their effects can be ameliorated, particularly by group prayer, between now and the time they occur.

I do not see anything as dramatic as New York City sliding into the Atlantic Ocean and I don't know whether the drastic earth changes such as those from earthquakes, including undersea ones, will be encountered by New York. California is a much more plausible target for those, since it includes major earth faults within its boundaries.

One must be careful not to interpret these dreams too literally. In most cases, the events portrayed can also be interpreted symbolically and I think this is the case with this particular dream. The fact that the same dream was experienced on the same night by both sisters certainly lends credence to it as being significant. But not necessarily literal.

You have asked about earth changes and I don't want to get diverted from that subject into interpretation of dreams. Yes, major earth changes are coming and, as you are well aware, have already commenced. They will continue with what I believe to be increasing frequency on a worldwide basis and with increasing severity. I want to emphasize that they are not intended as a form of punishment, although they will be painful, and we have created the conditions that have given rise to them. But it is not punishment any more so than experiencing vomiting and upset stomach is punishment for eating some tainted or spoiled food. It is simply a natural consequence. It is the body's way of dealing with such a situation that threatens its well-being. So it is also with Mother Nature.

I keep emphasizing this distinction because I know that many religious traditionalists will allege that the earth changes are God's punishment for mankind's disobedience. That is simply not the case and I say again that to assert that is to bring God down to our level when we should be seeking to rise to His.

Nature purifying herself occurs, of course, by natural means. Therefore, war and the results of man's inhumanity to man are not a part of this process. *The purification process will manifest itself through natural means, such as earthquakes, tornadoes, typhoons, hurricanes, volcanoes, floods and similar actions by Mother Nature without any help from humankind.*

I have also previously told you that if you are in danger from these earth changes, we will warn you in advance so that you can avoid them, because you have an important mission to perform for us on behalf of your fellow humans. Therefore, we still would like you to stay alive in the material world until you have fulfilled your mission. However, we do not intend to tell you what areas will be most severely damaged by the upcoming earth changes because we don't want to create panic nor do we want to sound like end-of-the-world predictors. The earth still has a long way to go before it becomes obsolete and can be abandoned. Look at all the souls on earth that still have to graduate from this school before moving on. Until that happens, we will not see the end of the earth because we will still have need of it.

Some speak of these times as showing signs of the "last days" according to the Christian Bible. Others predict the imminent "second coming" of Jesus Christ to earth in glory and majesty. That is not the way I view the future on earth. *I do not look for a second physical appearance by Jesus Christ on earth. What I do look forward to is the coming of what can be called the "Christ consciousness" into the hearts of all men, women and children throughout the earth.* When that spirit of love, caring and compassion has pervaded the earth, then we can say that Christ has come again to this small and otherwise insignificant planet in a minor solar system in a less than mainstream galaxy.

When we have raised our vibration to the divine level, then we have come to join God and God no longer needs to debase Himself by joining us. Don't allow yourselves to forget that when people die on this material plane, they don't die. They merely move on to another phase of existence until they later return to earth in new bodies, if that is still necessary. When we look at death, especially the deaths of large numbers of people, whether from natural disasters, wars, famine or flood, we should try to look at the situation from a more cosmic point of view. I am well aware that your human condition makes this very difficult for you to do but, to the extent that you can, it will help ease your grief for the loss of loved ones at any time and for any reason.

To summarize what became a little rambling, earth changes are coming and I expect more of them within the next seven years and even thereafter. They will be severe but can be ameliorated, though not entirely avoided, by prayer. Many people throughout the earth will die as a result of these changes—but remember that no soul is permanently lost. And the post-purification period will be something like a new Eden, because earth will again be more nearly like what it was supposed to be before we despoiled it.

Acting

Session 69 · October 13, 1993

Tonight I will talk about acting since you have just returned from a play rehearsal. In the material condition we all do a great deal of acting all the time—the question is, "Are we good or bad actors?" if you will pardon the pun. Most of the time we try to do what our society and our cultural heritage expect of us and that usually is reasonably constructive. If we are genuinely good citizens, the chances are fairly good that we will also be making at least some degree of spiritual progress at the same time. However, one can be regarded as, and actually be, a "good citizen" and yet gain little progress on the spiritual path. That is why I said "genuinely" a good citizen, rather than one whose good citizenship is driven by either ego or a desire to lord it over his neighbors. One who progresses spiritually the most in a given lifetime will be far more than merely a good citizen. He will sometimes, though by no means always, be recognized during his own lifetime as a saint, a sage, a holy man or woman or something equivalent.

Because "acting" is not a spontaneous activity but rather a highly disciplined, learned conduct, it involves a greater degree of self-control than is routinely found among humans while on earth. This kind of self-discipline allows you to make choices regarding how you will act toward others, whether human, animal or otherwise. And this same self-discipline will also prevent you from inadvertently acting badly toward others so as to reap negative karmic consequences.

As an actor, you are in control of how you portray the character and play the role assigned you. In the material world that is not of the theater, however, you get to choose the role you wish to play and it is then up to you to play it well. If you play it well and it is a good role, you can progress to bigger and better things—maybe even a lead role in the psychic equivalent of a Broadway play. It becomes your decision and your choice.

That is not the case with the person who is not an "actor" but acts in accordance with his or her spontaneous feelings. Because such a person does not possess the self-discipline of a good actor, he or she will often make stupid but costly mistakes inadvertently. Those mistakes will generate negative karma that could have been avoided by the exercise of a greater measure of self-discipline.

The person who acts on an instinctive, emotional level is bound to generate a sizable amount of negative karma, unless that person happens to be so innately good that his actions, even on such a level, are nevertheless governed by love, caring and compassion. You must understand that such an individual is indeed a rare creature and you will not encounter his like often in your material world. Therefore, *it behooves you all to learn some of the key skills of the actor and, especially, to acquire the self-discipline that is almost second nature for a good actor.*

Throughout this discussion I have been assuming that this self-disciplined person was also spiritually oriented and was seeking the highest spiritual and material good for all God's creation. But I must now point out to you that self-discipline can also be applied in furtherance of evil, and when that happens, the world has given birth to a monster—a spiritual monster. Remember, it is all a part of the risk that God took when he decided to give humankind the greatest gift in His power—the gift of free will. The Bible says that God made man a little lower than the angels. But the Hebrew word thus translated as "angels," is "elohim" and it is my understanding that that word, a plural grammatical form, is translated more properly as "gods" or "God." If correct, then God made man a little lower than Himself and free will was the key element in accomplishing that objective. So as long as humans have free will, and they will as long as there are humans in the universe, they will be free to choose to follow God's path or choose other, darker paths.

However, after learning the lessons which that individual spirit needs to learn, however painful and lengthy the process may be, each individual spirit will freely choose to follow God's path because that is the only path that will take him home. When I say "the only path," let me be very clear that I do not mean it the way some religious denominations do—namely, that *their* path is the *only* path to God. What I mean is that *there are many paths that lead toward God, the Light, and they are all acceptable routes on the way home.* What we have to guard against are those paths that lead *away* from God and home but sound too attractive or alluring to pass up. So my message is: "Don't be concerned about denominational exclusivity—God considers it rather sad and it will only lead down a wrong path if you follow it all the way. However, stop periodically as you proceed with your life on earth in order to look at the big picture of your life and in order to check your internal compass. Make sure that the path you have chosen will lead you to reunion with God and that you are not being taken in by some material bribe." I want to emphasize that, in this connection, I do not recommend paranoia but I do recommend mindfulness concerning who we are and why we are here.

༄༅

Confidence

Session 70 · October 18, 1993

The delay in getting back with us is not a problem. The important thing is that you did get back, and because you wanted to. What to talk about today? How about confidence? That is always a popular subject in your material world. There are many courses given on how to build your self-confidence so that you will be a success in the business world and make lots of money. The confidence I will talk about is of a different kind—but it is not inconsistent with self-confidence in fulfilling your role in the material world also. The confidence I want to talk about is, naturally, spiritual confidence. But what does that mean? It means transferring into the spiritual realm the kind of self-confidence that you try so hard to obtain for this short-time material realm.

Spiritual confidence tells you that you are a soul that is made in God's image and that possesses a spark of God's eternal flame. It also tells you that God loves and accepts you as you are, with all your imperfections, and that you are capable of reaching heights spiritually that you cannot even imagine. Spiritual confidence also enables you to appreciate your connectedness to all the rest of God's creation and to recognize that what you do to others, whether humans, animals or otherwise, you do to yourself. *When you possess spiritual self-confidence, you need fear nothing in the material realm.*

As you can readily see, spiritual confidence can carry you so much further than material confidence since the spiritual world is eternal and the material world is ephemeral. However, as I indicated, spiritual confidence can also be of great benefit to you in the material world. That is because you should never lose it after having acquired it in a particular lifetime. Also, by conducting yourself in the material world in a manner consistent with your spiritual confidence, you inspire trust, affection and respect—all of which are attributes most helpful in achieving success in the material world.

Spiritual confidence will also assist you in facing the earth changes that are upon you without panic or even fear. Knowing what and who you really are, you cannot be terrified by that great bugaboo that terrifies those who don't understand that they are eternal spirits. That bugaboo is of course death. To you who have gained spiritual confidence, death is nothing more than the closing of one door and the opening of another—perhaps the beginning of a great new adventure. So if it turns out that your destiny is to die in the course of these earth changes and as a result of them, you can still say with equanimity: "So what. I'll be back again." When fear of death is tamed, other fears tend to become even less significant.

I have already told you that the earth changes have commenced. That should also be quite apparent to all of you on your own. I do not intend to talk more about them because I don't want to scare people unduly, even though these earth changes will involve some pretty scary experiences for rather a lot of people. Still, I don't see much point in trying to resist them because that will accomplish nothing. I also don't propose to recommend wholesale moves of large numbers of people to what may seem to be higher, safer terrain. We cannot escape our karma and it is an act of futility to try.

Don't misunderstand my statement to mean that I advocate nothing more than a passive approach to life for the reason that everything is preordained. Not so at all! While certain major, worldwide events—such as the coming earth changes—are preordained because our conduct over many generations made them inevitable, most events affecting our day-to-day activities are not. So always remember your priceless gift of free will and exercise it but don't fight those problems that are beyond the human capability to solve. There is an old prayer or affirmation that goes something like this: "God, give me the strength to change what I can, the courage to accept what I must, and the wisdom to know the difference." That sums it up quite nicely even though I know it sounds like a cliché.

By the way, there is often much wisdom in what have become known as clichés. They were given that uncomplimentary title, not because they didn't often contain much simple wisdom but because they were used too often, too inappropriately and as a substitute for thought. Take a look at many little sermons that are now called clichés and, after considering them objectively and with fresh insight, judge for yourself whether there is wisdom there or not.

Back for a final few words on spiritual confidence. If you can achieve it in a given lifetime, the rewards are hard to overestimate. First, it represents major progress in your spiritual journey and is therefore extremely valuable in the most important aspect of your life. Second, it makes it almost inevitable that you will conduct yourself in this lifetime in such a way as to produce good karmic consequences later. And third, it will also help you be successful in this lifetime in the material world. That's quite a set of rewards, I would say. In so many situations, spiritual growth is achieved at the expense of material success and possessions since the two worlds are so often in conflict. But this example of spiritual confidence is an exception to that frequent conflict, or at least tension, between the spiritual and material worlds. Here you can literally have the best of both worlds. That makes spiritual confidence something that is very much worth striving for!

Force

Session 71 - October 21, 1993

What should today's subject be about? Let's start by talking about force. What kind of force? I don't know yet; I let it flow from me as the information wishes. [Right now I'm not completely sure whether this is Seneca or Michael talking, but I think it's still Michael.]

The term "force" has many connotations. It includes simple physical force, force of personality, force of reason, force of habit, and so on. What is the connection to spiritual messages, you may well ask. Well, the connection is that all forms of force begin with spirit and stem from spirit. Without spirit there is no force of any kind, just as without Spirit there is no creation. One flows from the other.

Since all forms of force have their origin in spirit, that means that they are to be used in a manner consistent with the ethical dictates of spirit—in other words for the good of all God's creation. Any less encompassing use partakes of selfishness and ego and is regarded as abuse, not simply use.

Start with simple physical force. It is needed to produce the necessities of life, and was even more so in times past. For example, someone had to chop down the tree for firewood to keep warm in cold weather and to cook the food to be eaten. Also force was needed to hunt animals for food, clothing and shelter. We may be some generations removed from those times and we may have more efficient mechanical devices for producing and harnessing that force, but the fact remains that simple physical force remains a necessary element of survival in the material world.

What about force of personality and force of reason? Though they are quite different, I will talk about them together. Force of personality is just what it says. You sometimes call it charisma and it is a very real manifestation of force. It is a kind of personal or emotional force that induces others to follow the lead of the charismatic individual. Again, such force can either be used, as in the case of Jesus, Paul and many others in all religious traditions, or it can be abused, as in the case of Hitler. I need not say it but I will anyhow—since this form of force is indeed a gift from the Divine, abuse of that gift will inevitably lead to serious negative karmic consequences.

Next I mentioned force of reason. That is also clearly a nonphysical form of force, but it is essentially rational, whereas force of personality is usually emotional in nature. Force of reason is usually the form of force that is used by the scholar, the analyst, the teacher. It too is very much of a Divine gift and is to be used with care so that it is not abused. To use force of reason for purposes of sophistry or to spread confusion or to mislead others carries with it the same kinds of negative karmic consequences as abuse of the charismatic gift.

Since all these forms of force have been identified as manifestations of spirit, what is there to say about spiritual force? Just what is it and how are we to use it best? As the source of all force, spiritual force is by far the strongest. That statement should come as no surprise to any of you. Moreover, spiritual force is basically what keeps us on the correct path to home while on our earthly journey. I should be careful, rather, to say "a correct path," for we already know that there is not just one single path that all must follow to get home. Instead, there are many paths, like the spokes of a wheel, leading to the same hub. I know I have used that analogy before and I undoubtedly shall use it again. It is especially apt because it puts God in the center, at the hub, while we circle around on the outside until we find and choose a spoke leading to the hub and then stay on it. And, again, ultimately we all do get there.

I will yet again mention one of my favorite concepts—mindfulness. *Being always mindful of the spiritual force within us, we are far more likely to use the other forms of force that have been made available to us, rather than to abuse them.* So much of our conduct is a product of mindfulness, because as long as we are mindful of who and what we are and why we are here, we are reasonably safe from the snares and temptations that this material world keeps throwing in our path—temptations to abuse other people, to abuse power and to abuse Mother Nature herself. As I use the term, mindfulness means a constant awareness, usually at a subconscious level. It does not require that our conscious mind be always focused on that subject, because if it did we would not be able to function effectively in the material world.

While spiritual force is by far the most powerful form of force in the universe, I must remind you that it is still subject to the dictates of your own free will. Notwithstanding the great spiritual force within each and every one of you, your gift of free will still enables you to opt to abuse these various manifestations of force if you so choose. You will pay a price if you do so, but you have the ability and the right to choose. That is what free will is all about and that is why it is such an awesome gift. We humans tend to take it for granted but in reality it enables us to function as little gods of our own if we choose to.

I am sure I will want to talk more later about other forms of force, such as the force of nature. Be assured that the force that manifests itself in natural phenomena on this earth is so enormously powerful that it makes all your human physical forms of force seem incredibly puny by comparison. When you heap abuse after abuse on Mother Nature, don't be surprised when she reacts with a strength beyond your ability to imagine.

Pain

Today, as I indicated to you earlier, I would like to talk about pain. While it may sound like an unhappy subject, there is more to it than initially meets the eye. Pain itself is unpleasant, but if it leads to something wonderful, then that will often make the pain worthwhile and short-lived. Perhaps the most obvious example of this in your material world is childbirth. The pain is excruciating but the result—a living child that is literally your own "flesh and blood"—is a magnificent compensation for the pain endured, not to mention the discomforts associated with pregnancy. Also, as you have been told, the memory of the pain fades rather rapidly with time or else you would have only one-child families—not an attractive prospect for the future of the human race on earth.

Pain is also often associated with the learning process and with growth. As for learning, we use the term that says some people can only learn things "the hard way." They do not take advantage of what others have done and learned before them. Therefore, they figuratively reinvent the wheel, and in that process they go through all the painful, as well as unnecessary, frustrating failures and false starts that the original prehistoric people did.

The same can be said for growth. Often there is pain as a young person grows to maturity—sometimes pain in bodily aspects but almost always pain in mental and emotional aspects. Growth of mind and spirit also involves pain, like any growth, but again the results make the pain worthwhile. As an open mind expands its horizons, pain accompanies the renunciation of old, fixed, comfortable ideas and attitudes. But again, persons undergoing this kind of experience will readily admit that the pain is worth it because the end result is so special.

I think I can summarize this question by saying almost categorically that, in the case of pain of the kinds indicated here, the affirmative results far outweigh the negative effects of the pain. In a lesser number of cases, that can also be true in the physical arena as well. Childbirth has already been mentioned as a prototypical example. Another kind of example could be accidentally touching a hot stove. Here the pain provides a direct and immediate warning that you are subjecting your body to something unacceptable to it. We also learn thereby to approach hot stoves with great caution and thus spare ourselves from more serious consequences later. In fact, physical pain is often a lifesaver. If we didn't get its message via our nerve endings, we would probably continue with the detrimental action or inaction because we would have no way of knowing otherwise.

I will even apply the same analogy to spiritual pain. If a person is sufficiently oriented toward matters of the spirit, he will get a very loud, clear message when he experiences spiritual pain as a result of a certain act or omission. He will hurt spiritually and that will tell him that he was engaging in conduct detrimental to spiritual growth and development.

So much of our lives consists of a kind of spiritual guessing game. As we experiment and observe the spiritual reaction to our various modes of behavior, we can then identify where we have deviated from the path of spiritual progress and what we must do to get back on it. Being only human, we stumble about a good bit, but by using spiritual pain as a guide we can usually find our way back to the path.

Of course, not all pain is a harbinger of spiritual growth and development or, if it is, its message is too subtle for us to handle. Therefore, I do not want to leave you with the impression that pain is an inherently good thing and that spiritually developed people consciously seek it. That would be nonsense. But since a considerable amount of pain is inevitable in most lifetimes, we would do well, when encountering it, to ask whether there is a constructive message or result associated with it. If we find that there is, it makes the pain more tolerable than might otherwise be the case. If there isn't, then we merely endure it as one of the trials and tribulations that goes with being human. Either way is better than mindless complaining about the unfairness of fate or going around feeling sorry for ourselves.

So you see, if properly approached, pain is not always a totally negative experience to be avoided at all costs. While there is no requirement to seek it out as if it were a virtue, we can respond to it in such a way as to make it a positive phenomenon in many cases rather than a negative one in all cases. Let us learn from it and let us treasure the learning and growth that often accompanies it.

⋑⋐

Fields of Flowers

Session 73 - October 29, 1993

Subject to start this evening off with—fields of flowers. That sounds like a strange topic but that is the phrase that came into your thoughts so that is where we will start. Fields of flowers is another way of describing the multitude of human souls with which each of you comes in contact during the course of a single lifetime on earth. Now, what do you do to these fields of flowers? Do you nurture them, water them, fertilize them and help them to achieve their highest level of being? Or do you dig them up, mow them down, or otherwise destroy them because you want to develop the land on which they lie as a shopping center or a condominium complex?

Putting the question in less allegorical terms, do you conduct yourselves solely, or even primarily, on the basis of what serves your own personal interests, usually of a material nature, without much regard for the effects upon others? And at the moment, when I refer to "others" here, I mean other people. Never mind the effect upon the ecology as a whole—that is another subject all by itself. Before you can really start to care about the environment in which you live—I often like to refer to it as Mother Earth—you first have to care about other people. That is why my fields of flowers represented only people and not God's entire creation.

If you are solely, or primarily, concerned about your own material objectives, then you may actually get your shopping center or condominium complex and the money represented thereby. But at the same time you must bear the responsibility for the fields of flowers that you have destroyed in the process. Do you really want to subject yourselves to those karmic consequences in return for something that is so temporary and fleeting? A prudent person who understands what the law of karma is all about will answer this rhetorical question with a resounding "No!" Yet in our lifetimes in the material world, we do things that, at least in part, are analogous to the destruction of that field of flowers.

How can we avoid doing this? The answer is simple. Our old friend, mindfulness, reenters the picture. By being mindful of the ramifications of what we are about to do, before we do it, we can avoid the unintentional destruction of a field of flowers, together with the resulting karmic consequences. What if we are mindful of the ramifications and choose to go ahead anyhow? Then we have exercised our free will accordingly and must ultimately bear even more severe karmic consequences. In that regard, the law of karma works much like your own criminal law here in the United States. Intentional wrongdoing is more severely punished than wrongdoing that results from carelessness or lack of attention.

Let's take a look at the brighter side of this analogy since we don't want to talk only about the destruction of fields of flowers by persons seeking their own material self-interest. What about those who nurture those fields, such as by helping little children to grow up with health, both physical and mental, sound values, knowledge that can be used constructively for the good of society, etc.? The karmic benefits of such nurturing of other souls, especially in the case of children during their most formative and impressionable years, is great indeed! I think this is especially true when that nurturing takes place with little fanfare or other ego involvement. The motivation should be the nurturing of the children, not self-gratification or self-aggrandizement.

I think the biblical reference to lilies of the field is what induced me to use fields of flowers as my allegorical starting point. The biblical statement uses the example as a method of asserting the extent of God's love for His human children. My statement uses the field of flowers analogy to assert that we must love and care about each other more than material wealth or success in order to earn beneficial karmic consequences rather than detrimental ones.

What else might we say about fields of flowers? Well, on a simple, straightforward basis, their beauty should help to remind us of the Creator who is responsible for such beauty and of our relationship to Him. On an even simpler basis, the beauty of a field of flowers should please our eye and appeal to our aesthetic sense. Physical beauty, whether in nature or in human beings, should give us pleasure as we go on our spiritual journey through a lifetime on earth. An awareness and appreciation of beauty, as each of us perceives it, can help to make the journey less arduous than might otherwise be the case.

Also, as I said before, not only is beauty something to be enjoyed in its own right but it also raises our level of consciousness to the God that created that beauty. When our consciousness is thus raised, it is easier for us to remember who and what we are and why we are here. The more often we remember who and what we are and why we are here as we proceed on life's journey, the more likely we are to follow a path back to our heavenly home, instead of being ensnared by the temptations and delusions of the material world. So I would urge all who may eventually read these messages—think of this message whenever you see a field of flowers and raise your level of awareness accordingly. It will stand you in good stead.

Train Wrecks

Session 74 · October 30, 1993

Today I put the thought into your head that I would talk about train wrecks. As you can see, I am choosing more unusual phrases as jumping-off points for my messages. After all, I have a sense of humor too here in the spirit world and even as one with a serious mission to try to help you help humanity understand its potential and utilize it.

Train wrecks—how does that subject relate to spiritual growth and development? Think about it. Train wrecks occur when the train either leaves the track that it is supposed to follow or when something improperly gets on the train's path just as the train is approaching that particular location.

As you can readily appreciate, when you leave a path of spiritual development that you have chosen to follow, your spiritual growth experiences a train wreck in that you retrogress—your progress toward your destination is delayed and you may experience painful consequences as a result of having jumped the track. Of course trains don't exercise volition when they jump the track; theirs is merely a result of the application of laws of physics. But when you jump the track, it is an exercise of your own free will so the responsibility for the consequences is therefore much greater. Included are those occasions when you may jump the track, at least temporarily, without necessarily intending to depart from the path of spiritual growth, as well as those occasions when you know that is exactly what you are doing. Unlike a train, however, you can also choose to get yourself back on track and proceed with your spiritual journey.

You must understand that, being human, you will jump the track numerous times in the course of a single lifetime and then get back on it, again as a matter of your own volition. Only highly advanced or illuminated beings, called saints in some cultures—can go through an entire lifetime on earth and remain on track for the entire period. When that happens, those beings no longer need to spend any more physical lifetimes in the schoolhouse known as earth. For the rest of us, the journey is one of stops and starts—more like a local rather than an express train. But for many, perhaps most of us, the journey is even slower because we jump the track and experience a train wreck from time to time; they get to their destination much more slowly than the local train that moves slowly but still stays on the track, and still more slowly than the rare express train.

What about the person who gets off his spiritual growth track and does not get back on, or at least not until much later, because he has been bedazzled by the material world and has come to think that that is all there is? Well, just keep using the train wreck analogy. The train that is no longer on its track simply isn't going anywhere! It cannot go anywhere as long as it remains off its track. There the analogy applies, regardless of the fact that the train is an inanimate object while we are free to choose. If we have jumped our spiritual track, as will happen to the best of us on occasion, we go nowhere spiritually until we choose to get back on that track. Yes, you can choose another track to your destination if you find one that is more suited to your philosophy and needs since there are many such paths, but as long as you are on no track, you aren't going anywhere.

This analogy is intended to show you that you can sometimes fail to make spiritual progress at various times in your life but you can always choose to get back on the track and continue any time during your life. Perfection is neither required nor expected of fallible human beings, or you wouldn't still need to be here learning. But if you have forgotten for a time who and what you are and why you are here and have, in effect, jumped your spiritual track, you always have the ability at any time of your choosing to get back on it. You can, but the poor, inanimate train can't.

I think something else I like about this analogy is that it fits my earlier assurances that eventually we all get to our final destination. If we want to continue to that destination, and at the deepest level of our being we all do want to do so, we have the ability to pick up our wrecked train, repair it, put it back on the track and proceed along the path. So you see that a message that starts with the peculiar subject of train wrecks ends with a message of hope for all. And as you know, that message of hope is something I have passed on to you before and will undoubtedly say again in various forms. *I do that because I believe that such hope is so important to all humans, but especially to those who have badly wrecked their trains, have low self-esteem and consider themselves unworthy of God's love or anyone else's. To those readers who may feel that way about themselves, rejoice because you are absolutely wrong!* You may have made some serious mistakes and committed terrible wrongs for which you must make amends, but you are still a bearer of the eternal flame and you will eventually be reunited with your Creator back home. It may take a long, long time, as measured in earthly terms, and it may involve a great deal of pain because of the karmic consequences, but you *will* arrive.

Enough of train wrecks for one message. I am actually having some fun starting off these most recent messages with a rather startling or unusual theme. May it help to get the attention of your readers! And may they thereby take the messages to heart for their own good and the good of all God's creation. That is my prayer as I know it to be yours also.

Understanding

I am glad that you enjoyed my message of yesterday. Actually the train wreck illustration turned out to be quite useful.

What shall we choose as the subject for tonight? Let's talk about understanding. Understanding is a complex term with many facets and levels. It can include everything from strictly intellectual understanding of a scientific problem or formula to a deep level of understanding of the spiritual forces that are unseen but nonetheless very much at work in the material world in which you live. In between there are many other levels and kinds of understanding.

I am not particularly interested in mere intellectual understanding because that has no moral or spiritual content to it and is therefore not a part of what I am trying to communicate through you, Bill. When we get to the level of empathic understanding of the distress or suffering of another person, that evokes some interest on my part. For empathic understanding, for lack of a better term, requires an acknowledgment, at some level of our being, that we are all one in spirit. Usually that acknowledgment occurs at a level well below that of the conscious mind because our conscious minds fight hard against that realization. As you know, our conscious minds focus on our status as an individual, unique and separate from all others, isolated and self-contained. But that is merely ego speaking, which fears the loss of its power over us.

When we reach down to the deepest levels of our being, we can see, even if only for a moment, that we are not isolated, self-contained individuals but part of the Eternal Flame itself. We know with an unshakable certainty that we are all part of the One and that whatever we do to any other part of God's creation we do to ourselves. That ultimate understanding is something that usually takes many lifetimes to achieve, and many more before we really believe it. And even then, while we are still on our journey in the material world, we experience and understand it only fleetingly before we are again diverted by our egos back to survival and success and achievement in the material world. However, when we can finally understand this profound truth and retain that understanding on a continuing basis within our conscious minds—*and live the results of that understanding*—then we are ready to graduate from this schoolhouse and need no longer endure the pains and difficulties of further lifetimes on earth.

The beginning of this kind of understanding comes with the control and taming of ego. Remember, ego is a device by which the conscious mind seeks to delude us into believing that this lifetime in this material world is all there is and that our objective must be to achieve the most power, money and pleasure that we can in that short time. Obviously a recipe for utter selfishness and the negative karma that accompanies it. In trying to mislead us along these lines, ego is dead wrong. The truth of the matter is that once we can get by the delusions generated by ego, we can have a much clearer perspective about our material lives and can live them more constructively, more spiritually and often even more happily from a purely human standpoint.

Some of the other more important dividends that accompany understanding are peace among men and a willingness to accept the fact that there are numerous paths back to our Father, and that our own particular choice is not the only choice. We are all trying to get to the same destination but we are too blind to recognize that simple fact. So we argue and proselytize and kill about whether we must go by car, bus, train or plane. When you view this matter, which has been a source of so much grief in the past and still continues to be today, you can readily appreciate how stupid and tragic our wars of religion have been and still are.

At a less deep level than the spiritual one, it is still possible and beneficial to understand other backgrounds, cultures, religions and viewpoints generally. One of the saddest things in today's world is the unreasoning fear, growing into hatred, of people who are "not like us." I don't have to give you examples. You have them right here in your United States as well as more obviously in places like Bosnia, Somalia, the Middle East and Northern Ireland. What a terrible waste!

Along with understanding there is usually a degree of compassion for "others" who may not be as fortunate as you are here in America. Once you are able to see and appreciate the common humanity that you all share—and recognize that the things that unite you are far more extensive than the things that divide you—love, caring and compassion can follow. And ultimately, we can achieve the realization that we are all part of God's creation, including everything that conclusion implies.

Search your hearts for understanding, and along with it, love, compassion and caring for each other. Your heart is the right place to look, not your mind for the mind, at least the conscious mind, is coldly rational while the heart is warmly emotional. And as you have figured out for yourself but which I will confirm, *listen more to what your heart tells you, for it is a more reliable barometer in guiding you toward what is spiritually beneficial to you.*

Tonight's message was much more conventional than yesterday's but it is nevertheless an important one for you to heed as you proceed on your spiritual journey. On other occasions I will give you messages that will start out with shocking introductions like the train wreck but those will likely be more the exception than the rule. While I enjoy some fun here too and continue to have my sense of humor, I must remind you that all the messages that you have received and will receive from Seneca and me are deadly serious. They are intended to help you to help your fellow humans as they all proceed on their spiritual journey, hopefully making further progress in each lifetime.

More About Foolishness

Session 76 - November 7, 1993

Yes, I have already told you that I would talk today about foolishness. Now there is a subject that could accommodate a great deal of discussion and still not run out of things to say, especially about your human conduct. Foolishness is not the same as illusion. In the latter case, we can say that at least the person believes that his illusion is real. With foolishness the believer in it doesn't even have that excuse. Foolishness should be detectable by normal operation of the human intellect but it doesn't seem to be. Perhaps that gives us a lead to what foolishness really is.

As I see it, foolishness is an unthinking or unexamined belief in erroneous points of view. Now why would anyone want to believe in something without even bothering to examine it or hold that belief up to the light to see if it is transparently mistaken? Yet millions of people in this material world of yours follow that practice every day. One major reason is conditioning. From childhood we are conditioned to accept certain beliefs without examination of their cores or true validity. Among the most obvious examples of this phenomenon are religion and patriotism.

We are usually brought up as children in the religious beliefs of our parents and we are taught that faith—their faith of course—is the faith that we should accept because it is the correct one. As children we have no basis or opportunity to examine the validity of this assertion and why should we question what our loving parents have told us? Later, when we reach the age of adulthood and are free to make our own choices, we often are afraid to examine the faith of our parents. First, we don't want to hurt them by rejecting what they believe, and second, we don't like to give up long-established habits.

If I wanted to be a little unkind, I could also add that the thoughtful examination of any important proposition is a difficult and often painful process that many of us are too intellectually lazy to even want to perform. So we wind up in a kind of limbo, where we follow our parents' religious practices, but with less than full belief, while at the same time we have not looked for a different set of beliefs that we can truly accept as our own. In so doing, we fall between two stools; we are neither fish nor fowl and we are dissatisfied, deep within ourselves, with our spiritual growth and development.

Patriotism is another set of beliefs that we are usually brought up to cherish. For some of us, patriotism may even rank ahead of religion in importance. Some might say: "People may argue about preferences in religious views, but you only can have one country to give your loyalty to." Patriotism at its height has been expressed as: "My country, right or wrong." But love of country does not necessarily carry with it an uncritical acceptance of everything that your country does in its relations with the rest of the world.

The true patriot, because he loves his country, will undertake to comment upon and seek correction of its flaws so that it will become as nearly perfect as possible. That is much harder and requires much more moral courage than merely echoing patriotic clichés. I want to emphasize that I am by no means criticizing sincere religious belief or love of country in these examples. What I am criticizing is the unthinking or unexamined acceptance—the blind acceptance—of everything that you are taught about both religion and country.

I have previously said that your relationship to God and His creation is derived primarily from the heart rather than the head. And that position still stands. However, I am not suggesting that you decline to use your critical mental faculties in examining questions of belief. Don't forget that these faculties are also part of what God has blessed you with. They are to be used on the journey and in the search for a path home, but they are also to be used with humility and without arrogance. They can confirm or correct what your heart tells you but, all by themselves, they cannot put you on a sure path back to your heavenly home. So use your heads but in conjunction with your hearts to help you make your way through your various lifetimes, but don't lose sight of which of your guidance systems is truly the more reliable.

Yes, I know you have started reading a little book about the Kabbalists (Jewish mystics) and I agree with their belief that God is known through the heart. To put it a little differently, you cannot get "there" on an intellectual basis alone for God so transcends human intellect that it is impossible to begin to comprehend him in that way. On the other hand, the boundaries of the human heart approach the infinite and it is via that medium that you can come to know God as completely as the human condition permits.

We started with a conversation about foolishness and its meaning as unthinking or unexamined beliefs. To come back to that, *I would encourage you all to examine periodically the core beliefs that you hold. Don't be afraid to chart new courses. It is a sign of your spiritual growth that you are able to examine beliefs, and where you find them no longer persuasive, to move on to new ones.* As you progress further and further along your spiritual journey, you will find old, limiting beliefs will fall away upon examination and you will see more clearly what beliefs and behavior will help you proceed most rapidly along your path. So don't be afraid to leave old familiar mental surroundings for a great new adventure toward the promised land.

I think I've said enough for one day on this general subject. I am sure that I will allude to it again in the future in some form or other.

War

Armistice Day, now known as Veterans Day, is a good time to visit us. Both Seneca and I, when we were in the material world, participated in numerous wars, though nothing as big or as destructive as those which you and your contemporaries have experienced.

That makes war a good subject for today's discussion. *War represents the ultimate in man's aggressive behavior and his fears as well. It embodies many of the illusory temptations that the material world—the world of ego—uses to divert you from the path of spiritual growth.* Some of these, as you know, are the desire for power, greed, domination, material luxury, etc. These lures to the individual spirit find their greatest combined expression in the aggressive behavior of the nation-state. War is itself an abomination because of the objectives of those who start one and because of the unnecessary slaughter of so many people, especially under present-day conditions. The latter may often represent past karma now being met but it also cuts short the lives (only on earth, of course) of so many before they have had a real opportunity to make spiritual progress in that particular lifetime.

But even war has its opposite side—that of the defenders. The defenders go to war because they have no other choice but to defend their nation or succumb to the ravages of the aggressor. Perhaps that is how the so-called "just war" concept, that theologians once were so fond of, originated. I am convinced that there are "just wars" and one in which your nation is attacked, as at Pearl Harbor, meets that test. However, beware of the temptation to characterize every war that your beloved country engages in as such. Many others are very muddy regarding their moral position. Most wars that you humans have fought throughout your history are not morally sanctioned and do not meet our "just war" test.

A good yardstick for trying to decide whether a given war meets morality criteria is to look at the motives of those leading it. You will notice that I said "those leading it" instead of "those fighting it." That was quite intentional because those fighting it usually have not had a great deal of choice in the matter. Also, watch for changes in the motives of those leading it because they may well change during the course of the war.

To me Vietnam represents a good example of what I have been saying, as well as a valuable lesson that I hope you will learn for the future. At the outset, the motives of the U.S. leadership were to protect the people of South Vietnam from invasion from the North, accompanied by Communist-fomented civil war in the South. At the same time the U.S., erroneously as it turned out, believed that the fall of South Vietnam would result in the loss of all of Southeast Asia to Communist rule — the now-discredited "domino theory." So even at the outset, the motives of the U.S., while fairly high-minded, were also influenced by national self-interest, at least as that self-interest was perceived at the time. Later in the war, however, motives became far less noble. Ego prevailed and President Johnson was determined to "win" rather than lose face. And things went downhill from there. Because of Vietnam, which he inherited, and his later ego-driven response, his was a failed presidency.

Unless a war is clearly a defense against military aggression from the outside, in which event the defenders are morally justified in waging war, start with the presumption that the war is not morally justified. That will turn out to be the case more often than not. Also, by starting with that presumption, you force the proponents of that war to explain what they are defending, from whom and why.

I made the exception to that presumption because I am not a pacifist who believes in nonviolent responses to military aggression. That is a personal view, and one that is probably in a minority here on this side. While I like to think that I am a reasonably advanced being, I guess I still have a good bit further to go. A real saint would almost certainly be a pacifist and incapable of taking human life for any reason, including saving his own. My own view, limited though I acknowledge it to be, is that while you are in the material world, you must survive in accordance with its rules while at the same time making the most spiritual progress that you can.

Perhaps what I am really describing here is a head-to-head conflict between spiritual progress and survival in accordance with the material world's rules. In such a case, I think the prevailing viewpoint here is that achieving spiritual progress is controlling and that survival in the material world must yield to the greater imperative. If I reflect on this question long enough, I too may become a pacifist as regards conduct in the material world — but I am not ready to yet.

Wars ultimately end, either by outright conquest or by some kind of armistice. Then comes the time to establish the foundation for lasting peace. If and when that is done, then the biblical beatitude "Blessed are the peacemakers" becomes truly applicable. The makers of a just, honorable and lasting peace are indeed blessed. They have earned good karma for their acts, they have made spiritual progress in that lifetime and, perhaps most important, they have helped create the conditions under which others can make spiritual progress. For while spiritual progress can be made even under the worst material conditions, peaceful conditions are by far the best setting in which spiritual progress by individuals can take place.

Heaven

Session 78 - November 15, 1993

Tonight I would like to talk about heaven. That should be quite a mouthful since the term "heaven" means so many different things to different people. Not just people of different religious traditions, but even to different people within an individual tradition. It ranges all the way from a pleasure-filled world of the Muslim paradise to the "emptiness" of the Buddhist. And it includes nearly everything in-between. Probably that is because we have never done a very good job of communicating, and you humans have never done a very good job of understanding, what is really meant by the term.

To some, heaven conjures up the childhood Christian version of angels with wings sitting at the feet of God adoring Him, while saved souls surround the throne playing harps and singing His praises. What nonsense! While that may have some appeal to young children, it is hard to believe that a surprising number of adults still retain that childhood—and childish—view.

In the first place, God requires none of the obsequiousness that seems to characterize the repetitious praises that are sent His way. He is so far beyond that level that it is almost absurd to think that such conduct evokes much more than a slightly sad shake of the head for the lack of understanding that humans possess about the nature of Divinity. *To a distressing degree, when we try to imagine what God is like, we make the understandable but ludicrous mistake of creating Him in our image.*

We show our own love of power and prestige, with the idea of other people kowtowing to us, praising us and trying to win favor by groveling before us. I think some of these attitudes manifest our worst characteristics, so why do we attribute such shortcomings to Him Who is perfect, the epitome of the spiritual, Spirit Itself?

I think it is because the real nature of Spirit is too difficult for the human mind, with its inherent limitations, to encompass except to the most limited extent. I don't mean that critically. I just think it is part of being human. But instead of accepting those limitations you try to extend your human understanding beyond its outer limits, and as a result you often come up with very distorted pictures of reality—especially the ultimate reality that is God.

Yes, you have been told that Jesus by his life and conduct taught us something about what God is like, at least in human form. He was free from sin, he loved mankind to the extent that he was willing to sacrifice his own human life for our sake, and he taught us a good deal about the fundamentals of living. But those lessons were meant for us while here on earth to teach us how we should govern our lives here in the material world in order to make the spiritual progress necessary to find our way back to our eternal home with our heavenly Father. These lessons tell us very little about the ultimate nature of God—mostly, I think, because we probably couldn't handle it. Only a few holy men and women at any time in history and anywhere in the world have been able, while on earth, to gain more than a momentary glimpse into the reality that is God.

Let's face it. Most of us don't do a very good job of following the relatively simple lesson that Jesus and other great sages, both before and after him, have taught us about how to behave in order to achieve spiritual growth. He summarized it very simply and understandably when he said that the Great Commandment is: "Thou shalt love the Lord, thy God, with all thy heart and with all thy soul and with all thy might, and thou shalt love thy neighbor as thyself." But have we? Our track record on that score is quite poor. Fortunately, we always seem to have a few role models in every generation to keep the spirit of that Great Commandment alive, but the great majority of the world's population, while subscribing to the words—in different forms, languages and traditions but in substance the same—does a better job of *professing* this Great Commandment than *living* it.

When we can't even seem to understand—really understand—and follow an instruction manual prepared and designed for humans, how can we possibly expect to understand the divine one?

That is one of the reasons why Seneca and I, and many of us here who are trying to help you in the material world, concentrate our messages on what it takes to achieve spiritual progress. We generally stay away from the province of the theologians, who try to tell us about the nature and attributes of the living and eternal God. While their intentions are generally honorable, there is, I believe, a certain hubris in their belief that they can even begin to approach the outer fringes of such an understanding. Mystics can come much closer than theologians because God is best found by looking to the divine spark within each of us, rather than by reading complex tomes written by scholars who have spent their lives translating obscure works by other ancient scholars with no greater insight than their own.

So we emphasize how you live over what you profess, or even what you think you understand. How you live and conduct yourself toward others, including all of God's creation, is a far better measure of the kind of spiritual growth and development that you will achieve in a given lifetime. Also, remember that how you conduct yourself is within your control in the material world, whereas what you understand frequently is not—and especially so when the subject is God, His plan, His will, etc.

Remain mindful of the fact that the ultimate goal of every human life is to make forward progress on the path back to reunion with God. That is our ultimate objective. That is our fundamental yearning. That is what we must do to end our feeling of incompleteness. When we get there—and notice again that I say *when*, not if—we will know the answers to these intriguing questions because then we will ourselves be a part of those answers.

Poison

Session 79 - November 18, 1993

Tonight I will talk about poison. It was a subject in your recent comedy play, though not intended to be taken seriously. My discussion of poison is serious.

Poison can affect the body, mind and spirit of a person while on the earth plane. We all know about poisons that affect the body by chemically interfering with natural bodily functions and, if the interference is severe enough, the person will die. Other lesser "poisons" also have an adverse effect upon physical good health, although they may not commonly be called poisons in standard parlance. One good example is tobacco in almost any form. It won't kill you as quickly as arsenic but its debilitating effects over a period of years entitle it to be classified as a poison, at least as far as I am concerned. But there is nothing new in what I am saying here. Physical poisons are a phenomenon well known to all of you.

What about mental poisons? Those are a good deal more subtle, although their effect upon the individual may be at least as profound as physical poisons. You have all heard the term "poisoning the mind" to denote the communication of information that is intended to influence other people with regard to a particular issue, idea or person. If the information is untrue or badly distorted as regards its truthfulness, then it may properly be considered as a form of mental poison. By its very nature, the term "poison" has negative connotations and that applies equally well to mental as well as physical poisons. Is there an antidote to mental poisons? Truth is probably the most effective antidote. If it is accepted by those exposed to the mental poison, it can go a long way toward neutralizing the ill effects of the mental poison.

I would sound a note of caution here about communicating negative information about others even when the information is accurate and is a fair summary. That is not spreading mental poison, with the bad karmic consequences that necessarily follow from doing so. However, by so doing, you manifest a lack of compassion for another human being—and therefore for yourself—for, as we have said before, at a soul level all human beings are joined together and what we do to others, we do to ourselves.

Spiritual poison seems like a much harder concept to grasp, and it is. Actually, it almost sounds like a contradiction in terms, an oxymoron, to speak of both spirituality and poison in the same breath. Yet there is such a thing and I will try to explain briefly what I believe it to be. Remember, I said earlier that poison—referring to physical poisons— interferes with normal bodily functions, and if severe enough, can even cause physical death. Well, the counterpart also applies in the spiritual realm. Spiritual poison can interfere with the normal workings of the spiritual self and bring about backsliding on the spiritual path to re-union with our Father. I think you can understand the concept but what are examples of spiritual poisons?

Some of the most obvious spiritual poisons are the serious sins enunciated in the Judeo-Christian bible. They include behavior patterns or attitudes such as pride, envy, hatred, lust for power, and a good many others. It is not my purpose here to provide a compendium of spiritual poisons, only to warn you that they exist and lie in wait for the spiritually unwary.

Another category of spiritual poisons, in my judgment, consists of beliefs as to one's exclusivity in God's plan. This can also be subsumed under the category of pride or arrogance because it is based on the belief that you (and presumably your co-religionists) have a special place in God's plan. This can take the form of belief in a Chosen People mythology, or a "salvation only my way" mythology or some equivalent attitude. It is a philosophy of "exclusivity" rather than one of "inclusivity."

As I have previously told you, there are many paths to our ultimate destination, not just one. And I have also told you that progress on the spiritual path is far more dependent upon how you live than it is upon what you profess to believe. There may also be something of an oxymoron there. How can one genuinely profess a certain set of spiritual beliefs and then conduct his life in a manner completely at odds with those alleged beliefs. *Your conduct is the most revealing manifestation of your genuine beliefs.* You can recite prayers all day but if you then go out and cheat your neighbor, all those prayers avail you little or nothing.

We know that there are antidotes for some physical poisons that will counteract the adverse effects on the body. We also know that truth is the best antidote to mental poisons that we may encounter from time to time as we pass through this lovely sandy little beach. What about spiritual poisons—are there antidotes for those? Yes, there are, and the use of those antidotes is within our own control. *In my opinion, the best antidote to spiritual poisons is a concoction consisting of love, caring, compassion and a healthy humility.* Protected and strengthened by these positive spiritual qualities, you need not worry about making dangerous detours from the path of spiritual development. Oh, of course you will stray once in a while—after all, you're only human—but you will never be in danger of losing your spiritual bearings or forgetting what your purpose here is.

I think that should be enough for tonight. Now that you know something about other kinds of poisons than the purely physical, you will be less susceptible to their interfering in your progress along the particular spiritual path that you have chosen as your route back to your Father.

Christmas Pageant

Session 80 · December 6, 1993

Our topic today should really take off from the beautiful Christmas Pageant that you and Enid attended yesterday in Fort Lauderdale. The message of that pageant, which we felt you relate to, was the unity of mankind, whether red, yellow, black or white. The emphasis also was on love and compassion, with the message that Jesus was not executed by either the Romans or the Jews but that he gave his life *voluntarily* for all of us. It is a reminder that, by following his example to the best of our limited abilities, we too can change our own little part of the world and find a path back to our eternal home. It really doesn't matter whether all or some or even none of the historical facts surrounding the life and death of Jesus are accurate; it is his *message* that is eternal and a guide for us—at least those of us who profess to be Christians.

Other traditions have their own versions of divine messages that are presented to their followers by saints and holy men. And these messages for the most part are consistent with the message of unity, love, compassion, etc. that Jesus gave us. They may be couched in different terms and sometimes they may even sound inconsistent because they reflect cultural and temporal biases. *However, stripped of their outer garments, the messages of the sages and holy men and women of all traditions and of all ages is substantially the same.* Their theology may be quite different but, from my point of view, that isn't really very important. Our focus should be on how we choose to live the lives we are given on this earth plane. If we also want to try to understand divinity and the divine plan, that's all right too—but don't necessarily expect to be right. You will learn more about the divine plan and your individual role in it later as you get closer to God on your return path. Eventually you will understand it all when you actually link up with the Divine Spirit.

In the meantime, concentrate your attention on how you live and how you interact with your fellow humans and the rest of God's creation. Remember, what you think, say, and do is a more accurate reflection of what you truly believe than what you profess. So take heed. Play your intellectual games if you wish, but always be mindful of the fact that you must walk the path back to your Father, not just talk it.

Another encouraging lesson from your attendance at the Pageant was the attitude of the participants who greeted you after the show. They were all smiles, wishing you a "Merry Christmas" and a "God Bless You." You could actually *feel* the goodwill that was flowing toward you from them. Remember this when you become discouraged by the negative events that you see in the world and by the ego-driven behavior of so many people that you encounter in the world. Ego and its illusions have not taken over the whole of planet Earth—nor will they!

There will always be people in the material plane that remember who and what they are and why they are here, and who live their lives accordingly. Just be one of them. I address that last remark to all who may someday read this material, rather than to any individual. Even in the worst and darkest of hours, the flame will continue to be tended by those on a path home or sincerely seeking such a path. Obviously the sincere seeker has farther to go than the one who is already on a path home but at least the sincere seeker has made the major move. He has identified his lodestar, his North Star, by which he can guide himself to one of the many paths that lead home.

Others may mill around in confusion—internal confusion, that is, because they may externally appear to be happy, successful, powerful, wealthy, etc.—while the sincere seeker has overcome the first and perhaps greatest obstacle. That obstacle, as you well know and as I will repeat many times more, is the lure of this material world—a preoccupation with all the objectives that I mentioned in the preceding sentence.

To put it into contemporary terms, your objective should be to extend the so-called Christmas Spirit to the rest of the year. You cannot hope to do it throughout the world but you can make a start in your own little corner of the world. And you would be surprised at how beginnings like that can spread like wildfire.

Although it is not a subject of polite conversation or cocktail party chatter, people throughout the world, but especially in your country, are groping for a deeper meaning to their lives than the material world alone offers. There is therefore a silent receptivity to spiritual messages and to matters of the spirit generally. Most people believe that they have spirits that are eternal. But what happens after physical death of the body has been confused by rigid notions of heaven and hell, along with a condemnation centuries ago of the doctrine of reincarnation that prevails in eastern religious traditions generally. *We see the beginnings of a spiritual awakening in the United States. It won't happen over night, it will be initially confined to small pockets of people, and it will be greatly accelerated by the earth changes that are nearly upon us.*

The Christ Spirit

Session 81 - December 21, 1993

You need not apologize for delays in communicating with us. This effort is, and must be, entirely voluntary on your part. We do not intrude; we come only when invited by you. We also know that you genuinely wish our communication to continue but you do tend sometimes to get caught up in your activities there. We understand that. We just urge that you try to stay in regular touch with us, for your own sake and that of those who may ultimately read these messages some time in the future. When, you ask? We will let you know, and it will be during your lifetime on earth.

Tonight's subject will start off with the spirit of Christmas since this is the season and the actual holiday is almost upon you. Maybe a more apt title for this message would be "the Christ spirit." Let's take the term apart and see where it leads us, while remembering that the same message may also be found in the teachings of other great holy men throughout history.

The message preached by Christ is — and note that I say *is*, not *was* — one that emphasizes love, caring, compassion, humility, unity and obedience to the will of our heavenly Father. The message eschews violence, power, false honors, outward piety unaccompanied by inner piety, and in general, the lures of the material world. The message also teaches forgiveness and a certain amount of unconventionality that we might well emulate in our own time. After all, he ate with sinners and tax collectors and others who were considered to be social outcasts in their own time. He forgave Mary Magdalene and even those who were crucifying him. He knew, even if most of us didn't, that he was giving his life voluntarily for the people of the entire world.

While he preached all these things, he was no hermit, but instead was a man who loved people, children especially. As anyone in the sales world knows, he had to sell himself before he could sell his message. His warmth and concern for people, along with a sense of humor that is not widely recognized in biblical materials, were well known to his many listeners as well as his disciples. Perhaps they didn't make mention of it in their gospels because they thought it would detract from his dignity, but it really emphasizes his humanity and his identification with us.

We sometimes bemoan the fact that the so-called Christmas spirit lasts for such a short time each year. But the fact that it usually comes back again the following year demonstrates that it continues to live in us, although usually at a subdued level during the rest of the year. I am talking, of course, about your United States, not other parts of the world that are overwhelmed by war and poverty, or even those people in your United States who are having a difficult time of it. The rest of you do seem to show a much more gracious and smiling face to each other during this season. My message to all of you who may read this, as well as to you individually, Bill, is to do your very best to preserve these attitudes and behavior patterns throughout the year. Not only will you be gaining in spiritual progress but you will also be gaining in human happiness at the same time.

The path home, while in the material world, is a slippery one—they all are—and we all slip off from time to time, except maybe for those enlightened beings who have come back here to help us. So don't be discouraged by the fact that you are less than perfect. Instead, just keep trying to improve, while remaining ever mindful of who you are and why you are here. Do this and you will slip off the path less often, and without having to make your way back onto the path so often, you will make greater progress along it. Recognize that ego is very clever and can try to use your occasional retrogression as a device for saying to you that you really can't handle the path, since you fall off, so why bother to even keep trying. It is a skillful ploy that ego is very good at but don't let yourself be taken in by either that gimmick or others like it. Unless ego can convince you that the here and now in this material world is not only real but is also all there is, it loses its influence over you and its place in your value system.

Ego requires separateness for its survival and is therefore threatened by thoughts of the unity of all humankind, never mind the unity of all God's creation. So it will resort to whatever tricks it can to get you to adopt its view of life. Mindfulness will be your most effective shield against the snares of ego. This you already know but others may not yet understand this truth.

New Beginnings

Session 82 - December 31, 1993

The new year provides an opportunity for new beginnings. That is why people make "New Year's resolutions," most of which go unfulfilled as the year progresses. But while new beginnings can take place at any time of your year, the beginning of the year seems like a particularly auspicious time to undertake such new beginnings.

❋ ❋ ❋ ❋

What new beginnings do we see for the world at large? Quite a few developments, but most of them are not conducive to spiritual growth and development. Times will continue to remain very uncertain throughout the world, in terms of things like aggression, weapons, human rights concerns, and the like. The world will muddle through this coming year but without making much, if any, long-term progress toward solutions to the many problems which it faces. Nationalism and even narrower forms of tribalism and ethnic conflict will continue to plague those who seek to promote the unity of mankind as a major goal of human progress in this world.

Enough of that. In spite of the large difficulties that the world as a whole faces this year, every individual can still take it upon himself or herself to make a new beginning and change that individual's life. To maintain that it makes no sense to do so because the world or the country is in such a mess is really what your young people would call a "cop-out." It is nothing more than an excuse, and not a convincing one, for taking the lazy way out and doing nothing different to improve the spiritual quality of your life in the coming year. Never forget that everyone counts—*every single individual*. As I have said before, you may not be able to change the world as a whole, but you can change that small portion of it that you inhabit, and become a role model for others to follow. And you would undoubtedly be surprised at how far the ripples would spread. So concentrate on what you *can* do, instead of bemoaning what you can't and thus doing nothing. You certainly won't build up positive karma by doing nothing.

You were just wondering momentarily about what happens when you die. It seemed out of place until you remembered that today's message deals primarily with new beginnings. That's why the thought popped into your head—yes, it came from us—*that's what the death of the body is, a new beginning, a time for a refresher course in the spirit world before you are considered ready for another try at the material world.* We understand that most new beginnings are rather scary, as well as exciting at the same time.

Just think of material world analogies. Weren't you a little scared when you moved to a faraway place, took a new job, got married and had children? Of course you were—you just don't like to talk about it or, in some cases, even admit it to yourself. Well, death is not that different. Although there is apprehension and uncertainty about the unknown world into which you are about to enter, if you have a positive spiritual outlook, you will also find it to be an exciting experience to be anticipated with interest rather than naked fear. Once you accept the fact that your spirit is immortal and that you have lived on earth many times in the past, and will again in the future, you will no longer fear death as the end of everything. Or maybe worse, as the time for God to "judge" you and admit you to a heaven or consign you to a terrible hell. Since humans are by definition imperfect or we wouldn't have to keep coming back, nearly everybody has failed to live up to his or her spiritual responsibilities in a given lifetime. And if God were to "judge" us on this basis, virtually the entire human race, except for illuminated souls who have reincarnated to help the rest of us, would be in big trouble. But that is not the way it is and the sooner we appreciate that fact, the less afraid of death will we be.

We also do a good deal of creation of our own reality. Therefore, if someone strongly believes in a fiery hell for his version of sinners, and if he considers himself to be one, he will encounter such a place upon his death—at least until he learns more about what the ultimate reality is actually like. Then he will cease to punish himself. As we have told you before, God is a loving and caring parent. He does not punish; He teaches. *We* do the punishing—of ourselves as well as others. Remember this truth and try to pattern your behavior after that of your loving, caring and compassionate God, in your relationships with other humans and with all of God's creation. I won't try to tell you that it is easy to do, but the spiritual progress it will bring is astounding. It will also have a profound effect upon your own human happiness and self-esteem.

৶৶৶

More About Heaven

Session 83 · January 5, 1994

What to introduce this new year with? Your thought was a good one. Let us start with the information that we gave you while you were lying in bed a day or so ago. You had thoughts going through your head and you knew they did not originate with you. So you assumed that they were somehow coming from either Seneca or me. You were correct that I was the source of those thoughts, through a kind of psychic leakage. I was not trying to communicate with you because that is something to be initiated by you. But maybe our connection has become so close that you can sometimes "tune in" to me even when you are not sitting at your computer keyboard and trying to make contact.

The thoughts you received were essentially these. *Heaven is within each and every one of you.* Jesus already told you that when he said "The Kingdom of God is within." All you have to do is sincerely look for it within yourself. No one is trying to hide it from you; it's right there in front of your very nose. You just have to be wearing the right glasses to see it. Of course the "right glasses" are figurative. But to continue the analogy, the right glasses are those which enable you to see through the snares and illusions of the material world to the substance beyond— glasses that enable you to separate the eternal from the ephemeral and to focus your attention, and your conduct, on the former.

Why is it that we tend so often to think of heaven in childish terms, as somewhere up in the blue sky out of sight? But even when we think of it in less childish terms, we still tend to think of it as a kind of place and always a place *outside* ourselves. I want to tell you that all those notions are wrong. First, heaven is not a place, or a location, in any meaning of that term. Rather, *heaven is a state of being, a state in which the individual's spirit, his divine core, is so closely linked with God, the Universal Spirit, or any other name you may choose, that they are joined in a single unity. The individual's spirit retains its identity but the link- age makes him what has been called a co-creator with God.* It is all within the deeper levels of being of each and every human being on the face of this small planet.

Knowing this, there is no longer any need for you to search for your own Holy Grail. Just locate it within yourself and polish it up. I realize that I am making it sound easier than it is. But once you look with clear eyes into your inner being you should have no trouble in finding it. The more difficult part is then to live what you know to be right and still be able to function in the material world. It is by no means easy, but hopefully it becomes a little easier to avoid the ego challenge of the material world if you realize that its attractions are only momentary puffs of dust with no lasting place in eternal history.

So while I encourage you to educate yourself more about the role of psychic communication in influencing attitudes, you do not have to read long scholarly tomes or follow difficult practices to achieve spiritual growth; all you really have to do is know who you are and why you are here and then live your life accordingly. Books and lessons are fine for trying to gain a deeper understanding of ultimate reality, but they can sometimes be dangerous by diverting people from practice to cold scholarly study.

Let me see if there is anything I want to add to this little summary. Oh yes, I think it was implicit in what I had said but it is important enough to be made explicit. *Because heaven is within each and every one of us and consists of the unique linkage described between an individual's spirit and the Divine Spirit, one does not have to die bodily in order to "go to heaven." One can "be in heaven" (as I have defined it) while still living in the body on the earth plane.* That ought to give you all some food for thought, and probably also a source of heated argument too.

The Challenge

Shall we begin this afternoon by talking about the sun? You are surprised? You shouldn't be. After all, without the sun to warm your planet, you wouldn't be here. Also the sun plays such a vital role in your survival that it was once worshipped as a god by early man. I want to talk about the sun because it brings light to the world. It brings physical light while we are trying to bring spiritual light. You should know (if you don't already) that without spiritual light, just as without physical light, your world would perish. Fortunately, as I have told you before, even in the worst of times there are always those spiritually endowed beings and their spiritually oriented pupils who will preserve the light and prevent darkness from taking over. Your mission is to become such a person in the remainder of this life and to serve as a messenger of these ideas to others.

It is quite a challenge but it is not beyond your capability if you decide to undertake it. It doesn't mean becoming a missionary in the sense of moving anywhere or preaching or any of that kind of stuff. It means being an anchor point for others who may also be spiritually motivated but are reluctant to acknowledge it in this materialistic age. It means living your life as an example of the love, caring and compassion that all humankind should display toward each other but do not. It also means being prepared to publish these messages, substantially as received, when the time is right. So you see, it is not all that bad. You don't have to move to darkest Africa or get a hair shirt or preach in the streets to hostile audiences. You just have to try to look after your own little corner of the world—to serve as a lens through which spiritual light may be magnified for the benefit of others.

The choice is of course yours. We here try to provide spiritual guidance to those who appear to seek it. But, as I have said many times before, we do not interfere. Free will is your gift from God and it always remains yours to exercise. You get to choose how strongly and extensively you take up this challenge, if you take it up at all. We think you will choose to do so, at least to the extent of your abilities. And we understand that the flesh is weak and the lure of the material world is very powerful.

All you can do, if you decide to take up this challenge, is to do your best. You won't always be a beacon of light, and you will sometimes backslide rather badly, for that is the human condition and you are nowhere near the stage of illumination even though you have managed to crawl out of the muck. So just do your best and don't berate yourself or get discouraged when you fall short. We will always be here to help and to provide advice, comfort and assistance. After all, keep in mind that, by taking on this challenge, you are already doing more to achieve spiritual growth than most people do in a lifetime!

You can undertake your challenge quietly and without fanfare. All you have to do is work harder at living the teachings that you have received from Seneca and me, and they are by no means original with us. You can be an example without anyone knowing that is what you are doing and why. That way you can also preserve your place in the material world without being dismissed as having lost your mind. Try it and you will see what we mean.

The more frequently you communicate with us, the more will we be able to strengthen you for your challenge. Of course, the more frequently you communicate with us, the more information can we give you for the guidance of those who will ultimately read the published version of these messages. So include regular contact with us as a part of your challenge — though admittedly a small part.

Even though this has been a short session, I think perhaps that I have given you enough to ponder for the time being. As I previously promised you, we will be passing along to you in future communications some new material, some of which may be quite startling to you. We want to be sure that you are ready for it. So far you have been a good, clear vehicle for our communications and we don't want to move ahead too fast and run the risk of spoiling that fine receptivity that you have developed to date.

Help

I see that you had a good visit with your son. He is on a sound spiritual path and will continue on that path for his entire lifetime. He is making good progress in his quest and will make even more as time goes on. As you agree, he is right to be a practitioner as well as a scholar in the intellectual sense. *Knowing* isn't enough; *doing* is also required. And he already knows that—something that most people don't realize until much later in life, if at all. You can be proud of this young man, though I hasten to add, in the course of this praise, that he is not by any means a candidate for sainthood yet.

You chose the key word "help" for this evening's message. Yes, I really helped you choose it (no pun intended). The term "help" has so many meanings and interpretations that it covers quite a broad area. I will confine my observations to spiritual help, since that, after all, is what I am trying to provide.

Spiritual help must ultimately come from within, even though a considerable amount can also come from external sources, such as these communications with you. They do represent spiritual help, both for you personally and also potentially for anyone who reads these messages and heeds them. I can already see some results in your specific case, Bill, although you still have a great deal to absorb and practice. You also have much more to receive from me and from Seneca in the coming years. All this material is to be prepared for publication when I tell you that the time is right.

All these messages contain moral imperatives that must be understood and practiced by you, and others who read this material, in order to achieve maximum spiritual growth in this lifetime. I see some progress on your part in terms of greater awareness, or mindfulness, about your interaction with other people. You are becoming more compassionate and thus less prone to judge others. You still have much more progress to be made but it is certainly a good start.

While still on the subject of help, you should know that Seneca and I are always available to provide spiritual help for you upon request. Such help can include guidance in dealing with questions in your own life, assistance in resolving moral dilemmas that you may face, assistance in achieving spiritual unity amidst the welter of religious denominations (I sometimes think of it as a kind of religious tribalism), and any other kind of spiritual assistance you may request. I almost said "require" instead of "request" but then I remembered that we do not intrude ourselves upon your consciousness; we communicate only when invited to do so, such as when our help is sought or when you wish information that may be available to us here.

The only exception I can think of is what I would call the "bleed-through," which occurred that night when you were in bed and were not trying to reach us. This occurred because the connection between us is now strong and vibrant—so "bleed-through" can occur under those circumstances. I for one am pleased, as I know you are, that we have achieved such a strong and clear connection. Even at my vibration level, I find it easy to communicate with you and that means that you are raising your own vibration level and therefore are making spiritual progress.

Spiritual help is available to all who sincerely seek it. Just as Seneca is your spirit guide, Bill, and has been from your birth in this life, so every human being on the face of the earth has his or her spirit guide. To you out there who may some day read this, *you* are the one who must make contact with your spirit guide if contact is to be made at all. My purpose is not to provide techniques for making such contact but, rather, to assure you that contact can be made if you sincerely desire it and can raise your vibration level high enough—through meditation, for example—so that your guide can make reasonably clear contact with you.

Spiritual help and guidance are thus always available if you want them. You don't have to follow the guidance that is given you—after all, you do have free will—but you know that it is much harder to ignore spiritual advice that you have asked for since you can no longer rationalize your way around the problem the way you could before you received the guidance.

I am not at all sure that this is a good analogy but I saw you thinking of the "Help" menu on your computer. It is there for the asking but it does not automatically come to the rescue. You have to call upon it or else it just sits there. Even when you do call upon it, it is pre-programmed into certain categories chosen by the programmer so you have to know what category your problem fits into before you can even ask for help successfully. But what can you really expect from a machine—even a marvelous machine, but one that does not have a mind? Your spirit guide, as a being that possesses a mind in addition to an enormous fund of knowledge, can respond to your requests for help even before they are actually communicated by your conscious mind. But the first part of the analogy still stands—the "Help" menu just sits there until you choose to activate it.

While our role is limited to providing you with spiritual help for your journey through this lifetime in the material world, you are not thus limited in your relationships with others. You are also able to provide material help to others—and I would go so far as to say that you have a duty to do so. Material help, as I use the term, means help in the material world, in the broad sense. I don't mean that you have to provide money or other material goods, though you gain good karma if you do. Material help can also include good advice or even a sympathetic ear. Material help can include healing of others who are afflicted by illnesses of body, mind or spirit.

You and your wife, Enid, are acquainted with this, for as you have been told elsewhere, you have both been healers in past lives. And you both have healing capabilities in this life. While some heal by laying on of hands and others heal by herbal and other natural remedies, you both heal by listening. It is a form of healing that is less obvious and less dramatic than some of the other methods, but it is healing nonetheless, especially for afflictions of the mind or spirit.

Continue to heal by listening. Those whom you help in this way may never know what you did. But that doesn't matter because you are not doing it for recognition or any other kind of material reward. You are doing it because you are aware of the unity of all human beings and you are doing it to make progress on your own spiritual path. As you heal by listening, you do make progress on your own spiritual path, so keep it up. It is also a form of healing that you can do quietly without fanfare or public awareness—and that is all to the good.

More About Earth Changes

What to talk about tonight? Earth changes seems like an obvious subject, what with the frigid weather conditions throughout much of the country and a major earthquake in southern California. If you had any serious doubt in your minds that they were really coming, these events should convince you. And this is hardly more than an introduction!

Earth changes have been building up for some time, almost like a volcano that builds up ever-increasing pressure beneath the earth's crust until finally it all erupts with a tremendous explosion and all the other accompaniments of an active volcano. The difference here is that we are dealing with a broad spectrum of natural phenomena. I can tell you with considerable confidence that when you encounter exceptional natural phenomena, you are probably experiencing an earth change event.

Hurricane Andrew was such an example, as are these two current events. Massive forest fires, such as those in California, may or may not be earth change events. If they were the result of arsonists or other vindictive or unbalanced people, then they are not. However, if they resulted from lightning strikes in those forests, then I would characterize them as earth change events. As you can see, events caused by man don't count but those caused by nature do.

What should people do under these circumstances? There are no easy solutions I can give you because no easy solutions exist. Mother Earth must purify herself from all the pollution that we humans have inflicted on her throughout our existence and there is no preventing or avoiding that. As you are also well aware, most of this pollution has come about in recent years (certainly "recent" in terms of the duration of man's presence on earth) and the penalty for such pollution—more accurately the "consequences," because I don't like the term "penalty" or its connotations—must be paid by persons now living, whose contemporaries are largely responsible for the worst of the pollution.

I don't encourage people to uproot themselves in an effort to escape the earth changes. Those whose karma it is to suffer and/or die as a result of them will anyhow. Those whose karma in this lifetime is to escape the consequences of the earth changes will be spared, wherever they may be. Note, for example, that some buildings were totally destroyed while others that were adjacent to them were left untouched or suffered minimal damage—whether in the hurricane, the earthquake or the forest fires. That should tell you something. Remember—*nothing happens by chance*. What you choose to call "chance" is merely a term to designate your lack of understanding of the forces that are at work to bring about the result that you attribute to something called chance.

We all do rather a lot of that—give something a name and thereby pretend that we understand what it is. Or perhaps by naming it we can brush it aside and not have to consider it further. Well, that's all that "chance" or "luck" is—a vehicle to hide our ignorance.

One potentially beneficial result from the earth changes is that it may cause people who have up to now been totally focused on the material world to direct their attention to spiritual matters. The earth changes can help to remind us humans of our mortality and vulnerability in this life in the material world. Once we realize how transitory is the physical world, with all its lures, possessions and temptations, then we may detach ourselves from it much more readily. Another beneficial effect, as illustrated by the earthquake, is that it brings people together. When faced with a common disaster, they seem to recognize their common humanity and strive to help each other. Of course it shouldn't have to take a disaster to remind people of this, but it does seem to, I regret to say.

I believe that this trend will continue as the earth changes continue and grow more severe. People will increasingly turn to their spiritual side, recognizing that the kingdom of heaven is within, and they will more readily recognize the unity of all God's creation and behave accordingly, not just during disaster periods. In this manner, spiritual progress for many people in this world will be achieved out of what on its face is unmitigated disaster.

I still haven't given you a definitive answer to what people should do in anticipation of the earth changes. The best thing I can suggest is more prayer, not in a vain effort to prevent the changes, but because prayer, like meditation, brings you into closer contact with your spiritual self. Any other devices or practices that will cause you to focus your attention and energies on the spiritual should also be utilized. I believe that this kind of emphasis upon spiritual values and conduct will be a far more effective way of avoiding the consequences of the earth changes than moving away or otherwise trying to escape physically.

However, I have to repeat that if your present karmic condition calls for it, then you will be injured or killed in the course of one of these earth changes. While that doesn't sound very appealing, you should be mindful of the fact that you have already lived many lives on earth and will live many more. If this one is destined to come to an end sooner than you might have liked, so what? There will be a next time, and in the meantime you may have paid off some heavy karmic debt.

For those people who are already spiritually oriented—and I include you and your family in that category, Bill—the earth changes will give you a greater opportunity to spread spiritual values, primarily by example. People who are scared because they can no longer control their natural habitat are more likely to be receptive to directing their attention to the spiritual, as compared with people who are, as you would put it, "fat, dumb and happy" with their material pursuits. That set of circumstances will afford spiritually oriented people throughout the world, regardless of religious denomination, a golden opportunity to achieve rapid spiritual growth by serving as examples to others, as well as by discussion along those lines. From the upheaval will come a kind of new beginning. I don't mean by that the destruction of all humanity and a new creation, of course, but rather a major shift in direction and emphasis, especially on the part of people in the "developed" or industrialized world. You can therefore expect that after the pain and suffering the end result will be good—sort of like the pain and suffering of labor followed by the birth of a beautiful child.

Movies

Session 87 - January 23, 1994

What to talk about? I see that you keep getting the word "movies" but are having trouble accepting that as the subject because it doesn't sound very unusual or exciting as a subject for today's message. Well, movies are a key reflection of the culture of a society. And they also influence the culture of which they are a part. As a result, they are in the rather unique position of being both an effect and a cause.

Movies present our values—what we deem important. They give a good indication of what we are willing to tolerate, accept, fight for and die for. They are *us* (it's OK! The bad grammar is intentional for emphasis), albeit often in exaggerated or distorted form.

Violence in movies reflects the violence that exists in our society. It doesn't really *cause* violence but it certainly enhances our willingness to tolerate and accept violence as a method of expressing frustration and alienation, especially on the part of young men. And even more especially in the case of young black men. Too often the violent outburst is a manifestation of an unbearable frustration that finally explodes into random, unthinking violence. Obviously that doesn't condone the violence, even though it may help us understand it a little better.

Amidst the negatives, there are also some positives in the movies. One of the funnier offerings that we saw with you a while back was Eddie Murphy's *Trading Places*. There the moral was in favor of the two young men who were being used as guinea pigs by the two selfish, uncaring old men. So when the young men got together and turned the tables on the old villains, the audience, amid its genuine laughter, felt good about the outcome. So all is not lost to the negative.

Life seems to have become more complicated in recent years. Compare present movies with those of the 1930s and 1940s, separate and apart from Hays Office censorship. I'm talking now about the content of those movies. The simple cowboy picture then versus now. Things were simpler then—simplistically simpler. The cowboys (or cavalry) were always the good guys and the Indians were always the bad guys, even though in many cases these stereotypes bore no resemblance whatever to actual reality. More recent times have seen more complex movies, not necessarily because life has really become more complicated but because we are now more willing to view life's challenges and dilemmas in varying shades of gray, rather than straight black or white.

Throughout it all comedies are still being made, some of which are very funny. These comedies show that humor is still alive and well in the American psyche. As you have said many times: "A sense of humor is a survival requirement for people" and as long as humor continues to be part of the American psyche, your society will survive. Comedy is the way in which we laugh at ourselves—our idiosyncrasies, our pretensions, our self-importance, and if you are fortunate, even your concern and preoccupation with material things.

Movies are also a way of testing how much of our basic humanity remains that is not covered by the hard shell that we all grow to hide our vulnerability. When we are emotionally moved by the plight of a character in a movie, we identify with that character and share his or her humanity during that short period of time. When we weep at a movie, we are demonstrating that we have still retained at least a measure of the compassion that we all started out with. We can take comfort in knowing that it has not become the hard, practical shell of the person who has decided to devote his or her energies almost entirely to the material world. *If we ever become unable to laugh and cry at movies, then we should worry about having lost our humanity.* And if we lose our humanity, we as the human race will have to pay a terrible price to regain that humanity. So let's make sure that we never lose it.

Let me say a word about movie violence. Those who truly enjoy it should stop and take stock of themselves. They are in imminent danger of losing their humanity and thereby becoming empty shells, biological rather then electronic or mechanical robots. Those who find thrills as they watch violence should remind themselves that we all have a dark side to our personalities. It is not important that it exists—that's a simple reality. *What is important is that we acknowledge the existence of that dark side and that we control it so that our actions reflect our positive values.* To try to eliminate it is useless and to try to pretend that it doesn't exist is dangerous delusion. The thing we must do is keep it under solid conscious control.

Even war movies have their redeeming features. While they show the inherent inhumanity of war, they also show sterling examples of teamwork, compassion, self-sacrifice and heroism. As we have all seen many times, wars, catastrophes and natural disasters bring out both the best and the worst in human beings. *If we are able to focus on the positive teachings that we can derive from movies — yes, even today's movies — then we can use the experiences that they present to us as opportunities for our own spiritual growth and development.* If we do not look beneath the surface, we will either stay away from them, deplore what is being portrayed in them, or adopt their worst features as acceptable guidelines for behavior. That would be an unmitigated disaster for anyone thus afflicted.

Paper

Session 88 - January 28, 1994

We are pleased that you enjoy and look forward to your visits with us. Seneca is indeed your spirit guide and I am now your teacher. We both love you and try to look after you and those you love too.

❋ ❋ ❋ ❋

Miracles do happen. They aren't really miracles but you call them that because you do not understand the processes that bring them about. Since we have chosen to look after you, that includes your family — and in the broadest sense of the word.

Enough personal information for the moment. How shall I start our message for tonight? You got the word "paper" in your mind and are wondering how paper fits into spiritual growth. Well, I guess I could start by saying that paper was mankind's most effective way of passing on the knowledge and wisdom of prior generations to those that followed. Oral traditions were remarkably resilient and successful but their coverage was necessarily too limited, especially as populations began to grow. The written word, initially on tablets, then papyrus, and finally paper became the vehicle by which prior accumulated knowledge was passed on. With the invention of the printing press, the paper method of spreading that knowledge multiplied fantastically.

Since paper is the medium used for the publication of books, among other things, paper has also become a most potent vehicle for disseminating spiritual knowledge as well as secular knowledge. Look today at all the publications you can find dealing at considerable length on various aspects of spiritual development. Look at what you are doing. We are asking you to reproduce our messages so that, when the time is right, they can be edited and reproduced in a suitable manner.

The time may soon be coming when interactive TV and computers will render the paper book obsolete but I certainly don't see that kind of obsolescence for quite some time. Thinking of paper brought to mind the old children's game of paper, rock and scissors. As you recall, scissors cuts paper, rock breaks scissors, paper covers rock. Maybe I am extending the moral of this game too far but it seems to me that the ability of paper to cover rock means that knowledge and ideas will ultimately prevail over brute force. As you see, in this little scenario paper represents knowledge, wisdom and ideas, while rock represents force and physical power.

You are also well aware of the maxim that "the pen is mightier than the sword." This bit of old wisdom is still valid, at least as long as you have the patience to wait until the penman knows what he is doing when he picks up his pen. That is really what this is all about.

I think I will try another subject because this one is becoming disjointed and I will not be disturbed if you do not in fact understand it.

Another subject—money.

✳ ✳ ✳ ✳

While I have said before that human happiness is not the purpose of a lifetime on earth, I have also said that there is no inherent virtue in poverty. Material resources are by themselves neither good or bad; it's what we do with them that determines whether we gain or lose in our spiritual quest. So don't feel guilty about being attracted to the idea of being materially rich. After all, you are already rich in many more important respects, such as your family ties and the degree of spiritual growth that you have already achieved, not to mention the additional growth that will take place if you are able to take our messages to heart and put them into practice in your daily life.

Violence

Session 89 - January 29, 1994

The interference you experienced last night was due to other communications on a very similar vibration that occasionally overlapped and caused you some confusion. We will try to make sure that does not happen again. We can shield this channel from interference and we will do so.

I am glad that you have come back to visit so soon again. It makes me want to give you some very helpful material but I must be sure that you are ready for it first. Maybe not quite yet. Yes, your impression that I understand your human condition and its shortcomings is correct. I do not judge. That is certainly not my place. Even God does not judge so it would certainly be presumptuous for me, now wouldn't it? As I have said many times before, God does not judge—or punish; He loves and He teaches.

Tonight's subject is violence. It is a sign of a social structure that has become too preoccupied with materialism and has lost its spiritual anchor. The problems of your American society illustrate this point to a distressing degree. Violent crime, drug abuse, alcohol abuse, the breakdown of the family, these are all manifestations of a loss of spiritual identity. It's not really "lost," just temporarily misplaced.

Deep within your psyche, you all know that you are primarily spiritual beings who are temporarily living in a material world in order to achieve spiritual growth and development. When you focus all your thinking and living on the transitory material world, you know at that deeper level of your being that you are incomplete—that something is missing. It is that absence of an anchor that leaves you rootless and unhappy, so you compound the problem by rushing into a frenzy of money, drugs, drink, sex, crime or what have you in an effort to escape from the feelings of alienation and incompleteness that plague you. *But of course you cannot escape—for the simple reason that you are seeking to escape from yourself and there is just no way to do that.*

At the same time, in the midst of all this materialism, there is a slowly but steadily growing awareness that man is first and foremost a spiritual being and that a life in the material world is merely a short journey to the schoolhouse to learn things not yet known—or perhaps known but not yet put into practice. Societies do move in cycles, as your one-time sociology professor said. And this very materialistic cycle that we are now experiencing here in the United States will soon change to a much more spiritual cycle. I expect to see a definite beginning to that next cycle around your year 2000.

When I talk about a more spiritual cycle, I mean a *truly* spiritual cycle. I definitely do not mean the kind of pseudo spiritual cycle represented by such abominations as the Spanish Inquisition or the witch burning in Salem. There was not true spiritual content there, just fear of people who were different. This next cycle in the United States will, I believe, be genuinely spiritual. While traditional established churches will welcome it and participate in it, the leading roles will be taken by those who are outside the traditional church establishments.

Churches of all denominations are too circumscribed by their creeds, traditions and power structures to be able to be completely open to the broader spiritual values that I am talking about. Nevertheless, they will be constructive partners in the process of encouraging a greater realization on the part of the American public of the spiritual nature of man. They may not be the leaders but they will not be obstructionists because they all, at bottom, sincerely seek to encourage the best in mankind and that best is mankind's spiritual nature.

Though we are still a long way, unfortunately, from world peace and an awareness of our common humanity, we can take hope from the ancient message of Isaiah about beating swords into plowshares. I am less familiar with other religious traditions but I am reasonably sure that they all have something similar since "peace on earth, goodwill toward men" is a universal truth that touches all legitimate religious traditions wherever they may have originated.

By disseminating these messages—which, of course, will only be read by those who are already disposed to believe them—you can make a small contribution to the rejuvenation of the spiritual life here in the material world, right here in your own country where the material world seems to wax strongest. Seeds spread in directions we know not, so don't be discouraged if, when I tell you to publish, you don't seem to get much response. Or later, when you don't get many sales. That should not be of great concern to you, at least not materially, since you already know that you are not supposed to profit financially from these messages. But you will indeed profit spiritually—much more important and lasting profit.

To answer your question, it is permissible for you to start editing this work even though there is still much more to come before publication will be appropriate. I still have much to communicate to you for dissemination to those with—I almost said "ears to hear" but I really mean "hearts to absorb." We will be together for a good long time yet so long as you continue to wish it. And I am quite sure that you will because I can feel it in your vibration. I thank you for the love that you feel for Seneca and me and I assure you that it is returned multifold. I also know that you are serious about fulfilling the mission that we have given to you. (I almost said "imposed upon you" but that is not correct for it was a mission that you willingly accepted.)

I sometimes have to remind myself that we do not ever interfere with your exercise of free will. Therefore, we do not "impose" anything upon anyone although we do seek willing allies everywhere. We appreciate your willingness to be such an ally and we will extend our protection to you as much as we can in a material environment. You already have, and will always have, our love and blessings—and because we know you want it, we extend those to your family and other loved ones.

Peace

Session 90 - February 2, 1994

Today I would like to talk about peace. Like a number of the words I have chosen to start these messages, "peace" has several meanings or levels. These include peace among nations as the most obvious, peace among members of families, peace within companies, governments and other organizations, and ultimately, inner peace, that which the Christian bible says surpasses understanding. But what causes or contributes to any or all of these forms of peace—or to the absence of peace?

In a nutshell, the absence of peace is in large measure due to man's preoccupation with the material. And within the material world, the key component of the absence of peace is power, including the desire for it and the absence of it. What contributes to peace, by contrast, is the focus on the spiritual—the permanent, the enduring—rather than the merely transitory. The individual who has achieved inner peace or is coming close to it has recognized that he is fundamentally a spiritual person who is on a temporary journey in the material world. He may wish to live comfortably while on the journey but he does not seek that most insidious of things—power over other people.

Political dictators do, ambitious politicians do, ruthless business executives do, and very wealthy people often do, because great wealth is often an instrument and manifestation of power over others. These people do not find inner peace, calm and contentment. They live with the fear of the loss of that power which is so vitally important to them. They are to be pitied. Perhaps a better expression would be to say that we should have compassion for them. In addition, if they abuse that power which they have sought so assiduously, then they earn much additional negative karma that they must work their way through at some future time.

What does this inner peace that we have mentioned consist of? Well, I think it is correct that it surpasses understanding—at least normal human understanding. It is a peace that comes from the knowledge—*knowledge*, not just *belief*—that we share the divine spark, know who we are and why we are here, and have experienced, even if only momentarily, union with God and the mind-boggling awareness of His unqualified and unbounded love for us. That does not mean that we who are fortunate enough to have experienced this do not still get distracted by the problems of the material world on our journey through it.

You yourself know this well, Bill, for you have been distracted and will be many more times. But whatever the distractions and problems, you know deep within your being what your relationship to God is and that will always sustain you. The same is true for any others who may read and heed this material. Bill is a good channel for me but he is very human, just like the rest of you, and anything he can achieve in terms of spiritual growth can also be achieved in this lifetime by the rest of you. I won't let you "cop out"—to use one of your colloquialisms—that easily by saying that you are not up to that standard. Of course you are! The very fact that you are reading these messages should indicate to you that you are seeking spiritual guidance and that you are up to the necessary standard.

The inner peace that you will feel when you focus upon your spiritual being is well worth the effort, I can assure you. It puts your mind and spirit above all the discord and pettiness that plague the material world. Remember Jesus' statement that the kingdom of heaven is within. That is what he was referring to and it is as close as we can get while making our journeys through the physical, material world. Regular meditation can help put you in the right frame of mind for the necessary realization to occur. But however you may induce that realization, that is what you want to occur.

When it does, it changes your life, not necessarily that visibly to the outside world because you must still survive in the material world. But you will have greater serenity, calm, compassion, patience and tolerance of other people, your brothers and sisters in spirit, and their human shortcomings. You can then be an oasis of calm in the midst of a desert. Don't be too disappointed if it doesn't always happen that way. As I mentioned earlier to Bill, you too will often be distracted by the material world but you will retain that inner peace and serenity at the core of your being. Peace—it's wonderful!

✿ ✿ ✿ ✿

When mankind can achieve the kind of inner peace that I am talking about, outer peace throughout the world will necessarily follow. But not until individuals learn and believe who and what they are and why they are here. Until then, the lures of the material world—especially that of power over others—will continue to keep your world there from achieving the long-sought and sometimes utopian goal of universal peace.

That's enough for now. Keep your mindfulness quotient high, Bill, and you can more frequently achieve this state of inner peace and union with God that you have at least once achieved.

Wisdom

Session 91 - February 3, 1994

What should today's topic be? Let's try wisdom, although I may have talked some about it before. Even if Seneca or I have, there is plenty more to be said about a subject of that scope.

Wisdom is a combination of knowledge, maturity, experience, and basic intelligence, all infused with a divine spark. All the other elements, put together, may get fairly close to true wisdom without the addition of that divine spark—but they don't quite make it. The reason is rather simple. True wisdom requires the participation of the God-consciousness within each of us. Some of the other elements can be missing but not that one. For example, a person can possess true wisdom without necessarily being unusually intelligent. The same is true with knowledge or experience or maturity. But *nobody* achieves true wisdom, as contrasted with a mere facsimile thereof, without that additional element, the infusion of that divine spark. The truly wise man or woman has discovered or had revealed to him or her what that person's place in the universe is—at least for this present lifetime.

How can we distinguish true wisdom from the facsimile that we are often confronted by? I won't tell you it is easy because it is not. The best way, I believe, is by observing the allegedly wise person to see how he conducts himself generally. If he comes through as a loving, caring and compassionate human being, then you can be reasonably sure that his wisdom is genuine. If that is not the case—if he is otherwise arrogant, self-important, domineering and the like—then you can be reasonably confident that his "wisdom" is counterfeit, or at best a poor facsimile.

Note that one of the biblical references to Jesus was as the "Wisdom of God." And the name Wisdom is often capitalized there to denote a living being. So it should be clear to all of you that wisdom is of God. Without God there isn't any. Literally, of course, without God there isn't anything. I mean it, of course, to refer to God's active participation in the process of acquiring wisdom. I don't mean his complete absence because that is impossible.

Another characteristic that I would associate with genuine wisdom is humility. The truly wise man knows that his wisdom is not his own product but that he is reflecting the views of a higher power—perhaps not as directly as the prophets of old but somewhat along those same lines.

Because of its tie to the God-consciousness, wisdom can sometimes come in the form of inspiration. Assume that a person has been struggling with a problem, as we all do from time to time, and suddenly, out of an apparently clear blue sky, the answer as to how he should best proceed comes to him. That I would regard as a kind of "instant wisdom." That is not the usual form that it takes but it can happen and it has happened to a number of people here in Punta Gorda Isles.

Let me speak for a moment about the applications of wisdom. It is a most active characteristic and requires actions to implement decisions that have been wisely reached. Almost by definition, the action taken to implement wise decisions must be useful and constructive. *Wise decisions cannot be implemented by improper or immoral means; that would fly in the face of the wise decision-making.* The old maxim that the end justifies the means is still as false as it was when it first was invented. I may sound rather absolutist about this but I think that maxim has been used to excuse terrible conduct against fellow humans, all in the name of a higher end. It just won't fly with me. And I actually think that most moral philosophers have long rejected that proposition. So maybe here is one place where I am in agreement with the scholars and theologians.

I also regard wisdom as active rather than passive. The wise person feels compelled to share his wisdom with others for the good of all—and to act upon his wisdom for the good of all. If you encounter passivity in an allegedly wise person, the chances are that person does not possess genuine wisdom. At best he possesses only a loose approximation and at worst he is nothing more than a fraud.

୧୨୨

Hunger

Session 92 - February 9, 1994

We do try to help you, even in worldly affairs, and you are getting much better at absorbing our guidance and then recognizing it as such. It is one of the fringe benefits for you of our relationship. When you were lying in bed last night, you also received an indication that my topic for tonight, or whenever our next meeting occurred, would be hunger. I even started to talk to you about it but you had no facilities there for writing it down, so I'll start again.

Hunger is normally thought of as something associated with grave poverty or famine—insufficient food to sustain normal, healthy physical life, and of course that is true. But, as you well know, hunger has a non-physical meaning as well, such as when a person "hungers" for recognition, appreciation, cultural opportunities or, ultimately, spiritual growth. That hunger is also very real and, of course, it cannot be appeased by mere physical food. It requires food for the soul.

At some level of their being, all humans have a deep and abiding hunger for spiritual growth—for reunion with their spiritual home. They all know that, without the spiritual dimension, their lives on earth are empty and pointless. They experience that feeling of emptiness, of incompleteness that occurs when something essential is missing. They may not know what is missing but they recognize that something important is.

Many people who realize that material possessions are not the objective of life may expand their interests to art, music, theater, literature and other forms of culture—food for the mind. *But the void cannot be filled by food for the mind alone, although that helps some. What is also needed is food for the spirit.*

That is where the sincere seeker obtains a big advantage. He at least knows what kind of menu he is looking for, even if he does not yet know precisely what is on that menu. Others may jump from menu to menu looking for one that will fill the void within them. Eventually, they will come upon the spiritual menu and will feel its strong pull, though they may still sample quite a number of dishes on that menu before deciding upon their main course. (I don't want to push this analogy too far, although I know that you like analogies and I find them helpful in explaining things so that they will be more readily understood.)

As long as you are human, you will never lose that hunger for spiritual food. You may cover it up, even bury it, scoff at it or whatever else, but you cannot get rid of it. It all comes back to the fact—and it is a fact—that man is fundamentally a spiritual being, rather than a physical one, and he cannot escape from his basic nature, no matter how much he tries to deny that basic nature.

When those of you who read this material find yourselves disturbed by feelings of incompleteness or emptiness, remind yourself of what I have said here and seek out spiritual food for your souls. Again, the fact that you are even reading these messages indicates that you are already a seeker or very close to becoming one. You also then have the advantage of knowing that what you are seeking is spiritual sustenance, not physical, cultural or whatever else.

Knowing that, you can then focus on the many religious traditions that exist in the world and see what fits best with you. Or you can do what many seekers do namely, pick and choose the best features of many traditions and maybe add a few features that you adopt from these messages. As I regularly repeat, there are many paths that will take you back to the same hub—our Creator who has given each of us a little piece of Himself.

Always make up your own mind as an adult regarding what you choose to believe. Children are not in a position to do that and, for the most part, do not really have the capacity at that stage of their young lives. But adults do. Beware of cults, by whatever name they may present themselves. Anyone who demands that you surrender to him or his organization your God-given free will is not your friend or guide; he is more likely to be a dangerous fanatic or a self-seeking hypocrite. In either case, stay away! While it is good to study and learn about as many religious views as you care to, the most important voice to listen to is that still, small voice within you. It comes from the heart, rather than the mind, and it is a voice you can trust. Don't let it be drowned out by the noise that you are all surrounded by in daily life.

As you get closer to understanding who you are and why you are here, your spiritual hunger will abate some because it is being fed. But it won't abate completely until you have rejoined God and become a co-creator with Him. And you don't want it to abate until then, because only then will you have reached your ultimate goal. And let me assure you that being filled with spiritual food is so much superior to being filled with physical food that the difference is indescribable. Also, as you well know, with physical food you are hungry again the next day or in a few hours. With spiritual food, on the other hand, you may never be hungry again once you have filled up on it. Something to think about and strive for, eh?

I guess if I talk about hunger, then maybe I should say something about thirst. Thirst is much more severe than hunger. After all, as you all know, you can go for quite a while without food but only a short time without water. Thirst is more urgent. Although it is usually used to refer to the absence of water to drink, it also has acquired a non-material meaning as well, You are all familiar with the scholar's "thirst for knowledge." Sometimes I wish the term were a "thirst for wisdom." They certainly are not the same although some would pretend that knowledge equals wisdom. Of course it does not and we should be sure to remember that distinction so that we are not intimidated by the pundit with many degrees, and perhaps much experience, who may or may not be wise at all.

As far as experience goes, you reminded me of the story of the old stodgy doctor who had not kept up with advances in medicine and who was arguing with a young doctor who was familiar with the latest techniques, medications, etc. In arguing about a particular case, the old doctor sought to intimidate the young doctor by asserting, "Young man, I have twenty-five years of experience in dealing with these matters." To which the young doctor replied, "No, doctor. You have one year of experience repeated twenty-five times." I don't think the story needs to be elaborated on; it speaks pretty well for itself and it has a good message that you would do well to pay attention to. Since you are ultimately responsible for yourself, both physically and spiritually, you should take responsibility for major decisions made regarding your physical or spiritual well-being and never abdicate them to another, expert or not. Listen to the experts you consult but then make up your own mind, because the responsibility is yours.

Athletics

Welcome back, old friend. I now consider you to be an old friend, even though our acquaintance is relatively short from the standpoint of linear time. It is quite obvious that you sincerely wish to continue, and even expand, our contacts and communications. Even though you really didn't need it, it was helpful for you to have Paula reinforce the authenticity and validity of our communications. You are quite right in your belief that she is indeed a special person and quite advanced in her own spiritual quest.

Today's subject: athletics. Perhaps it is the Olympic Games, which I hear in the background on your television, that gave me the clue, but I think that is a fine starting point for a message. The Olympic Games represent perhaps the best manifestation of the unity of mankind in spite of differences in race, color, religion, ethnicity and anything else. They honor the common humanity of all people on your small planet. Young men and women compete in athletic events in a spirit of friendship and sportsmanship. Of course, most do not win medals, but that is of secondary importance.

What counts is the participation in a world-wide spirit of fellowship, even though regrettably that spirit is short-lived. Though it lasts but a short time and occurs only at lengthy intervals, it shows you what you can ultimately achieve in relationships among people throughout the earth. And all you have to do is remember the common humanity that you share. *Just focus on the things that unite you rather than those that divide you.* For example, you all have two eyes, one nose and mouth, all located on one head, two arms and legs, hair on that head (if you're lucky), and all other physical attributes in common. You don't seem to have any trouble recognizing other species for what they are, even though they don't all look alike, so why should you have so much trouble recognizing the unity in yourselves?

A few words about athletics generally. Athletics are inherently good since you should honor and take care of your body as the "temple of the soul" even though it is such only temporarily—in any given lifetime. Also, a healthy body makes it easier for us to connect and communicate with those of you who may seek contact with us. So sports, athletics and physical activity are good things to participate in. But, unfortunately, they too can be corrupted by greed and ego, and they have in the United States. Professional sports have become big business, with enormous salaries paid to excellent athletes who may in many cases have little else to commend them. Television revenues continue to drive professional sports more and more into being just another part of "show business" as you would call it.

Now look at college sports. Big money there, too, resulting in extensive recruitment of athletes by sports-oriented colleges even though some of those athletes are not even remotely equipped for college studies—another example of exploitation resulting from that poor combination of greed and ego. Even children's athletics have become corrupted. Witness the Little League parent who demands that his or her child perform superbly—or else. Or the one who curses the opposing team, especially if they are playing well. I don't think I need to go on in order to convince anyone that athletics in the United States has become something far different from what it was originally meant to be. The idea of "a sound mind in a sound body" is more like a discarded poster than a reigning truth these days.

What can you readers of this message do about it? Just avoid falling into the same trap. If you have children that engage in sports, remind them of the true value of sports—a healthy, strong body, playing by the rules, sportsmanlike conduct (which is tantamount to ethical conduct), and the ability to lose a contest graciously and with dignity. It will also help if you remind them that the physical life is a temporary journey and that the purpose of that journey is to achieve spiritual growth, although there is nothing wrong with achieving material success at the same time. But it is important that they keep their priorities straight, and that is where your reminder can help.

I must admit that I tend to prefer competitive sports that do not involve bodily contact because it is too easy to hurt other people in such sports as hockey or football. Even here there are gradations. In ice hockey, for example, hurting your opponents seems to have become an art form—and one that is fed by screaming fans who cry out for mayhem in the heat of the contest. That just brings out the worst in everyone—the fans and the players. Football is not very far behind in this respect. Probably boxing and wrestling are the worst because there the gladiators are supposed to be trying to knock each other out or pin each other to the mat.

Track and field sports, on the other hand, do not have this disadvantage—at least not in most cases, although there are infrequent exceptions. The same is true for swimming, diving and other sports of that kind. Many of the winter sports now taking place at Lillehammer are also in this category—skating, skiing, and the like. Sports are not intended to be a method of projecting your aggressive tendencies on to others in a manner that is considered socially acceptable. *Sports are intended to build both your physical body and your character.* That's the real message here.

Sports should also be a reminder of the existence of beauty and grace in the physical world. When you watch figure skating, for example, independent of the ugly Tonya Harding situation, you cannot help but be impressed by the grace and beauty with which the individual skaters and the pairs perform. It should remind you that man is supposed to be a noble creature even while in the material world and going to school there. I know that it sometimes does, but all too often it brings out your baser characteristics.

My advice to those who participate in athletics, as well as those who merely observe them, is to adopt the positive features that they demonstrate and reject the negative features that have corrupted so much of them. Your own focus on your fundamental spirituality will help you to keep these things in perspective—even amid the roaring crowd.

Suffering

What shall I talk about today? Let's see what comes into your head. Suffering? Well, all right, although I may have talked about that previously, or Seneca did. Suffering is of course a mental, as well as a physical, phenomenon. You already know that. What you may not know is that suffering can also occur on the spiritual side as well. Physical suffering implies pain, hunger and thirst, illness, and other negative events that directly affect your human body in an active and generally constant manner. Suffering has an element of the continuing about it, whereas pain alone may be very temporary, as from a skinned knee.

Mental suffering is very akin to physical, except that the subject matter is your human mind, rather than your human body. But the other elements are present and the extent and severity of the suffering may be just as great, though not necessarily as visible, as in the case of physical suffering.

But then I added another category—that of spiritual suffering. I think you would like some explanation about what that is and what to do about it. After all, matters of the spirit are the assignment that both Seneca and I share with you. Spiritual suffering, while even less visible than mental suffering, is usually deeper and more intense. That should come as no surprise to you since you already know that man is fundamentally a spiritual creature, even when heavily camouflaged in a human body. Therefore, spiritual suffering can logically be expected to be the most severe of all, though not necessarily on the surface. *Spiritual suffering results from our separation from the source of our spirituality.* You can describe that source either as the divine spark within each of us or you can refer to God as the source. It all amounts to the same thing. At the deepest level of our being, we sense that connectedness, and when the connection is broken, even temporarily, we suffer spiritually. I really should have said "when the connection *appears* to be broken" because it cannot, of course, *actually* be broken. But it certainly can be badly neglected and covered with lots of debris—and in too many situations in your material world, that is exactly what happens. Humans become so preoccupied with the conditions of the material world that they forget their fundamental spiritual nature. And the emptiness or incompleteness that follows from such a course of action leads to spiritual suffering.

Suffering does have some positive aspects too, although it may not seem to be the case while it is happening. But consider! Physical suffering can lead us to reflect on things we have always taken for granted—for example, the miraculous nature of life itself and the remarkable capabilities of our human bodies and of the earth that sustains them. Mental suffering can remind us (no pun intended) of the wonderful powers of the human mind, including our ability to reason, to create, to analyze, and to be conscious of our own individual selves. And spiritual suffering can serve to remind us of our fundamentally spiritual natures, including why we are here and what this material world represents for us as a way station on our spiritual odyssey. As you can see, good things can emerge from suffering of all kinds—not that I am trying to suggest that suffering is inherently good, but only that we can derive good from negative things if we retain our precious mindfulness.

So far I have been talking about our own suffering. What about the suffering of others? Again, our exposure to the suffering of others can play a major role in enhancing those crucial attributes of compassion and caring. As I have said before, love, caring and compassion are indispensable characteristics of spiritual growth. Only by nurturing these attributes and seeking to expand them—ultimately to encompass all God's creation—can we progress on our spiritual journey home. Thus, while we would not have it so, we can nevertheless enhance our own spiritual development by using exposure to the sufferings of others as a vehicle for expanding our own love, caring and compassion for the victims of that suffering.

For some reason, when you thought of suffering, you also thought of the very different meaning in Jesus' admonition to his disciples: "Suffer the little children to come unto me." Here of course it meant, "*Let* them come to me." That in turn led to another thought on your part, the comment made by your friend, Paula, to the effect that little children are born much more spiritual than adults and begin to lose it when their tongues are unfrozen. That's not exactly what she said but the underlying thought is there. She is basically correct in that observation. *Except for unavoidable ego and the notion that each of them is the center of the universe, most spiritually negative behavior by children is learned rather than innate.* I don't know but maybe that is also what Jesus had in mind when he said we had to become like infants again, or be reborn, in order to enter the kingdom of heaven. Yes, *as you grow in spiritual power, your responsibilities grow correspondingly. So be mindful of your thoughts and words as well as your deeds so that you do not project negativity—powerful negativity—upon anyone else or upon yourself as a kind of mirrored response.* That insight of Paula's was sound and you would all do well to act (including thought and word) in accordance with that precept. You could all make considerable progress in healing various physical ailments that have spiritual root causes.

Courage

Session 95 - February 18, 1994

Subject for tonight—courage. As you well know, courage is not the absence of fear; on the contrary, without fear there is no true courage. *Courage is overcoming your fear in order to do what you know must be done.* Physical courage and moral courage are, of course, different but the basic attributes are the same.

Some of the best examples of physical courage occur during difficult situations, such as in wartime or in natural disasters such as fires, floods and earthquakes. The hero who rushes into the burning building to rescue the small child had to overcome his fear of losing his life in the fire. In some cases he may rush in without consciously thinking of the fear, and then overcome, but that is nevertheless what he did, perhaps on an instantaneous basis. The hero on the battlefield—who overcomes his fear of death and does his terrible job because his buddies are relying on him—is another representative example.

Moral courage is at least as commendable, even though the hero's life may not be in danger at the time. *Moral courage includes doing what you know to be right even though your peer group thinks otherwise.* It is extremely difficult for humans, who are very social creatures, to take stands that go against the "conventional wisdom" of their peer group, their age group, their social group or what have you. In some respects, moral courage may even require a higher sort of dedication because it is so much easier to avoid moral issues than it is to avoid battlefield conduct. However, if a person acts in accordance with what he sincerely believes in, while hurting no one and respecting differing views, he cannot properly be faulted, we believe.

Many issues in your material world are not "black and white" as some would make them appear. Many involve judgments based on particular circumstances. I am not making a speech in favor of what has come to be called "situation ethics," which sounds more ambiguous than traditional ethics, but I am saying that there is a good deal of room in your material world for honest differences of opinion. Abortion is a good example of such an issue.

Perhaps the only absolute that I would come up with in regard to moral or ethical behavior is the simple precept that you do no harm to any other human being or to the rest of God's creation except, in the latter case, as reasonably needed for your use—but not abuse. If you apply this rather simple test to the broad spectrum of moral and ethical issues that you are confronted with on a daily basis, you will almost always make the right decision on how to proceed. In doing this, you will be guided by your fundamental spiritual nature, rather than your misleading ego. You will also be making good spiritual progress during this particular sojourn on earth. *The precept is simple; following it as a way of life is what is hard.* In its essence, it is no different than the "golden rule" that we should do unto others as we would have them do unto us. Simple to state and to understand, yes. But to practice? Meditate on it.

Courage also consists of living your spirituality in the midst of a materialistic world. You don't have to make a lot of noise about it. As you have been told before, you don't have to say anything to shock your friends and neighbors—just be a role model who puts his beliefs into practice. That is really the best kind of missionary, rather than the one filled with rhetoric—at least for most of us.

Courage also includes the ability to persist when circumstances look bleak and when there might be a temptation to "throw in the towel" and join the rest of the crowd in its unending pursuit of pleasure in this lifetime. Too late these people find that the mad pursuit of pleasure or money or possessions, or even the highest example of negativity, control over others, alias power, is not fulfilling. The spiritual emptiness is still there, just below the surface and demanding to be released. So even when things are difficult and the temptations of materialism are great, remain mindful of who and what you are and why you are here.

Then persist in your spiritual quest. You will certainly be rewarded in terms of spiritual growth—and maybe materially too.

Having talked some about courage, I don't really need to say anything about cowardice. That is the opposite of courage and it of course applies in both the physical arena and in moral and ethical areas as well.

In short, having the courage to believe in yourself, to know yourself as a fundamentally spiritual being who is merely passing through a lifetime on the material plane, and to persist in your spirituality in the face of everything negative—from greed to mockery on the part of those deluded humans who are pursuing a transient materiality—will guarantee you spiritual progress in this lifetime. And there is no inherent contradiction between spiritual progress and material success either. Motive is what counts and, in the quiet of your own soul, you know what your motives are for the various actions that you take. So don't try to delude yourself because you may be able to delude your conscious mind (after all, it specializes in delusions) but you cannot delude yourself at the deepest levels of your being.

I think that is enough sermonizing for one evening. However, I don't take back anything that I told you and *I would strongly urge that all who may read these messages do their utmost in trying to live their spirituality and to persist in it despite outside conditions in the material world.*

More About Happiness

Session 96 - February 23, 1994

What would I like to talk about today? Let's try happiness, although I know that has been discussed before. Happiness is generally perceived in the material world as being the highest objective to which people can reach—and from a material world perspective that is correct. As you know, though, that is not the case when viewed from a spiritual perspective. From the latter perspective, spiritual growth is the objective of life in the material world. That is why you reincarnate repeatedly—in order to learn the lessons that you must learn *and practice* in order to progress on your spiritual journey back to reunion with your divine source. There is no inherent conflict, however, between spiritual growth and human happiness as long as your human happiness does not require, in each individual case, that you do harm to others—human, animal or ecological. In fact, making spiritual progress, once you understand that is your objective here on earth, can be a source of great human happiness. In an enlightened sense, personal happiness and spiritual progress go hand in hand.

Let's talk a little about human happiness in the material world. What does it consist of? Of course, it varies from individual to individual. For some it means power—usually the power that comes from wealth, position or political strength. But that is a false happiness, an illusory one. Since man is still fundamentally a spiritual being, he cannot escape his own spiritual demands, or more accurately, the spiritual demands that his innermost being makes upon him. He can mask them, cover them up, try to ignore them, pretend not to feel them, but he cannot escape from them entirely.

Amidst his wealth, position and power, the still, small voice within will call out to him, often when he is alone and not surrounded by the noise in his material life. So his human happiness under these circumstances is really an illusion, a face that he presents to the outside world but one that he cannot truly believe in himself. The extent to which he comprehends this depends on his own sensitivity and vibration level. At the grosser vibration levels, he may come pretty close to actually believing his own materialistic propaganda, but at higher levels, he will recognize the illusory nature of what he thought was happiness if it is not accompanied by the spiritual dimension that is essential.

As I have said before, there is no inherent virtue in poverty, human misery or other negative features of life on earth. Sometimes they are necessary in order for an individual to learn the lessons that he would not otherwise learn—and in that respect they are like a spiritual kick in the pants to get one's attention. But not everyone needs that kind of jolt to become mindful of his spiritual calling and to start living it.

Genuine human happiness necessarily involves inclusion of the spiritual dimension. Knowing and living your spirituality gives you a great deal of happiness, even under circumstances where your material condition would appear to be less than ideal. However, it also works the same even when your material condition is close to ideal, such as when you have health, wealth, close family ties, and all the other benefits of life on the material plane. *The basic message here is to enjoy your life in the material world to the extent that you can—as long as you remain mindful of your spiritual calling and keep your motivation clean.* That is to say, you can have power, wealth and position as long as you did not do negative deeds to obtain them and as long as you do not abuse them when you have them. Again, no incompatibility there as long as the motives are spiritually clean.

You have previously been told, by Seneca or me, that spiritual growth, not human happiness, is the purpose of life on earth. While that remains true, you can see from this message that enlightened people on earth—I am not using the term "enlightened" here in the true Buddhist sense but in a much more modest sense—can enjoy both. Just stay mindful and you will have no problem of conflict between them. However, if you encounter a conflict between them, remember your priorities and act accordingly, although it may be a difficult choice for you to make in individual cases.

The theory that your friend (who once was a sister in a past life) Paula expressed about the effects of growing spiritual power is correct. *As your spiritual growth increases, you do acquire more spiritual power and must therefore be more careful how you use it—whether projected toward others or reflected back at yourself. Negative thoughts and words, as well as deeds, have greater force than before, whether projected outward or inward.*

It is something like the difference between driving a little four-cylinder Volkswagen beetle and driving a V-8 muscle car. You have to drive more carefully with those eight powerful cylinders under the hood or you are that much more likely to either hurt others or hurt yourself. Since you are making spiritual progress as a result of our communication, as well as your improving life style, you are gaining in spiritual power and must therefore be more mindful of how you utilize it.

Spiritual power is a normal phenomenon—all humans possess it in greater or lesser measure. You just don't know the manner in which it is propagated or focused, so as a result it is easier for most people to deny its existence. Just use the analogy of electromagnetic radiation. Before its laws were identified, manifestations of it would have been regarded as magic or witchcraft or something evil and fearful because its laws were not understood by the science of the times. We now know that everything material consists of particles/waves that vibrate in certain manners. Well, that is also true of spiritual power sources too. Eventually, as you humans become more familiar with your spiritual capabilities and less oriented toward the material world, you will improve your ability to utilize and control these capabilities for the good of all. In the meantime, do the best you can, remain mindful of your spiritual power, and persist in your search for spiritual progress as you learn the lessons you reincarnated to learn.

Aging

Session 97 -February 27, 1994

Our subject for tonight is aging. It is, after all, a subject of great interest to you and your friends since you are at an age where you must necessarily appreciate your mortality—at least of this particular body. If you already have a firm belief in the immortality of your soul, or spirit, by whatever name you may choose to call it, you are well ahead of the game by comparison with all too many people in your age group. If you believe in reincarnation of the body, then you are still further along.

I feel most sorry for those who believe that this one lifetime is all there is and that their immortality is measured by their children or their accomplishments on earth during that one short period. What a depressing thought! I don't, of course, mean that you shouldn't love your children or try to do constructive things for your civilization. It is just that there is so much more that I hate to see you missing it, at least while in the flesh there. I also feel sad for those who accept the immortality of their souls but nevertheless believe that, on the basis of one very brief performance, they will be judged for eternity and either saved or damned. The kind of fear produced by such a set of beliefs is enormous and you can be sure that it is, and has been, a very effective tool for controlling the multitudes for centuries. It is not true, however. It represents an abuse of power by religious authorities that goes way back. People who believe in this point of view may discover its fallacy when they pass from body into spirit, but all too often they encounter in spirit what they expect to. And that can be mighty frightening if you have some of these strange belief systems. It is part of the remarkable capacity that humans have for creating their own reality. If it's a reality of love and compassion, that's wonderful. But if it's a reality of pain and damnation, that's terrible. And so unnecessary.

Stop and examine your beliefs. This is one area where I believe your hearts and minds can both join in coming to a common conclusion. You, Bill, have said that you do not consider it logical that we, who are God's children and made in His own image, should be saved or damned on the basis of one tiny stay on earth that is shorter than the blink of an eye on any cosmic scale. You have also said that it simply doesn't *feel* right. That is not the conduct of a loving and caring Creator toward His creation. You are absolutely correct.

If others would understand and accept reincarnation and its ramifications, as Seneca and I have been trying to explain to them, so many more people would conduct themselves the way they should. They would know that whatever they do to others they do to themselves and that they ultimately have to work out with those other persons the karmic consequences of what they have done. *The karmic law of cause and effect, once accepted as valid and applicable, goes a lot further then any fear of punishment to induce people to reflect their finest spiritual attributes rather than their worst.*

How does this relate to aging? Well, the aging process tends to make humans reflect on what lies ahead behind the door that we call death. To most of the young of every period of history, there is a belief that they are indestructible. It's true of their spirits, but they think it's true of their bodily selves as well. It is usually later, when we find that we can't do as many things involving our bodies as we used to, or want to, that we become very conscious of the process of aging. You enjoy joking with friends who complain about having birthdays by telling them that it's when they are *not* having birthdays that they are in big trouble. With the aging process should also come a greater awareness of the spiritual dimension of life and a reduced emphasis on the attractions of the material world. Of course this is by no means always the case but it still occurs quite often. I am of course talking in generalities here. For example, your son and many other young people have focused on their spiritual nature instead of allowing it to be overwhelmed by the lures of your materialistic society. So take my statements here as generalizations rather than as universal truths.

Apart from your awareness of your bodily mortality, aging should also carry with it the benefits of experience—experience that most young people may not yet have learned. As you experience more of life on earth, you may discover situations where people with all kinds of material power and possessions are nevertheless empty and unfulfilled. It can help you to resist the lures and attractions of materialism.

Sometimes with age there also comes a measure of wisdom. But what is wisdom and how would you define it? In this context I would define wisdom as the ability to distill the right course of thought, word or deed — the spiritual course — from the multitude of competing courses that are regularly presented to you in the material world. I think I would include the concept of mindfulness as an attribute of wisdom. As you well know, I put great emphasis on mindfulness in my messages to you. I do this very intentionally, because mindfulness of who and what you are and why you are here is a prerequisite to consistently choosing the correct spiritual path among the many choices crying out for your attention.

So tell your friends — many of them already know it — that what are often called the "golden years" can also be just that in terms of spiritual growth and development. Make good use of them to develop your own calm and serenity. Work on acquiring patience — a continuing lesson for nearly all humans, including you too. Aging should not be looked upon with fear and unhappiness.

Many peoples in different times and cultures revered their elderly as sages and repositories of the wisdom of the ages. Though that is by no means the case in your modern American culture, you can still make it a part of your own cultural background. Reflect on your life as you reach these golden years. Be honest with yourselves about your strengths and weaknesses and undertake even now to correct the latter.

Above all, do not fear what has been called "God's other door" because it is indeed the door to a very different but much more fulfilling kind of existence. There you can help those still on earth, grow in spiritual stature yourself, and earn good karma until it is time for your next trip to the schoolhouse known as earth. Eventually you will get promoted beyond that level and then you will wonder why you ever feared the death of the body in any single life.

More About Foolishness

Session 98 - March 3, 1994

Tonight I would like to talk about foolishness, a subject with a lot of room for discussion. In the material world you often say, "One man's folly is another man's wisdom." I think that little saying is an attempt to assert a kind of relativism that has no substantive merit. It would make everything subjective and while it is true, especially in the material world, that many decisions are matters of individual preference rather than natural law, there are nevertheless some areas that do fall within what may be called "natural law." In the realm of spirit, this same degree of flexibility does not exist. We have much clearer guidelines regarding what is right and what is wrong and they are universally accepted by us here—at least while we are in spirit. Once we reincarnate, we forget what we learned here and must learn it and practice it anew in the material world to demonstrate that it has become an integral part of our being.

While foolishness is obviously not something to be sought, there is an enormous difference between foolishness and malice. The person who does foolish things may have consequences to pay but they do not even begin to approach the karmic consequences of those who do the same thing out of malice. *As in so many other examples that Seneca or I have given you in prior messages, motivation is the critical element in determining the moral (and therefore karmic) consequences of our thoughts, words and deeds.*

It is also true that since our *deeds* have the greatest impact on others they have the greatest karmic consequences, both positive and negative. (These rules work in both directions; that's only fair.) This does not mean that you can afford to indulge in negative thinking or speech without paying the price for those as well. The price in karmic terms is not as high as in the case of deeds but it is by no means negligible. Also, as I indicated in an earlier message, as you gain more spiritual power, the impact of thoughts and words, whether positive or negative and whether projected outward or mirrored inward, becomes much greater. So continue to remain mindful of your thoughts and words as well as your deeds, for they too determine your karmic balance sheet.

Foolishness is also a term applied to entertainment where a person plays the clown or fool or whatever in order to provide people with an opportunity for healthy laughter. This kind of "foolishness"—if that is even the correct term (it probably isn't)—is very positive because it relieves the tensions of daily living in the material world. I might also add, as you well know, that laughter and humor are attributes that are peculiar to the human race and they are what you have called "a survival requirement" in this complex material world in which you must make your way. In addition, humor is very helpful in dispelling some of the fog generated by ego, because the person who can laugh, and particularly at himself, is far less susceptible to the lures of ego.

Foolishness, unlike malice, is not always hurtful to others. In many cases the consequences of a foolish decision or course of action may affect only the foolish person himself, and there may not be serious consequences. Malice, however, is different. Almost by definition, malice is hurtful to others and is intended to be so. That is why it carries such heavy karmic penalties. Included under the category of malice is revenge. This is an inherently negative concept that hinders spiritual growth and that can undo much of an individual life's spiritual progress.

It is extremely easy to delude yourselves into thinking that "getting even" is admirable, particularly when the injured person is someone else and not yourself. You may even delude yourself into calling it a matter of honor to seek revenge for wrongs done to you, your family or friends. As a former human living in the material world, I can fully appreciate this enormous temptation—and the rationalizations that are used to justify it. *But I must tell you, unequivocally, that revenge will earn you only negative karmic consequences that you may have to pay dearly to work through.* Revenge flies in the face of the recognized unity of the human race—or at least I hope that by now you who read these messages will have arrived at that conclusion. It also rejects so many of the beautiful messages that Jesus left his followers, as did other great religious leaders of different times and places.

Revenge is really an outgrowth of hate and that is perhaps the greatest negative force in the universe. *Just as love is the greatest positive force (with love of God at the apex of that triangle) so hate is the greatest negative force.* I certainly don't mean to minimize the human capacity to hate or the many circumstances that will bring out that capacity. You have only to look at your own world today to see it at its worst—and Bosnia isn't the only example, I can assure you. You have to work hard to reject that temptation and it is by no means easy—but whoever told you that spiritual progress would be easy? Why do you think it takes so many

233

lifetimes before we can graduate from this earthly schoolhouse? It isn't easy but it is most assuredly worth all the effort and sacrifice required to substitute love for hate and forgiveness for revenge. Try it and you will be surprised that you will feel so much better about yourself when you make those substitutions.

Spirituality

Session 99 -March 6, 1994

Tonight I would like to talk about spirituality. I realize, amid your puzzlement about this choice of topic, that it encompasses the subject for many books rather than a single message. Nevertheless, I still want to say something about it.

Spirituality means, to me: "matters pertaining to the spirit." An apparently simple, maybe even simplistic, definition. But is it really? We can start by saying that it means matters pertaining to the spirit, as contrasted with the flesh. That's certainly valid. But where do we go from there? How do we go about purifying the spirit so that it is ready to return to its Source and Maker? Not so easy a question, is it? And why must spiritual purification take place in the context of material lives? Why can't it be done on a purely spiritual, separate plane of existence? That is really just another way of asking: why do we have to go through all these many reincarnations here on earth before we can graduate?

I have to give some thought as to how to answer that question for you in a way that you can understand. Perhaps we could say that as spirits lose their intimate connection with their Divine Source, they acquire "blemishes"—maybe you could call it a kind of spiritual acne. Usually these blemishes are the result of a preoccupation with the material, although in some cases it may even be a kind of rebellion against the demands that God imposes upon His children. However it happens, the spirit must take actions to clear up the blemishes, if he wants to, before he can be readmitted to his ultimate home.

How does one clear up these spiritual blemishes? That, I believe, is where material life on earth enters the picture. Because in most cases (and we need not concern ourselves with the others now) the blemishes were generated by excessive materialism, usually aided and abetted by ego, it is in the material world that they must be dealt with—that is, cleansed. Obviously, the being in question first must recognize that there are blemishes on his spirit, and second, he must want to cleanse them away, so to speak, before the question even arises about *how* this is to be done. Once the individual gets that far—and that does represent a great deal of progress even though you might not initially think so—then he must go through the cleansing process on earth. In a way, this too is a matter of karmic law; since the blemishes were generated on earth, they must be cleansed on earth.

How to cleanse? I know that you enjoy somewhat picturesque analogies so I will use the analogy of the car wash. You can't simply go though the car wash once and come out spiritually cleansed—at least not usually. *To become spiritually cleansed, you must apply spiritual values and thinking as you live your life in the material world.* It is a lengthy process, but then again, the rewards are also great. You must try to live in the material world the way you know, at the deepest levels of your being, that you are supposed to interact with your fellow humans and all the rest of God's creation. You must try to act as if you *really understand* that everything you do to others you do to yourself. I say "try" because you won't always succeed, but as you get better and better at it you will find yourself sloughing off more and more of the spiritual blemishes. Ultimately you will clean them all off and then you will be ready for the next great adventure. Exactly what and where I am not at liberty to say—but I can at least assure you that it will be infinitely more exciting and rewarding than any lifetime on earth could possibly be. So there, that should give all you readers out there something to look forward to!

How did spirit ever find its way into flesh? Well, calling on some reading you did long ago about Edgar Cayce, he had the right general idea. Sensation is the answer. *Spiritual beings do not experience the pleasures (or pain) that go with materiality. Spirits found that they could experience these sensations in the bodies of material beings, such as animals, and they enjoyed it so much that they became trapped there and forgot who they were and where they belonged.* As you should know by now, and I will continue to repeat many times, the lures of the material world are many and strong. That's nothing new.

Remember when you were having a can of root beer and I expressed regret that I couldn't enjoy the taste of it that you were experiencing on that hot day? Well, I miss it too at times, but fortunately I can easily overcome any temptations from the material world that I may encounter in my present situation. But there was still that little bit of nostalgia. So when you succeed in avoiding the lures and temptations of the material world, take heed that you don't become too complacent lest you be ambushed by those same temptations when you least expect it.

I said I was only going to talk about one little segment pertaining to spirituality, and I think I have. There is so much more to be said on the subject, but I think a *useful and simple approach would be to view spirituality as a counterbalance to materialism. Materialism focuses on the temporary and illusory "here and now" while spirituality focuses on the eternal and unchanging.* It can serve as your North Star, your guide through the travels of a lifetime in the material world, while still keeping your eye on that North Star so that you know where you are and where you are going.

Persistence

Session 100 - March 9, 1994

Today I would like to talk about persistence, both in the material world and in the world of spirit.

Persistence in the material world is generally considered a virtue and so it is—as long as the objective toward which your persistence leads you is an affirmative one. Otherwise, of course, it can result in terrible karma. Persistence in efforts to do good and help people is therefore commendable—after all, you don't give up at the first rebuff. On the other hand, persistence in evil objectives, or even very selfish ones, can only create negative karma that must ultimately be worked out. For instance, both Hitler and Stalin could certainly have been called persistent in the way that they both stubbornly clung to their objectives. But since the objectives in their cases were unequivocally evil, their persistence merely increased the karmic burden that they must bear. *So by all means be persistent—but first be sure that your persistence is directed toward a worthy objective that will earn you positive karma.*

Persistence can also help you to achieve material success in this world, and there is nothing inherently wrong with that. As long as you don't achieve your material success by hurting others.

Persistence is also a virtue when applied in the pursuit of spiritual growth and development. Remember that those who seek spiritual progress in this life are relatively few and far between. I don't mean to suggest by that statement that most people are "bad." What I am saying is that most people don't focus their attention very often on the subject of spiritual growth. And all too often, in those occasional moments when they do, they are likely to be in a religious house of worship and echoing whichever "party line" that particular religious institution is promoting as its version of Truth. I would again remind you that there is nothing wrong with going to a formal religious institution of your choice and if it helps bring you a little closer to God, however briefly; that is not hypocrisy at all. What you must be careful of is the narrow exclusivity that is too inherent in denominational religion. So even though you may find it useful to attend a church, synagogue, mosque or stupa of your choosing, keep in mind that you are most likely to find a path suitable for you by private seeking.

Persist in following the teachings of the great sages throughout history. Concentrate, for example, on the message of Jesus, rather than on questions about, or the nature of, his divinity. If you all acted in accordance with the messages of your own religious traditions, with their emphasis on the unity of all life, and especially all human life, your badly mixed-up world would be a far better and happier place.

Even when you seek to find your own path of reunion with Divinity, keep in mind the fact that you are never alone—or lonely. Persist in practices of meditation and prayer, remembering that prayer is nothing more than a private, two-way conversation with God, our Father.

To those who will some day read these messages, persist in your belief that these are not messages out of Bill's subconscious mind, but rather they are messages from another independent entity who cares so much about humanity that he is using Bill as a channel to communicate to all persons of goodwill his advice on how to live in the material world and progress spiritually on the journey back to our Creator. That is a special assignment of mine and I am using Bill as my channel to communicate these messages—at least to that segment of mankind that believes in things of the spirit and wishes to grow in spiritual stature while pursuing their odyssey of life on earth.

ॐॐ

More About Peace

Session 101 - March 14, 1994

Thank you for taking time out of your busy worldly activities to meet with us tonight. Also, continue with your editing efforts; it will make your job much easier later when the time comes to publish.

Tonight's subject is peace. That is really a subject for an encyclopedia, or at least a fat book. But I will make it the subject for a short sermon tonight. Peace—a term that conjures up so many mental images that it is hard to know where to start. The most obvious place is with peace on earth among nations. We can then shrink the scope to different groups within nations—ethnic groups, religious groups, racial groups, tribal groups, etc. Ultimately we get down to bedrock—namely, peace between each of us and his neighbors. Here I mean "neighbors" in the broadest sense, rather than literally. *If we can achieve peace as individuals with all those around us, then we can successfully expand that peace to encompass the greater scope and achieve peace on earth. All it really takes is a decent respect for those who are different from ourselves.* If we start with that as individuals, it can then extend to clans, tribes, ethnic groups, races, nationalities, religions and any other categories that we find it convenient to group people into. Just imagine what peace on earth would mean for the spiritual progress of all of us in this little schoolhouse called Earth!

Another extremely important form of peace can be described as inner peace. Jesus was referring to that inner peace when he told the disciples, "My peace I give you, not as the world gives . . . ." How do we describe that inner peace, and more importantly, how do we achieve it? I think I can say that it goes with what I referred to in an earlier message as spiritual confidence, and it is a feeling of unshakable serenity and calm that its possessor feels, even in the face of the buffeting that inevitably comprises a portion of a life on earth.

How do we achieve that highly desirable condition? I believe that we can achieve it *if we genuinely believe, at the core of our being,* that (a) God loves each of us unequivocally just as we are, shortcomings, flaws and all; (b) negative things that happen to us in an individual lifetime are not random accidents but lessons to be learned by us or the working out of karmic debts incurred in past lives; (c) our purpose here on earth is to develop spiritually to a level where we can make our way home and rejoin our Creator; and (d) ultimately we all get there, although the process may be longer and more painful for some than others because some of us are slower learners and do not exercise our free will to achieve spiritual growth as we should. With these beliefs firmly ingrained in your deepest being, you can withstand anything that the material world can throw at you and still retain that sense of serenity that goes by the name of "inner peace." As I think you can readily see, this kind of peace goes far beyond what is commonly called "peace of mind"; it is more accurately described as "peace of the spirit." Believe me, it is worth striving for because, as I said, with it you are like the Rock of Gibraltar and even stormy seas will crash harmlessly against you.

Another way in which you can achieve this state of inner peace, at least temporarily, is through the process of deep meditation. In such a meditative state, you may be fortunate enough from time to time to achieve a state of communion with God, at least briefly. You know it has happened to you, Bill, at least once, and the resulting sense of peace, calm, love and compassion was indescribable. Even though it doesn't usually last long, as in your case, it leaves you touched in such a way that you are never quite the same afterward. The more frequently and the more deeply you meditate, the more frequently are you likely to experience this magnificent relationship.

I rather think that is why hermits and other holy men spend their entire lives in meditation and prayer, seeking this experience on as continuous or repeated a basis as possible. For those of you who have chosen to live in the material world rather than escape from it as hermits, that alternative is not realistically available to you. Nevertheless, I would recommend that you try to make time, on as frequent and regular a basis as your individual circumstances allow, for deep meditation in the hope that from time to time you will encounter the communion experience—literally, not just symbolically.

That was a pretty strong message tonight. Should I add another subject to it since you feel up to it? I will take advantage of your invitation to continue. Let me talk a little bit about force. It seems like an odd choice after talking about peace. Force is in some respects and in some forms the antithesis of peace. But that is just one aspect of force. You humans tend to think of force as something applied by someone or some group to compel others to do what that person or group wishes. You perceive it as an exercise of power over others and usually in the most spiritually negative sense. And as you use the term, you are correct.

Remember, however, that force is also another term for energy, and that opens up much broader and more affirmative horizons for the use of the term and its substantive content. *I have already told you that energy is the primal substance in the universe.* It constitutes material objects, life in the material world and all that occurs in that world. However, energy also makes up the world of spirit. You know something about the energy makeup of the material world, though not as much as you would like to think you know. Mother Nature still has plenty of important secrets that your scientists have not yet discovered.

As for the laws of energy of the spirit world, you humans know almost nothing about them. Since they don't lend themselves to your so-called "scientific method," it is far simpler for your pundits to brush aside their very existence rather than admit their ignorance. That will change as spiritual energy becomes more manifest in the material world. I see that happening and the existence, though not the laws, of spiritual energy should become more apparent as the earth changes occur and continue to grow more severe. Eventually, though not in the very near future, as people on earth become more spiritually oriented and proficient, you will begin to learn something of the natural laws applicable to spiritual energy. Then you will see that the world of spirit was not something you had to fear and avoid, but rather that the world of spirit is the real and permanent world while the material world is the illusory, temporary and transient one—just as the Buddhists maintain.

Value

Today I would like to talk about the subject of worth or value. *Everything in this material world is worth something or has some value to something else. There is nothing that is completely useless and serves no purpose whatever.* That is part of the wonder of God's creation. Of course it includes things that you humans would not consider valuable because they annoy you or cause you difficulty or inconvenience. You might even call it part of the magnificent balance of nature.

Let's talk for a minute about the turkey vulture, a bird that is prevalent in your part of Florida and is regarded as ugly. In addition, vultures have been given a bad name in your speech and literature. Yet this gentle bird—not pretty or colorful or musical by your standards—is nature's garbage collector, particularly of road kill. The useful role of the turkey vulture is recognized by your ecologists but how many other "nuisances" aren't. Many other examples could be given about other species, ranging from tiny bacteria to giant creatures. It is a useful reminder that every creature has a role, even when that role is not to your liking, for this is not a random universe that resulted from blind chance combinations over eons of time.

So everything has some value in the overall picture. What am I trying to say with that? I think I am trying to tell you not to tamper too much with nature as your science advances in terms of its capabilities. I recognize that you must "tamper" some, such as seeking to control or eradicate the most virulent human diseases that derive from bacteria or viruses, but I am nervous about what you might do with your new-found abilities in genetic engineering. I recognize that it is your intention to use these capabilities to improve the quality of human life and to ease suffering—to use these capabilities to do good—but I must warn that you do not always know what "good" is. There is still an element of hubris in what you do along lines such as these.

On a less frightening front, let me mention the efforts by the state of Florida to deal with water problems by bringing in trees from other parts of the world, only to find that those trees became more serious problems than the ones they were brought in to overcome. You must remember that you do not have either the knowledge or the wisdom to see the ultimate effects of the "ripples" you may create in the water. Another example that was mentioned to you during your tour of the Nature Conservancy in Naples recently was the Brazilian pepper tree that now infests the mangroves and is virtually impossible to eradicate. I hope you will learn from these and other lessons to be very careful when you play around with Mother Nature—and that includes genetic engineering and biotechnology generally. I do not suggest prohibition of such endeavors for knowledge is intended to be used. But I do suggest that greater care be taken in the future than has been the case in the past.

Let me talk a little about the balance of nature because I fear that population growth, and all that goes with it, may be the largest and most dangerous form of natural imbalance that this earth is confronted with in the foreseeable future. Population growth threatens to outstrip the resources needed to sustain such growth at the levels of comfort to which people aspire. And as populations grow, especially in the least affluent portions of the globe, the gulf between haves and have-nots grows ever wider—not because the haves have so much,but because the have-nots have so little. *Birth control is therefore one of the most serious problems of human survival over the long run.*

I am not predicting that the human race will grow so numerous that it will become extinct because it will not be able to find or produce the means to survive. But I do predict that, if means—acceptable means—are not found to bring world population into balance with natural resources, then the instability that we now see between wealthy societies and impoverished ones will continue to grow worse, with very negative results from the standpoint of both material conditions and conditions for spiritual growth. As you know, spiritual growth is indeed possible under terrible material conditions, but it has a greater opportunity to flourish where people are not in a constant struggle for bare survival in the material world.

Of course I must also remind myself that when humans become too comfortable materially, they are in danger of falling into the ego trap of believing that here and now is all there is. So maybe what we need is an intermediate condition somewhere between selfish consumerism on the one hand and abject poverty on the other. Again, it sounds to me like balance is the key concept here. Maybe that is one of things that the great Greek philosopher, Aristotle, had in mind when he urged that we seek the "golden mean." That sounds like another vote in favor of balance in all things. *If we are able to remain mindful—again, my favorite word, it seems—of the need for balance in all things, we can make our way through our lifetimes in the material world and at the same time achieve progress on our spiritual path home.*

Can I suggest a reason for the enormous population growth that has been occurring in recent times, you ask? On the surface it would be possible to say that mankind has made progress in reducing infant mortality through vaccinations, greater knowledge of diet, etc. But shouldn't we ask why so many spirits seem to need human bodies these days as compared with the past? It begins to seem, when looked at from this standpoint, as if we have a large number of souls that have failed to graduate at the former rate. As a result the schoolhouse is becoming very crowded, the resources available are becoming scarcer, and maybe the student-teacher ratio is getting up there. But why the backsliding—if indeed that is the explanation—or even part of it? Generally we backslide when we let ego get out of control and take charge of our lives on earth.

That is what has been happening. We as humans have tended to become so caught up in our human, worldly affairs and accomplishments that we have, to a greater degree than before, tended to forget who and what we are and why we are here. So we haven't had the graduating classes that would have reduced the need for seats in the schoolhouse—i.e., human bodies.

That will improve, due in part to the upcoming earth changes. Those changes will go a long way toward refocusing our attention on our fundamentally spiritual nature and on our reasons for being temporarily clothed with human bodies. Then we shall see a major revival of emphasis upon things of the spirit, not to the exclusion of material enjoyment by any means, but in a better balance than is now the case. As always, the hope is there because this small planet will not pass away or become uninhabitable until it has served its purpose—which is another way of saying until we all graduate.

Enough for now. That should give you something to ponder about. I told you we would soon be getting into some interesting and significant material. Well, we've started—not that the prior material isn't significant. It certainly is, but it is material that you already know, deep in your being, is true; you humans just have to start living it instead of merely professing it.

ꙙꙙ

Friendship

Tonight's subject will be friendship. Friendship is a slightly attenuated expression of love. It carries with it none of the sexual overtones that the term "love" does in your American society. But we do have feelings approximating love for those people for whom we have strong feelings of friendship. You should not be embarrassed in the least by this statement. I have told you before, and will again, that love is the most powerful force in the universe, except for prayer, which is a special form of love directed at God. Since friendship is an offshoot of love, it too is very powerful and commendable as well.

Friendship carries with it many responsibilities, including the obvious ones of loyalty, assistance when needed, support, companionship, and the like. The attributes that are encouraged by friendship are all positive ones. Sometimes negative ones can sneak in, like possessiveness, but that is not an indicator of true friendship.

Just as love desires the best interests of the loved one, so does friendship desire the best interests of the friend. Possessiveness is not compatible with that. Possessiveness is actually a form of selfishness — a negative attribute — and therefore not a characteristic that accompanies genuine friendship. If possessiveness is present, the friendship is not real, even though the possessive person may delude himself or herself into thinking it is. Possessiveness is in its own way an attempt by one to exercise control over another, and this, we have previously told you, is one of the most negative manifestations of ego that exists in your world. And the karmic price is high. So if you find yourself approaching attitudes of that kind, put them quickly behind you.

Friendship is a two-sided coin. If there is genuine friendship, which is the only kind I am talking about since any other kind would be an oxymoron, it applies to both the parties equally. If it happens to be a group friendship, rather than one just between two people, the same point applies. It cannot by its very nature run only in one direction. Each of the friends will provide the mutual support in times of grief or difficulty that the other friend or friends need.

Friendship also carries with it the burden of honesty toward the friend. I say "burden" because it can often be very difficult to be honest with your friend when he asks you awkward questions and you know that the honest answers will be painful to him. Yet you must understand that you do not truly help your friend if you try to shield him from hard truths that he must learn in this material world.The painful but honest answers—they will come naturally between true friends—that sometimes must be given can be eased somewhat when communicated with sincere compassion and open concern for the well-being of the friend. Sycophants of all kinds are quick to tell others, especially in positions of power, what they think the other person wants to hear. In so doing, they not only earn negative karma for themselves but they also mislead those whom they are supposedly counseling into erroneous decisions or actions. Is that what you would consider the act of a friend? Of course not.

Friendship does not carry with it unthinking support when the friend is wrong. To do so would merely cause him to persist in his error. The old slogan, "My country right or wrong," when applied personally to friends, is just as mistaken. Blind loyalty does not serve the best interests of the friend. Constructive criticism, compassionately offered, does the friend a far greater service both in terms of his spiritual growth as well as in coping with the tasks of the material world.

Whether they are consciously aware of it or not, friends do concern themselves with each other's spiritual side. Remember, at the deepest levels of your being, you always know that you are fundamentally a spiritual being, temporarily clothed with a material body. Since you know this, even though not usually at the level of your conscious mind, you will be concerned about your friend's spiritual progress in a given lifetime. It may seem strange to you while in the material world, but you will have such a concern for your friends although you may have a hard time describing or defining exactly what it is. And in the case of friends, even more than with other people generally (even though you should there too), you will always be ready to forgive errors and misconduct.

You will remember that you have not been appointed to judge anyone but yourself and you will also remember that perfection is not a part of the human condition. Recognizing your own shortcomings and spiritual backsliding on occasion, you will apply to your friends, and hopefully to a broader segment of the population, the same measure of understanding and forgiveness that you would wish for your own transgressions.

Ideally, you would make major spiritual progress if you could come to think of the entire population of the world as your "friends" and could relate to them as such. Alas, that will be a long time coming but if you can apply that thought to your own little community, you will gain greatly. As you already know, with a genuine friend you don't have to see or communicate with that person frequently in order for the friendship to be enduring and solid. When you do see the person, it is as if the months or years had never intervened and you are as close as you ever were.

Perhaps love, in the agape rather than Eros sense of the word, is still a bit too much for most humans to handle at this stage of their general spiritual development. If so, then friendship, something we all need in making our way through this material lifetime, is a somewhat attenuated version of love, but one that is acceptable (at least in terms of nomenclature) in your rather confusing collection of values. As is so often the case with my messages, the names don't matter a great deal. What counts is the conduct. So conduct yourself as a friend to all if you can, or to as many as you can, and you can call it friendship. Maybe I will call it love but I won't shake up you readers out there by telling you.

Cruelty

Session 104 - March 24, 1994

As I told you earlier, tonight I will talk about cruelty. Unfortunately, cruelty exists in many forms. Physical cruelty is the most obvious but mental cruelty runs a close second. We see physical cruelty take the form of cruelty by people toward other people, toward animals and other living creatures, and toward the Earth itself. Mental cruelty is somewhat less obviously visible, though often it is only thinly disguised, if at all. What I am trying to do here is identify why people engage in cruel behavior. What motivates them and what are they trying to accomplish or communicate to the rest of us?

First, let me say that *all humans are capable of cruelty toward others.* That is simply a part of the imperfection that goes with the human condition. Face it so that you can control it, rather than trying to deny its existence and then be taken by surprise by it. It is another way of reminding yourselves, as you have been reminded before, that we humans have a dark side to our personalities. We must recognize and acknowledge it so that we can keep it under control.

To get back to my question of what motivates acts of cruelty, I think it is a form of misplaced and highly negative exercise of power by one person over another. As you already know, power over others is one of the great temptations of ego and one of the sources of severe negative karmic consequences. The ability to be cruel is a manifestation of power by the stronger over the weaker. Of course I don't mean the stronger physically; I mean the person in the stronger end of the particular relationship. Power creates a very heady sensation and it seeks outlets. Cruelty is one of those outlets, albeit one of the more negative ones. You have heard the expression "drunk with power." Well, a heavy dose of power can produce sensations akin to the consumption of an excessive amount of alcohol. And you know that, in many cases, the intoxicated person thinks he can do anything—from flying through the air to being invulnerable to anything.

Not only is the commission of acts of cruelty an exercise in the use of power—or rather, the abuse of it—but it is also a reminder that the dark side of the cruel person's personality has taken control over his spiritual side. In effect, ego has overcome spirit (at least temporarily) for that particular entity. Remember also that the price for such an abuse of power will be high and will have to be compensated for, either later in that lifetime or in a subsequent life.

The same general comments apply also to mental cruelty. That is more likely to take the form of interaction between a boss and a subordinate, or a dominant spouse with the other spouse, or any other relationship in which one person is clearly dominant over the other or others. It isn't always as obvious as physical cruelty but its karmic consequences are nearly as severe. The reason is that in cases of mental cruelty, generally the person engaging in the cruel conduct is in a dominant relationship to the other and is, in essence, demonstrating his power over that other person. Occasionally there may be a cruel response to such an abuse of power but that is rather infrequent. What I mean is that a subservient spouse, having had enough, will respond to a cruel remark by lashing back with an equally cruel remark. Or an employee, having reached the limit of his endurance, will lash out at his boss' cruel comment with a cruel response, even at risk of his job. As I said, however, that is infrequent and, in light of the circumstances under which incidents of this kind occur, the karmic consequences are not very severe. After all, this is not the exercise or abuse of power over others; it is an attempted defense, rather, against such an abuse by the other person.

As in so many situations, we come back to motive as the primary criterion to be used in evaluating the moral status of an ostensible act of cruelty. Amputation of a hand as punishment for theft, as provided by the Koran and which is the law in some Islamic states, would be considered cruel and morally reprehensible. On the other hand, amputation of a hand that is gangrenous and that must be amputated to save the life of the patient would not be. The motive for the act in the second case is a positive one.

In the mental area, the expression of some harsh truths to a friend may or may not be cruel depending on the motive for the statements. If the motive is in the best interest of the recipient, then there is no cruelty involved. On the other hand, if the motive is to enable the speaker to feel superior to the recipient, for example, then the harsh truths are cruel, even though they are just as true in both cases.

The terms "cruel" and "cruelty" by their very nature carry with them negative connotations. Therefore, before using the terms—that is, before determining whether a given act or statement is "cruel"—it is necessary to examine the motives of the actor. In some cases the motives can be easily ascertained, sometimes even from the nature and circumstances of the act itself. In the mental area, it becomes more difficult sometimes to ascertain the motive of the speaker but usually there is enough external evidence to make it possible for you to make a determination that will be accurate in the great majority of cases.

Besides, it is not our job to go around judging others. These criteria are intended to enable each of you who reads these messages to evaluate *your own words and deeds* in the quiet of your own inner being and without deluding yourself as to your motives. You may be able to delude your conscious mind. After all, your conscious mind is the seat of ego and is quite expert in self-delusion and dissembling. But at the core of your being, you cannot delude yourself about what your motives were when you said or did what you are now trying to evaluate.

What else needs to be said about cruelty? *I regret to say that cruelty is a characteristic that is unique to humanity.* You do not find it in the animal kingdom. Of course animals kill each other for food, or territory, or other reasons associated with their own survival. But they don't torture or otherwise engage in what we have described as cruelty in this message. It takes a rather highly evolved creature to be able to engage in acts of cruelty. That sounds on the surface like a contradiction but it isn't. *Because cruelty, as used in this message, is essentially a moral failing, it is necessarily limited to human beings since human beings are the only beings on this planet with "moral" values as such.*

As both Seneca and I have said before and will say again, when people in large numbers finally realize who they are and why they are here on earth, cruelty will diminish and finally disappear from the face of the earth. But that time is not imminent, I am afraid. And all you can do is to set an example for your own little corner of the world and let the ripples spread as they will.

Quiet

Session 105 - March 28, 1994

Tonight I would like to talk about quiet. Yes, I really did say "quiet." Quiet is rather easily defined as the absence of noise, with noise referring to actual sound or other mental distractions.

Quiet is a state to be sought by everyone on a regular basis. In the first place, it provides surcease from the constant intrusions of the material world and therefore provides some rest for the spirit. Also, it gives the person an opportunity to take stock of himself and his life and to regain perspective on what life in the material world is supposed to be all about.

Keeping this perspective in the forefront is a necessary prerequisite to avoiding the snares that the material world—the world of ego—lays for all of you. Again I come back to what has become one of my favorite words: "mindfulness." This will do a great deal to protect you on your journey through your various lifetimes.

It is in the quiet times that beings like Seneca and I can contact willing people on earth. As you yourself know, Bill, when you communicate with us, you go into a quiet room, close the door, and enter a meditative state. You don't have to go very deeply into this state because our connection has by now become very close and we can come through to you without delay when you call upon us. Also, the connection is now so close that sometimes we have a little "bleed-through" when you feel our presence and communicate with us even though you have not initiated the contact.

Quiet is also the time when the small, still voice may be heard. All too often, it is completely drowned out by the noise levels of our daily struggle for existence. But that small, still voice is the voice of either your own divine spark or of your Creator Himself seeking to communicate with you. Such communications, if only you can hear them and then act on them, will resolve many questions you will have throughout your life concerning how you should handle a variety of situations that you are confronted with. You will learn from this small, still voice what the spiritually progressive course of conduct is, even though your conscious mind may not be able to perceive it or, worse yet, may not consider it important.

One of the best reasons for people to attend a house of worship of their choice is that it gives them the opportunity to spend a little quiet time in an effort to look within and achieve, even momentarily, actual communion with God, as contrasted with the symbolic or ritual communion offered by some of the Christian churches.

Quiet is an adjective that I associate with spiritual calm and serenity. It seems to me that a characteristic of mystics who have achieved regular or repeated communion with God while still in the flesh here on earth is a quiet serenity. They know what the rest of us are still trying to learn. With some contemplatives, silence is a part of their way of life. For you who must make your way in the material world—and that is nearly all who may read these messages—total silence is neither feasible nor necessary. Just take a little time out of your busy day to reflect quietly on who you are and why you are here. Such reflection will provide you with the most effective inoculation against the disease known as ego and its consequences.

I believe it is the Book of Ecclesiastes that contains the statement that there is a time to speak and a time to remain silent. Though said in quite a different context, the statement remains applicable today—and literally. *Each of you needs to find, or make, a brief period of daily silence during which you reflect on your life in the flesh and your spiritual objectives.* If you can get into the habit of doing that, it will stand you in good stead.

Guilt

Session 106 - March 30, 1994

Tonight we will talk about guilt. Yes, I indicated that would be my subject earlier today. Guilt, as I said to you while we had a brief connection this afternoon, is a form of spiritual acid. It is painful, it is corrosive and it leaves scar tissue—all on a spirit level, of course. But you should understand that guilt is a condition that you inflict upon yourselves; God does not deal in guilt. If you are even a moderately spiritual person, you know deep in your soul when you have done something you shouldn't or have not done something you should.

While guilt, like pain, cannot be regarded as inherently good (it really isn't), it can have some beneficial effects, just like pain. Pain tells you something is wrong, either physically, mentally or spiritually. Well, so does guilt. It's just another alarm system and I would consider it as more subtle or finely-tuned than pain. *If you feel guilt at any time, your inner being is telling you to stop and take stock of what you have recently done or are considering doing* (I use the term "done" and "doing" here to include thoughts and words as well as actions, because as you know, they too have karmic consequences).

Guilt can therefore be used by you as a rather sophisticated spiritual early warning system. If you respond quickly and satisfactorily, you can wash away the guilt before it has done much spiritual damage, maybe even entirely. If you ignore the feelings and shove the entire situation out of your mind, then the guilt grows deeper, whether you are consciously aware of it or not, and the damage done is that much greater, I might remind you that, in such instances, so are the negative karmic consequences that you must later deal with.

You have to work to separate self-imposed guilt (for acting contrary to your basic spiritual nature) from guilt that may be imposed upon you by others under material world conditions. The latter is something to be avoided. You will encounter numerous situations in your journey through a material life in which other people will try to manipulate you in various ways by making you feel guilty if you do not comply with their wishes or demands. This can be particularly true in family situations. Spouses manipulate each other, parents manipulate children and children manipulate parents—that's just a simple fact of material life, and I would add that it is usually not done maliciously. Perhaps we could simply call this kind of conduct just another manifestation of ego that plays such a large role in the material world and that you must constantly seek to keep in its proper place.

You don't have to worry too much about the externally imposed guilt feelings—unless they are accompanied by internal confirmation. Then you will know that you should do something about it. Otherwise, just ignore them as another attempt by someone else's ego to manipulate your conduct.

I would like to say a few words about what guilt is not. It is not a form of punishment from God, as some might have you believe. As you have previously been told, God does not punish; He teaches. What your limited human minds may perceive as a punishment from God is in reality only a means of teaching important truths to His children on earth. So don't be taken in by those who would attach to God characteristics that belong to humans—and not even the best characteristics of humans.

When you all reach the point in your lives on earth where you never feel guilty—internally imposed, that is—then you may be very close to experiencing your last required learning experience on this planet. You will be about ready for graduation. I might also have said that, when you never experience self-imposed guilty feelings, you have so anesthetized your spiritual self that you cannot feel its early warning message. I did not say that because it is not true. There may be a few people who could fall into such a category—one where they have an enormous amount of spiritual ground to make up—but that is not the case with the great majority of humans on earth at this time. Certainly you will err and fall short; that indicates your imperfect human condition. But you will still feel that prod of conscience at the core of your being that I have called guilt. The further advanced you are spiritually, the more sensitive you will be to these feelings when you fall short, and you will then be more likely to correct the situation that initially gave rise to the guilt pangs.

Do not dwell on feelings of guilt—instead, do what is necessary to eliminate the cause. To dwell on feelings of guilt is a form of self-abasement and that too is another example of ego taking charge. God's children know who and what they are; they know their shortcomings and they sincerely try to make spiritual progress in each lifetime on earth. They know, or should know, that beating one's self about the head and shoulders, as you would put it, is not a constructive approach to anything.

Again, mindfulness enters the picture. If you stay mindful, you will usually be alert to situations of this kind and will be much less vulnerable to the ego trap.

Hope and Fear

Session 107 - April 3, 1994

Tonight I would like to talk about hope and fear. The two are substantially opposites of each other. Both look to the future but one does so with anticipation and optimism, while the other does so with foreboding and dismay. They color our lives in the material world more than we would like to admit, especially in the case of fear.

Hope, in my opinion, is predicated upon a view of the world as a friendly place, watched over by a loving and beneficent Father. Even though bad things happen since there is negativity in the material world, the person of hope looks to the future as having brighter possibilities. That person may also recognize the bad things that happen as important lessons that need to be learned in order to advance spiritually. The person of hope can then put his negative experiences into a more spiritual context and derive positive benefits from negative events.

Even in the material world, you sometimes have the opportunity later to see that what appeared to be a negative event was in reality a blessing in disguise. For example, suppose you were suddenly and unexpectedly fired from your job after twenty years with the same company, and the firing was politically motivated. At the time you were shocked and horrified. Five years later, having found another job that turned out to be far superior in all respects to the old one, you look back and realize that the unfair firing was a blessing in disguise. You acknowledge that you would otherwise have stayed in that job with that company for the rest of your working life, probably under-paid and under-appreciated. In most cases the "blessing in disguise" phenomenon is not that obvious— even later—but the person of hope knows that there is purpose in this universe and that enables him to withstand adversity and look to the future with optimism.

The person of fear, on the other hand, starts with a world viewpoint that sees the world as either hostile, or at best, random. In either case, he looks ahead with trepidation because he believes that he must look after himself against all others. He may well be a person who does not believe in the existence of God, or if he does, his image of God is that of a fierce, angry, vindictive but all-powerful old man who seems to enjoy strewing obstacles in the paths of poor humans. He may well be quite paranoid but of course he does not consider himself to be so. He sincerely believes that "they" are out to get him.

I have not decided in my own mind whether the person who believes in a hostile world is better or worse off than the one who believes in a random world. At least the hostile world has some semblance of meaning, even though twisted, whereas the random world is essentially meaningless. In the latter concept, the world has no purpose, we have no purpose, everything just happens. It would seem to be a world devoid of moral content and one could only wonder why he was here. He might even decide that the sooner he gets out of it, the better off he will be.

What I have just described may be a rather dramatic way of saying that hope is a positive attribute while fear is a most negative one. As you have previously been told, so much of the strife in the world stems from fear—usually fear of people who are not "just like us." *Fear emphasizes the differences that exist among the various segments of mankind. Hope focuses on those things that we share in common.* With hope as your dominant characteristic, you can handle the slings and arrows of the material world because you believe that something better lies ahead. With fear as your dominant personality characteristic, you hide from those who are different, you try to confine yourself to interaction with others like yourself and you keep your horizons incredibly narrow. You are afraid of diversity instead of regarding it as a source of richness and strength.

The message here is simple—be harbingers of hope rather than messengers of fear and you will not only make progress on your spiritual path back to your Father but you will also be much healthier and happier people during your sojourn on earth. It's really as simple as that. The choice is yours, because how you perceive the world around you and the unseen world of spirit is within your control. Take charge and be positive in your outlook—it works.

Enough for now. As always, our love, protection, blessings and prayers go with you and all your loved ones. This is not just a routine closing statement. Be assured that we really do try to look after you and all your loved ones but we must do so without interfering with your and their exercise of the great God-given gift of free will. Good-bye until next time.

Fasting and Feasting

Session 108 - April 6, 1994

Tonight I would like to talk about fasting and feasting. As you know by now, I like to pick a subject as a starting point for my messages and then go from there. Sometimes the starting point seems a bit startling when you first see it. At other times the message goes off on a very different tack from the starting point. We'll see what happens with this rather unusual starting point.

Fasting and feasting are both well-known terms in the material world. Fasting tends to be used to describe not eating by choice, rather than by necessity. "Going hungry" or some similar term would normally be used to describe the involuntary kind of non-eating. Fasting in many religions is associated with purification rituals, such as the Jewish provision for fasting on Yom Kippur and the Moslem requirement for fasting from sunup to sundown during the month of Ramadan. Native Americans included fasting as part of the preparation for a vision quest, and there are numerous other examples that could be cited.

The important point is that *fasting is a form of retreat from the material to the spiritual.* It is a way of reminding ourselves that, though we require food and drink to survive in the flesh, we are also spiritual beings who seek to make spiritual progress on the path back to our Father. Fasting is a good way to enhance mindfulness of who and what we are and why we are here. I don't mean by this that you should fast all that often but it is a good idea to do so every once in a while. How often will depend on how mindful you are of your fundamentally spiritual nature on a normal day-to-day basis—i.e., without fasting. Besides, occasional fasting can also help you lose some weight and that would be a good thing for most Americans.

I would also recommend that, when you meditate, you do so before a meal rather than after. It can still be done after a meal without a doubt, but especially in the early stages when you are trying to get into the good habit, it is easier to meditate if your blood supply is not busily occupied in digesting your current meal.

This started off as a message about fasting and feasting so I should say something about feasting also. I don't have to tell you anything about physical feasting; you certainly know that it is a vehicle for the celebration of happy or noteworthy occasions. It can be a wedding or a family gathering or a holiday celebration, etc. But what about "spiritual" feasting? What do I mean by that?

Spiritual feasting is the counterpart of physical feasting, except that the subject matter of the celebration is a spiritual event or accomplishment instead of a physical one. For example, suppose a person you know and like has come to realize his fundamental spirituality and has turned away from excessive emphasis on material goods, money and power. That would be an occasion for spiritual feasting. And if you had a hand in bringing the change about, then you can feel good and know that somewhere in the spirit world, a toast is being offered for your accomplishment.

Material feasting is fine for the kind of special occasions like those mentioned. Just make sure that it doesn't degenerate into mere gluttony. If you keep feasting all the time, regardless of what you call it, you will soon begin to look like King Farouk, the former king of Egypt. As a young man, he was slim and strong and handsome; as he grew older, he became fat and ugly and gross. Did this also reflect his spiritual odyssey? You can come to your own conclusions on that, but just keep in mind that the body is the temple of the soul and should be treated with the respect due to such an edifice.

I have talked about physical fasting and spiritual feasting. Is there a place for something that could be called "spiritual fasting?" Let me think about that a little. Since physical fasting is usually part of a purification rite or preparation for same, spiritual fasting is also a counterpart in the spirit world. But what do I mean by that and how does it work?

Spiritual fasting involves a kind of recognition of spiritual humility in the face of spiritual progress. As you make spiritual progress, and you will if you pay attention to these messages and live them, it is important that you not become complacent about that fact—even though it is a fact. Complacency is another rather subtle manifestation of ego and it produces attitudes similar to those condemned by Jesus on the part of the Pharisees. Spiritual fasting can help you avoid that ego snare, even as you make the spiritual progress that you are seeking in each lifetime.

I think I have said enough tonight to get your attention on the subject of fasting and feasting. Isn't it interesting how only one little letter of the alphabet separates these two opposite conditions? Maybe that should indicate to us that there is some nexus between them. That sounds like it could be a subject for a later message—or maybe the nexus is to be found somewhere in tonight's discussion. You see, now you get puzzles too. Anything to hold your attention and maybe let the messages sink in more readily.

❂ ❂ ❂ ❂

I think that should be enough for now. Good-bye until next time and, as always, our love, blessings, protection and prayers go with you and all your loved ones. I know you already know this but I still like saying it.

☙ ❧

Roller Coasters

Session 109 - April 9, 1994

As you already knew, today I would like to talk about roller coasters. It sometimes seems that God, when He designed this material world, called upon the services of someone who had experience in designing roller coasters for amusement parks. Your recent experience, Bill, is an illustration of this proposition.

A few days ago, within the space of a single afternoon, you went on an emotional roller coaster ride. First, you visited a garden shop with your wife, where you saw a wide variety of gorgeous plants and flowers that brought to you a sense of wonder at the beauty of nature. Seeing manifestations of that beauty in somewhat concentrated form can do that to a person. For those who may be uncertain about whether there is indeed a divine Creator, the beauty that you can see in nature every day, if you have your eyes open for it, can help convince you that such perfection is not the result of mere chance combinations of molecules on some kind of random basis. For what it's worth to the skeptic, I can add my own assurances too.

Later that same day you received some information that made you furious—the roller coaster on the downward leg. What happened to you is a very common occurrence among humans—that is, the experience of wide emotional swings within a very short period of time. That's why I refer to it as an emotional roller coaster. It also indicates the need for more internal work.

Your objective should be to achieve a level of calm and serenity with respect to both the good things and the bad things that you may be exposed to. That not only keeps you off the emotional roller coaster but it also helps remind you that the events of this world are temporary and insignificant in the cosmic scheme of things. By maintaining a general demeanor of serenity, you distance yourself emotionally from the impact that the events of your daily life have upon you. You acquire a measure of what the Buddhists would call "detachment" from the churning of the material world. The advice that they generally give to that effect is good advice, even though it is rather difficult for western temperaments to accept and adopt.

My suggestion about seeking serenity does not mean that you should lose your humanity while on this planet. I would not suggest that and I doubt if you could do it anyway. Take joy in the good things that happen to you and your family and friends and weep with them for the bad ones. That's fine. But you can still do so with an inner serenity that reminds you that both the good things and the bad ones are transitory and that they carry within themselves lessons for you to learn. *Again I will point out to you that the world is not a random, meaningless series of events governed by no law or intelligence. If you accept my statement as true, it follows that all the things that happen to us happen for a reason—either to teach us lessons or as a result of the choices we have made through our own exercise of free will.*

Another lesson for you, Bill, that may also have application to others. Some of the information that initially made you extremely angry was in error. Or you made a mistaken interpretation of what had been passed on to you. That distinction doesn't really matter; what does matter is that you jumped to an emotional conclusion before verifying the facts. It is true that you took no action on the subject prior to checking out the facts but you certainly went on an unnecessary roller coaster ride. I would also add here that anger, even if deserved, is never a constructive or affirmative state of mind. It detracts from your clarity of thought and it lowers your vibration level. So it is important that all of you who may read these messages learn to control your anger until you can reach the state where you can avoid even experiencing it. That is why I have gone into this experience of Bill's in this much detail—not just as a lesson for him but as a lesson for all of you.

I see that you have a question about the effect of body chemistry upon your emotional behavior. I know that humans like to think they are always in control of their bodies, not to mention their minds. However, it is true, and a bit humbling to realize that in some respects and on some occasions, you are actually prisoners of your body chemistry. However, if you examine this question at a deeper level, you will find that your spirit—sometimes described in this context as your mental attitude—greatly influences, if it does not actually control, your body's behavior, including its chemistry.

Even modern medicine recognizes the mind-body interaction as having real effects upon a person's physical health. Well, I will say it a little differently. If you are spiritually confused and stumbling around in that part of your being, the chances are very good that you are also experiencing physical problems of equivalent severity. When you examine the question at a deep enough level, you will conclude, as I have, that mind affects body, rather than vice versa. That should come as some comfort to you to know that your spirit is really in charge of your body—though your conscious mind of course will seek to deny it since your conscious mind is the location where ego holds sway.

Truth

Tonight I would like to discuss truth—a very large subject that I will of course refrain from trying to cover in any detail. What is truth? That's what Pontius Pilate asked Jesus and he neither knew nor cared what the answer was—he was merely being a cynic and taunting Jesus. Well, we take the subject much more seriously because it is an essential element of spirituality. Truth is allied to integrity and it represents a cause that many people in the material world have been willing to fight and die for, if necessary, over the years. That's fine but it still doesn't tell us what truth is.

Let me see how I can describe or define it so that it can be easily understood. *Truth emanates from God, just as the divine spark within each of us emanates from God. By the same token, truth is eternal and unchanging and never wrong.* When capitalized, Truth is often used as another name for God. Well, truth (lower case) is something like a younger brother of Truth (capitalized). That is to say, truth is an attempt in the material world to reach for the eternal. You don't quite get there in the material world because it is so full of illusion. Even if you did somehow get there on occasion, you probably wouldn't be able to tell, due to the noise level and disturbances that abound in the material world.

Another way to try to say it is that if something is true, it is of God. Now I am not talking here about material facts being true. They are true or false according to your rules of science and experience—or at least you think so and conduct yourselves accordingly. *I am talking about moral and spiritual truths when I say that truth is of God.* And I would also add that, at the deepest levels of your being, you recognize those truths, even though your conscious mind may be so confused or diverted by the illusions of ego that you don't even recognize it when it hits you in the face. That is also why I encourage you to listen to the still, small voice within that speaks to you in moments of quiet meditation. That is a voice that comes from the deepest levels of your being, your divine spark, or in some cases from God Himself.

In a rather peculiar way I might say that truth is a little like pornography. That should shock you some. But I am of course referring to the famous statement by a Supreme Court justice who said in effect: "I can't define pornography but I sure can recognize it when I see it." The same kind of comment could also be applied to truth—see?

The opposite of truth is falsehood. What do we have, and what do we do, if a decent person sincerely believes something to be truth when in reality it is falsehood. Since humans on the earth plane don't do a very good job in distinguishing truth from falsehood, my advice would be to treat any sincerely held belief by another with respect and courtesy since he may be right and you may be wrong. And neither of you will know who is really right on the question while you are still in the material world. This is particularly important in the area of religion, where so many terrible things have been done by people to their brothers and sisters in the name of God. As I have previously said, the arrogant conviction that your point of view has a monopoly on truth is just that—ego masquerading as human arrogance.

My truth, as both Seneca and I have said before, is that your conduct is what truly reflects your belief system, rather than what you profess to believe. I have never been able to figure out how professional gangsters can commit the most heinous crimes and genuinely believe that, if they are Catholic Christians, they can confess their sins to a priest thereby and be absolved. You can't confess your way out of the karmic consequences of your thoughts, words and deeds. The books must be balanced, either in this lifetime or later.

Should I also talk about something else now that I have touched on truth? If you wish to continue, I will talk a bit about commitment. Commitment to what? That's the real point. Commitment is generally a positive characteristic so long as the subject matter of the commitment is morally and ethically acceptable. In most respects, therefore, commitment and persistence, which I talked about earlier, are kissin' cousins in terms of their common characteristics. Commitment, however, seems to me to partake of the element of identification with the object of the commitment, while persistence is more process-oriented. For instance, a commitment to God would mean to me that the person in question has undertaken to do all in his power to help bring about the kingdom of God on earth. The manifestation of that commitment will be his conduct toward his fellow humans and all the rest of God's creation. His persistence will be demonstrated by continuing along his course even after encountering disappointment, rejection and negative conduct from others with whom he interacts.

If you who read these messages and are receptive to them can make a commitment to do your best to conduct yourselves as the fundamentally spiritual beings that you are in your daily contacts with other people, animals and Mother Earth herself, even in the small corner of the material world that you inhabit and influence, you can make a great deal of spiritual progress in your present lifetime. And you may be surprised by what your example may trigger in others and how far the ripples may eventually spread.

Fatigue

Session 111 - April 17, 1994

Today I would like to talk about fatigue. You have felt some lately and wondered what was causing it. In the physical sense, fatigue occurs when you try to do more than your body considers appropriate under all the circumstances. A fair synonym for fatigue is weariness, although fatigue is usually more associated with the after-effects of action. Clearly, when you are suffering from fatigue, you know it. There is no doubt in your mind, although you may wonder why. Is there also a kind of spiritual fatigue that occurs in people's lives? If so, when does it occur and how do we recognize it? Also, what can we do about it?

Unlike physical fatigue, spiritual fatigue does not result from trying to do too much in the way of spiritual progress. You can't do too much in that direction. Moreover, that would only lead to spiritual exhilaration, not fatigue. The circumstances in this instance are very different between the physical and spiritual worlds. *Spiritual fatigue results from doing too little toward achieving spiritual growth, rather than too much.* Spiritual fatigue is more in the nature of spiritual anemia, a matter of inadequacy rather than excess. So while in many other areas that we have talked about, the analogy among physical, mental and spiritual remains fairly constant, here it is reversed.

If spiritual fatigue results from doing too little rather than too much, how do we recognize its occurrence? When it happens to us physically, we readily recognize its effects, even if we don't always identify its causes. But what about when it happens spiritually? If we are at all sensitive, we can recognize the signs of spiritual fatigue by feelings of spiritual restlessness. We may also feel a sense of incompleteness about life here in the material world. By looking closely at ourselves, we can then identify the cause as spiritual fatigue. We have to look closely, however, because there may be other phenomena that will mimic those symptoms.

Also, it takes a fairly high level of sensitivity to your fundamentally spiritual nature for you to recognize what is happening. If you are not at all sensitive to your spirituality, you won't ever identify the subtle feelings that indicate spiritual fatigue. The most you will experience is a vague, indeterminate sense of dissatisfaction, with nothing to attribute it to. By the same token, in such a situation, you can't expect to be able to do anything about it since you won't even know what "it" is.

For those who are sufficiently advanced in their spirituality to recognize these feelings for what they are, you can rather easily cure your spiritual fatigue. You do this, of course, by bringing your fundamentally spiritual nature more directly and extensively into your material life. You don't have to make a lot of noise about doing so; you can do it very quietly by changing your conduct in this lifetime into a pattern that reflects your true nature. As you can see from this discussion, the real trick is in identifying the fact that you are suffering from spiritual fatigue.

Once you have determined that to be the case, the course of action to be taken to cure the ailment is easy. Of course, *implementation* of that identified course of action may be a good deal more difficult if it requires major changes in the way you conduct yourself in the material world. But that won't usually be the case. *If you are spiritually sensitive enough to know what spiritual fatigue is, the chances are very good that you have been living a life that does not require drastic externally observable changes in order to bring a proper measure of spirituality into it.* Try it and you will see.

We are beginning to approach the latter stages of this first book. Soon I will make a major change in subject matter—from how to live in the material world in order to achieve spiritual growth to a clearly different subject or series of subjects. When that happens, you will know that your first book is complete and ready to be prepared for publication. Incidentally, I like the subtitle that you decided to give it. No, I didn't put that thought into your mind; it was your own. Don't make the mistake of thinking that the guidance provided by Seneca and myself extends to everything you think. You really do a considerable part of it yourself. You know that you are by no means our puppet. We try to guide and help you, while also protecting you, but you are the spirit in charge there. After all, you have your own spiritual progress to make in addition to disseminating our messages. So give yourself some credit for your own good ideas and good deeds.

As a final note, Enid is earning excellent karma as a result of her compassion for the animals at the wildlife center. Sometimes I think that if people behaved toward each other as well as they often behave toward wildlife in trouble, life on earth would be much better.

Surprises

Session 112 · April 20, 1994

Yes, tonight I would like to talk about surprises—a surprising topic, perhaps. Surprises of course can be either pleasant or unpleasant but in either case they represent an unexpected event. Something that you expect does not come as a surprise—only something you don't expect. So what? In the material world, there isn't a great deal you can do to avoid surprises of either kind, since you have only a limited amount of control over your surroundings or the conduct of others. In the spirit world, there are far fewer surprises because those in that world have a much clearer idea of where they are and where they are trying to go—at least if they are reasonably advanced beings. Lower levels of the spirit world may function much more like the material world, largely because the inhabitants there, like those in the material world, still have so much more to learn.

How should we handle the surprises that occur all the time in the material world? The good ones are easy. Just enjoy them and be grateful that you have some good karma accumulated; that is most likely the cause of the good surprise. For the bad surprises, I would advise you to remember that they are either lessons to be learned by you or they are the results of conduct by you earlier in your present lifetime or in a past life. You can take some comfort from the fact that they are not merely random occurrences that have no meaning; they do have meaning. Also, you can take considerable comfort from the fact that a single lifetime in the material world is no more than a short dream—the blink of an eye in the cosmic scheme of things.

I might also apply some of these same comments to misfortunes that all humans are subjected to at some time or other in their lives. It helps to look at it as a repayment of past karmic debts that helps balance the karmic books, and also to regard life in the material world as the illusion rather than the reality. *That I can attest to—it is life in the world of spirit that is the world of reality and the material world is a world of illusion—albeit a necessary one—for learning to take place.*

You are getting more curious about when this book will be finished so you can go ahead with publishing efforts. Well, don't be too impatient; it won't be long now. And it would now be permissible for you to make your first preliminary contact with a publisher, while pointing out that the book is not yet complete, but is close to it. Your editing efforts are timely and will save you work later on when you convert your manuscript into the format desired by the publisher. Don't worry—I'll let you know when this book is finished so we can start the next one. Also you will see a marked change in subject matter.

What else do I want to tell you tonight? Do I want to talk about fire? The thought occurred to you, so maybe I should say a few words about it. As with so many things in the material world, fire can be a great boon or a great tragedy, depending on circumstances and how it is used. It provides the means of cooking your food and heating your homes—or at least it did in earlier times and indirectly it still does. By the same token, it can also burn down your houses, kill people and destroy property in large amounts.

Fire is also often used in purification rituals, though much less so now than in the past. The analogy between fire as a spiritual purification process and fire as a steel smelting process is an interesting one. In steel smelting, the iron is subjected to intense heat in order to burn off the impurities and leave the material stronger than it was before—as steel. The same can be said of some of the trials and tribulations that humans encounter while on earth. *Misfortunes can therefore be a means of purification—and one that results in a stronger, more spiritual being, even though most of us would not intentionally choose to undergo hardships and misfortunes as a form of spiritual weight-lifting.*

This has been a somewhat rambling discourse but I think the main point is that we should look at our material misfortunes as spiritual smelters from which we emerge stronger and purer in spirit if we approach them properly. That puts a positive approach on events that, from a material world standpoint, may seem to be unmitigated disasters. But if you remember what the material world really is, you can then put its occurrences, both good and bad, into proper perspective.

Wealth

Session 113 - April 25, 1994

I see that you have been working hard on your editing efforts because you somehow "feel" that we are approaching the end of the first book. We are, and you will know when that occurs. Tonight I would like to talk about wealth. As with so many of your terms, wealth also has many meanings. First and most obvious in the material world, though actually least important, is material wealth. It can enable you to live comfortably and enjoy the many pleasures that abound in that world. Again, there is nothing wrong with wealth, or the enjoyment of it, so long as it was not acquired at the expense of others and is not abused after it has been acquired. You already know that. It is the other kinds of wealth that I want to talk about tonight, and particularly spiritual wealth.

Before we get to spiritual wealth, let me talk a little about other non-material kinds of wealth. You have previously been told that you are richer than Croesus in terms of the love and friendship that you experience with your family and friends. That is a most important illustration of non-material wealth. There is also the matter of reputation that I have talked about before. That is another precious example of non-material wealth. That kind of wealth remains with you regardless of what the stock market does or any of your other investments. The latter can be here today and gone tomorrow, as I have already told you. But the non-material items of wealth remain. That shows that such items are so much more durable and lasting than mere money or possessions.

Now let's talk about what I mean by spiritual wealth. Spiritual wealth, I believe, consists of the knowledge that God loves you individually and accepts you with open arms unconditionally as you are. That knowledge I would describe as spiritual wealth. To take it further, God also wants you to return to your spiritual home and achieve reunion with Him. When you have been able to accomplish this—and remember that eventually you all will—you will then become a co-creator with Him and you will have achieved infinite spiritual wealth. It simply can't get any better than that!

That is the kind of wealth that is everlasting and so far transcends any and all other kinds of wealth, both material and non-material, that it is indescribable. But I can assure you that when you achieve it, you will indeed know it. Your happiness, in enduring terms rather than mere human terms, will be greater than you or any other living being can hope to imagine. Now there is something to really strive for with all your might and main, isn't it?

As has been the case so often with these messages, you help yourself when you adopt a bird's eye—or is it a God's eye?—view of your life in the material world. From that vantage point, you can see where you are spiritually and where you wish to go. You can even get some idea of how to get there and you can identify some of the most difficult obstacles along the way. These obstacles take many forms but they can usually be grouped into the category of "manifestations of ego."

With that kind of perspective, you can make your journey in the material world a reasonably pleasant one on the whole by building up your bank account of good karma and by recognizing that the negative things that happen to you have meaning and purpose. With such a perspective, you never lose sight of your goal, nor are you distracted from it—other than momentarily—by the temptations of the material world. You know who and what you are, why you are here, where you are going and, generally, how to get there. In effect, you have a road map back to reunion with God. The trip may seem long, there will be obstacles along the way and you will sometimes falter. But with the road map engraved on your soul, you will get to your destination.

That concludes this book. We have much more to convey to you for the benefit of humanity, but that completes this first task of yours. Now it is up to you, with our help, to disseminate these teachings. Go with God.

✌ ❦

Epilogue

Have the messages changed my life? Not very noticeably to the outside world, although I think I have become more patient and compassionate and less judgmental. But internally—which is where it really counts—the changes have been extensive, although I still have a long way to go. For instance, one message tells us that God loves each and every one of us unconditionally just as we are, warts and all. If we can get ourselves *to really believe* that mind-boggling statement, how can it not affect—and profoundly—our attitudes and relationships with each other?

You, the reader, must draw your own conclusions about these messages and what they mean to you. Regardless of your view regarding the source, I urge you to focus on the content because that is where the real significance lies. The very fact that you are choosing to read them, and hopefully not just out of curiosity, is a good indication that you are sincerely interested in achieving spiritual growth for yourself. I hope you will find help and guidance here. God bless.

Index